Against Equality of Opportunity

Against Equality of Opportunity

Matt Cavanagh

CLARENDON PRESS · OXFORD

*This book has been printed digitally and produced in a standard specification
in order to ensure its continuing availability*

OXFORD
UNIVERSITY PRESS

Great Clarendon Street, Oxford OX2 6DP

Oxford University Press is a department of the University of Oxford.
It furthers the University's objective of excellence in research, scholarship,
and education by publishing worldwide in

Oxford New York

Auckland Bangkok Buenos Aires Cape Town Chennai
Dar es Salaam Delhi Hong Kong Istanbul Karachi Kolkata
Kuala Lumpur Madrid Melbourne Mexico City Mumbai Nairobi
São Paulo Shanghai Taipei Tokyo Toronto

Oxford is a registered trade mark of Oxford University Press
in the UK and in certain other countries

Published in the United States
by Oxford University Press Inc., New York

© Matt Cavanagh 2002

The moral rights of the author have been asserted

Database right Oxford University Press (maker)

Reprinted 2004

ISBN 0-19-924343-3

Cover illustration: Jesse Owens © Hulton Archive.

Acknowledgements

I would like to thank Balliol College and the British Academy for their support in the early stages, and the following for reading or discussing earlier versions of the book: Bill Brewer, Peter Goldie, David Howie, Christopher Lake, Joseph Raz, Janet Radcliffe Richards, Alan Ryan, and David Wiggins.

Contents

Introduction

I. THE QUESTION

If you ask people what we should be doing to make society a fairer place, the chances are they will say something about equality of opportunity. But what do they actually mean by this? That is the question this book tries to answer—what we mean when we talk about equality of opportunity. Clearly we mean something to do with the way jobs should be allocated. But what exactly? If you press people on what they mean by 'equality of opportunity', the appearance of general agreement soon evaporates. For some, 'equality of opportunity' turns out to mean that the best person should always get the job. For others, it means that everyone should start in the same position, or enjoy the same chance of success. For others still, it means something much narrower—simply that things like race or sex should not matter when it comes to getting a job. Does it really make sense to think of all these views as merely different interpretations of a single ideal? Probably not. It is like asking people what they want out of life: they might all *say* the same thing—'happiness'—but this is just a kind of shorthand for their real answer. For some, 'happiness' turns out to mean pleasure, for others, it means being successful in the pursuit of worthwhile ends, for others, it means having some kind of balance in your life, and so on. These are not merely different ways of interpreting an ideal, they are different all the way down; they have nothing in common except that they are all answers to the same question. 'Happiness' has simply come to stand for the answer to that question, whatever it happens to be. The same seems to be true of 'equality of opportunity'. The fact that we all use the same form of words makes us think we must agree on *something*: we agree that whatever it is exactly we believe in, 'equality of opportunity' is a good way of describing it. But this sense of a shared central idea is an illusion. The fact that we all converge on a certain form of words does not mean we actually agree on anything substantial.

However, perhaps this is a little too pessimistic. If someone says they believe in equality of opportunity, that might not tell us exactly what they believe, but it does seem to tell us something about what kind of view they have. We can probably assume, for example, that they don't believe in either pure *laissez-faire* or a centrally planned system of job allocation. That is, they probably don't think the state should let employers hire however they want, but equally they probably don't believe in going to the other extreme, in which the state would take over the whole mechanism for deciding who should do which job. Neither extreme would generally be thought of as just another interpretation of equality of opportunity. However, that leaves us with the space between these two extremes, which includes almost every respectable view, including those I have already mentioned: first, the view that the best person should always get the job, which I will call *meritocracy*; second, the view that everyone should start in the same position, or enjoy the same chance of success—which is in fact two separate views, though I will bracket them under the general heading of *equality*; also, third, the variety of views which try to combine meritocracy and equality; and last, the narrower view that things like race or sex should not matter when it comes to getting a job.

The last of these views occupies a different place in this book to the other three. The book is called *Against Equality of Opportunity*, but if this last view really was all that 'equality of opportunity' was supposed to mean, I would not be against it. Indeed, once this last view is properly separated from the others, it is pretty hard to object to (though I do argue, in Part 3, that we should understand it more narrowly than we might at first think). When I describe myself as being against equality of opportunity, what I have in mind are the other three kinds of view: meritocracy, equality, and the variety of views which try somehow to combine meritocracy and equality. I think this justifies the book's title, since these do seem to be what most people mean by equality of opportunity. (The single most common view today is probably one of those that tries to combine meritocracy and equality, the view that the best person should get the job, but that everyone should have an equal chance of becoming the best.)

But if my real target is only the first three views, why not simply call the book *Against Meritocracy and Equality*? The reason is that one of the things I want to draw attention to is precisely the confusion and vagueness surrounding the term 'equality of opportunity', as well as the problems which face the various different actual views when it is finally made clear exactly what they are. But I am less interested in opposing the idea of equality of opportunity itself—if there is such a thing—than in opposing certain particular views which go under that heading. In the end it doesn't matter whether the ideas of merit and equality, taken separately or together, successfully capture *everything* people think they mean when they say they believe in equality of opportunity. (Perhaps no single idea, or even any coherent set of ideas, could do this.) What matters is that these two ideas certainly appear, separately or together, clearly or vaguely, in the way most people think about the question of how jobs should be allocated; and this is the question I am really interested in. My aim is to challenge these common ways of thinking about it, and then to suggest some answers of my own. And when it comes to suggesting my own answers, I am similarly more interested in whether the answers I suggest are correct, than in whether they represent a better way of understanding equality of opportunity. This is not an entirely cosmetic point. It is perhaps one of the biggest problems with the whole debate that it seems to be constrained by the assumption that the answer must be *some* form of equality of opportunity —or at least some theory which could be so described.

The aim of the book, then, is to take one of the big questions facing us today—the question of how jobs should be allocated—and do two things: first, show what is wrong with the way most people think about this question, and second, offer an answer of my own. However, I should probably explain how the book is structured around these two aims. From what I have said so far, the reader might expect a brief and energetic tour through existing views, followed by a long and meticulous exposition of my own. What they will get is very different: different in terms of structure, and almost the opposite in terms of balance. As far as structure is concerned, any positive suggestions I have to make are made along the way, rather than separately in a second part of the book. And as for balance, these positive suggestions are merely sketched, to provide points of contrast with existing ways of thinking; the bulk of the discussion is taken up with trying to understand those existing ways of thinking, in order that we might finally break free of them. Indeed, I don't think it would even be possible to run through these views more quickly. Even the most simple sounding views turn out to require a good deal of preliminary untangling before they can be properly assessed. Consider, for example, meritocracy—the view that the best person should always get the job. People generally associate meritocracy with the idea of *competition*, but that idea can be understood in at least two different ways. On the first, the purpose of competition is to give everyone the chance to earn the right to a job. On the second, the purpose is not to *create* winners and losers, by giving people the chance to earn rewards, but to *reveal* who the best person is. This is far from the only complication. Another is that whichever version of competition people believe in, they generally aren't clear about the *point* of competition: whether the point is that competition is fair, or merely useful. And a whole further layer of complication concerns how the different parts of people's views relate to one another. Most egalitarians, for example, seem confused about whether equality is desirable in its own right, or whether it is simply a necessary part of fair competition (the 'level playing-field'). Similarly, those meritocrats who accept equality as a necessary part of fair competition are generally unclear about what *kind* of equality should play this role: whether everyone should merely start in the same place, or should literally have an equal chance of success, and so on.

A large proportion of the book, then, is devoted to trying to unravel these complications, so that we can come to understand the different versions of meritocracy and equality more clearly. Once we understand them, it is easier to show where they go wrong. However, because of the size of these two tasks, the first interpretative, and the second critical, I spend less time than I might have in trying to set up my own alternative view. On the other hand, the positive aspect of this is that much of the book—the interpretative part—should be useful even to those who simply will not be shifted from their meritocratic or egalitarian intuitions. I hope that after reading this they will be in a better position to understand why they believe the things they do, even if they can't bring themselves to stop believing them.

No doubt some of them will be thinking that a philosophy book could never have done more than this anyway—that is, could never have done more than clarify what their options are, as opposed to helping them find the right one. For this kind of reader, moral principles just aren't the kind of thing we can be wrong about. Or, if we want to talk about right and wrong, we must mean right or wrong *for me*, right or wrong *for you*, and so on, rather than *objectively* right or wrong. But to the extent that I have held back from telling the reader what the right answers are, this is not why. I do not share this corrosive modern scepticism about the very idea that there might be right answers in this kind of area. I agree, of course, that in a sense it is 'up to me' what principles I believe in: I should try to make up my own mind, and (most of the time at least) no one should try to influence me in any other way than by engaging me in rational argument. But this is not the same as saying that I can't be wrong. It is true of almost all matters, not just morality, that I should try to make up my own mind about them, and that other people should leave me free to do so. Yet it is always a separate, further question whether I can be wrong. I happen to believe that fundamental moral principles—either those that deal with how we should live our lives as individuals, or those that deal with how we should organize our affairs as a society—*are* the kind of thing we can get wrong. Indeed, much of this book is devoted to trying to explain why the standard views in this area are just that—plain wrong. Clearly I do think there are right and wrong answers, and that philosophy can at least help us to identify the wrong ones. It can help by showing us when an answer is based on confusion, or logical error; or simply by drawing out its implications, so that we can see whether it is really so attractive an answer after all. Now, this might not take us all the way to the truth. When we clear away all the fallacious and obviously unattractive answers, there might still be a confusing variety of possibilities left in the frame. But we do not have to see this as a problem. To believe in right and wrong answers is not to assume that there will always be one, and only one, right answer.

These days, of course, merely saying this much—that some answers are clearly wrong, and wrong objectively, not just wrong *for us*—is guaranteed to upset or enrage large parts of one's audience. This is a strange state of affairs, and it would probably take a psychologist or sociologist to explain, as much as a philosopher.[1] I certainly cannot hope to tackle it here. But I want the reader to be clear from the start about the kind of book they are reading. It is the kind that sees the 'tidying up' aspect of philosophy not as something we do for its own sake, but as part of an attempt to get closer to the truth.

2. THE BACKGROUND TO THE QUESTION

This book, then, revolves around a single question: the question of what would be the fair way for jobs to be allocated. But before I can start trying to answer this question—before I can even start trying to clarify what some of the possible answers might be—I need to say a few things about the background against which the question is asked. This is the aim of this second section of the Introduction. The third and last section then gives a brief outline of the argument of the book as a whole.

2.1. Is this the right question to ask?

The question is what would be the fair way for jobs to be allocated. This is a question which seems to concern us more than ever. First, because the proportion of people who spend at least part of their lives in the job market is greater than ever. Second, because work has become more central to the way we understand our lives, and success or failure in our working lives means more to us, in terms of how we think about the success or failure of our lives overall. On the other hand, since fewer jobs today are jobs for life, each particular job we get, and therefore each particular hiring decision, might seem that much *less* important. But the fact that we spend less time in any given job simply means that we go through more jobs, and therefore more hiring decisions, across our working lives as a whole; so it doesn't really make the question of how these decisions should be made any less important.

Nevertheless, there is an old and venerable objection against even *asking* this question.[2] The objection is that it simply distracts us from the real questions, which are, first, why there aren't enough jobs to go round, and second, why some jobs are so much better than others, both in themselves and in how much they pay. If this was what really bothered us—that there aren't enough jobs to go round, and that some jobs pay so much better than others—then it should hardly be our first priority to change the basis on which jobs are allocated (whether from old-school-tie to merit, or from merit to everyone's having an equal chance, or whatever). We should be more interested in trying to make sure there are more jobs to go round, and in trying to reduce the disparities between them. This is, however, one particular objection to equality of opportunity that I do not share. I do not agree that the debate isn't even framed around the right question. There are simply two different kinds of question here—one question about how many jobs there are and what they are like, and a second question about fair allocation. These two questions reflect two quite different kinds of concern. Moreover, the two kinds of concern are complementary rather than competing. Anyone who is interested in fair allocation is likely also to be interested in how many jobs there are to go round. Arguments about fair allocation tend to start (reasonably enough) from the premise that having a job is very important to people, and this clearly tells in favour of arguing that there should be more jobs to go round, as well as in favour of arguing that so long as they remain scarce, they should be allocated fairly.

However, although these two concerns are complementary, it would be a mistake to assume that they are not truly distinct—for example, to assume that the problem of fair allocation is simply subsidiary to the problem of scarcity, and that if we solved the problem of scarcity, the problem of fair allocation would simply go away. Remember the second question which this old objection accuses the equal opportunity debate of neglecting—the question of why some jobs are so much better than others. If there were full employment, then everyone who wanted a job would be able to get one, but there would still be the problem that some jobs were better than others (and better in themselves, even if it were possible to remove disparities in pay). This reminds us that the question of fair allocation is not just a symptom of an unjust world: it would remain a real question even in the ideal world where there were more than enough jobs to go round.

2.2. *Top-down and bottom-up theories*

One thing that emerges from the discussion in the last section is that when we talk about equality of opportunity, sometimes we are talking about people's chances of getting *a* job—any job—and sometimes we are talking about how a particular *kind* of job is allocated (as, for example, we might ask whether everyone has an equal chance to become Prime Minister). The fact that there are these two quite different contexts to the debate is always a potential source of confusion. Another and equally important source of confusion is the difference between what we might call 'bottom-up' and 'top-down' theories of equal opportunity. Bottom-up theories focus in the first place on how individual employers should make decisions about who gets jobs. Top-down theories, by contrast, start from some view about what the overall distribution[3] of jobs, or job prospects, should look like. When we talk about equal opportunity, we tend to shuttle between these two quite different ways of thinking. Consider, for example, the demand for equal opportunity in regard to race. Sometimes this demand relates to the way employers are perceived to treat black applicants; at other times it relates to how black applicants are faring in general—which is of course affected by how employers are treating them, but is also affected by a large number of other factors. Even those of us who realize that these are two quite different ways of approaching the issue of race nevertheless tend to think it doesn't matter. We assume that we will end up in the same place whichever end we start—that is, whether we start at the micro level, thinking about how each individual decision should be made, or whether we start at the macro level, thinking about what we want the resulting pattern to look like. But this is not quite right. It is true that whichever end we start, whatever we say will have implications for the other end as well. Any theory which applies in the first place to how employers should make decisions will have implications for what the overall distribution of jobs will look like; and any theory which tells us what the overall distribution of jobs should look like will usually require us to change the way employers make decisions in order to arrive at the desired distribution. But this doesn't mean it makes no difference which end we start. Consider the thought that things like race or sex should be irrelevant when it comes to getting a job. If we took the bottom-up approach, we would understand this to mean that employers should not actually make decisions on grounds of race or sex; whereas if we took the top-down approach, we might understand it to mean that the overall distribution of jobs or job prospects should not be *correlated* with race or sex. The second is a far more demanding view, since the overall distribution of jobs or job prospects could be correlated with race or sex for all sorts of reasons besides through employers actually making decisions on racial or sexual grounds.

To take another example, consider next the idea of equality: again, if we are applying this to jobs, it makes a difference which end we start. If we accept not only that there will never be enough jobs to go round, but also that some jobs will always be better than others, we might think that the only way to treat everyone equally would be to give everyone an equal chance of getting any job. But in fact even the most fervent egalitarians would accept that there are some jobs which can't be done by just anyone. (Would you really want just *anyone*—never mind their unsteady hands, or psychotic tendencies—to have an equal chance of becoming your dentist?) These limitations would not cancel each other out: there will be some people who are capable of doing almost any job, and others who are capable of doing very few. If we persisted with a bottom-up egalitarianism —arguing, in relation to each particular job, that everyone who wanted it and was capable of doing it should have an equal chance of getting it—that would not translate into everyone having an equal chance overall. Indeed, if we are talking about people's *overall* prospects—factoring in what kind of job they end up with—then this first inequality, the fact that while some people are capable of doing almost any job, others are capable of doing only a few, is exacerbated by a second inequality, the fact that the jobs which the latter group can do are generally the worst kind. So giving everyone an equal chance of getting any job they are capable of doing would leave the less qualified not just with less chance of ending up with a job, but with far less chance of ending up with a good job. If by contrast we start with a top-down approach, the picture is very different. If we start from the idea that everyone's overall prospects should be equal, it will be clear that we should weight people's claims on each particular job according to the quantity and quality of the other options open to them. (Of course, even this would not produce perfect equality, since people differ in what kinds of jobs they *want*, as well as in what kinds they are fit for, but even top-down egalitarians tend to think that this is one inequality we aren't obliged to compensate people for.)[4]

Perhaps the one view where it doesn't seem to matter which end we start is meritocracy. If we start by thinking about how employers make decisions, saying that they should make them on merit, we seem to end up in pretty much the same position as if we had started by thinking about the big picture, about the desirability of having the overall distribution reflect people's relative merits. But even here, where there is no difference in end result between bottom-up and top-down approaches, we still need to bear in mind that there are two different routes to arriving at the same end result. When we come to assess the arguments for meritocracy, some of them might only make sense if we understand them as being motivated in the first place by thoughts about the big picture, and as having merely derivative implications about how employers should make their decisions; while with others the opposite might be true.

At this early stage my main aim is simply to clarify the difference between the top-down and bottom-up approaches. It should be clear from what I said in Section 1 that I am not interested in getting involved in an argument about which of them is the *right* approach, at least not in the sense of the right way to understand equality of opportunity; as for the wider question of whether one of them is just the right approach, full stop, I don't think this is something we can decide in advance. However, it is worth saying something here about the differing assumptions which are implied by these two ways of approaching the question. The top-down approach, which starts by asking *What should the overall distribution of jobs look like?*, seems to imply that we can think of jobs as if they are sitting there in a big pile waiting for us to decide how they ought to be distributed. If we take the bottom-up approach, we are more likely to think about the way jobs are actually allocated—by real people making decisions about who is going to work with them or for them. We are then more likely to wonder whether there might not be very good reasons for leaving people free to make these decisions for themselves. By contrast, on the top-down approach, which encourages us to think of jobs as if they are sitting there in a big pile waiting to be distributed, there is a tendency to see decisions about jobs exclusively from the point of view of the applicants, and to forget about the employers altogether. Now, I have said that I am not interested in arguing in advance about which of these two approaches is the right one. But I will say this. In a liberal state, there has to be a general presumption in favour of leaving people free to make their own decisions, and this presumption doesn't simply disappear when we switch from, for example, thinking about an applicant making a decision about which jobs to apply for, to thinking about an employer making a decision about which applicant to hire. In both cases people will sometimes make decisions in the wrong way, or simply make the wrong decisions, but none the less there are good reasons why we should leave them free to make these mistakes. It is true that in the applicant's case there is more of a sense that the decision affects him alone; but this doesn't mean that the argument for freedom is completely absent in the other case. We must have *some* degree of respect for people's freedom to make decisions about who is going to work with them or under them, even if the case is not quite so clear-cut as when we are talking about their freedom to decide what kind of work they want to do. If we are tempted by a top-down approach, we need to be careful that it does not lead us to forget this basic point.

Moreover, to the extent that there is any real division between left and right over equality of opportunity, this is where it lies: it is not that the left believe in equality while the right believe in meritocracy (since, as I have said, if you are the kind of person who believes in either, you probably believe in both), but that the left assume that there must be *some* kind of overall distribution or pattern which the state should be trying to impose here, whereas the right are much more sceptical about the desirability of imposing anything on anybody.[5] On this particular division, I side with the right. I don't think we can simply *assume* that there is some grand social aim at stake here—especially if we are not yet sure exactly what it is. And we should certainly not allow this assumption to obscure the genuine questions which the right raise about the extent to which the state can legitimately interfere with the way individual people—whether employers or employees or anyone else—make their decisions. We should not set up the debate as if there is no one who has any prior claim as to how jobs should be allocated, in advance of some impartial discussion of how they *ought* to be allocated. So long as we intend to persist with anything resembling a market economy (and the equal opportunity debate better had make this assumption, if it wants to keep people interested), the owners of private sector companies must be in *some* kind of privileged position when it comes to deciding who gets jobs in those companies—even if ultimately we decide that they do not have the right to hire just whoever they want.

2.3. *The libertarian objection*

There is a further argument, besides the simple appeal to freedom, which tells against talking about jobs as if they were sitting there in a big pile waiting for us to decide how they ought to be distributed. This is that a private sector employer has some kind of *property* right over jobs in his company: since he is the one who is going to pay the wages, his right to hire as he sees fit is just an example of his more general right to spend his money as he sees fit. This right is not merely different from the right to freedom discussed in the last section: the two rights are often held by different people. In large companies, for example, the right to freedom, in deciding who is going to work with you or for you, is held by the managers; whereas the property rights are held by the owners or shareholders. It is then a nice question how these two different kinds of right should be balanced. However, I am going to ignore this complication, because I am interested in the question of where the *state* fits in to the picture. From this point of view, all we need to know is that there are two different reasons against intervening. The first arises from the need to respect people's freedom to make their own decisions about who is going to work with them or for them, and the second arises from the need to respect property rights. From the state's point of view it does not matter whether these rights are held by different people, nor, if they are, how they should be balanced—to what extent the shareholders should respect the managers' freedom to hire as they see fit, or vice versa. The important thing from the state's point of view is simply that any argument for intervention will have to be strong enough to defeat both kinds of right.

Unlike some people, I think we need to take the idea of property rights seriously here. This might not seem all that surprising, given that I have already declared my sympathy with the right over its concern for freedom: after all, the appeal to property rights is generally also associated with the right. However, I should make clear that I am not suggesting that we simply give in to all the right's concerns; I am only suggesting that we have to take them seriously. In fact, the property rights argument does have obvious limitations. The first is that it does not apply at all to public sector jobs. The wages of public sector employees are paid for out of public funds, so if we are to speak of property rights in this area, those rights must belong to society as a whole; in which case it is perfectly proper to talk about public sector jobs as if they were sitting there waiting for us to decide how they should be distributed. (Or at least, this is perfectly proper as far as property rights are concerned: we still need to appreciate that public sector managers retain the other, non-property-based right, the right to have some freedom over who is going to work with them or under them.) But to point out this limitation hardly counts as pointing out a *weakness* in the property rights argument. Libertarians, for example, would not deny that the argument doesn't apply to public sector jobs. They just aren't interested in the public sector—other than to argue that there shouldn't be one, or at least that it should be as small as possible.

A more serious limitation is that the property rights objection only really applies to those theories of equal opportunity which are fully determining—in other words, those which would completely specify how every decision should be made (if we are talking about a bottom-up theory) or what the overall distribution should look like (if we are talking about a top-down theory). The view that everyone should have an equal chance of getting every job, for example, is such a view. But not many theories of equal opportunity are like this: most seek only to *restrict* employers' freedom, rather than removing it entirely.

Of course, libertarians tend to object to these theories too; but it is more difficult to accuse these theories of simply *ignoring* the employer's point of view. These theories are quite consistent with believing that employers have certain rights against interference. What the libertarians have to show is that these theories somehow don't fully appreciate the extent or stringency of those rights. The argument might run something like this. Employers' property rights over jobs, as we have seen, are just an example of their more general right to spend their money as they see fit. Now, according to the libertarian, the only legitimate restriction we can place on the way people spend their money is to require that they not spend it in a way that violates anyone else's rights. In the present case, *at most* this allows us to require that employers not discriminate against people on the basis of things like race or sex.[6] It certainly does not allow us to require employers to do anything positive to *help* the disadvantaged.

This is exactly the same kind of argument which the libertarian uses against redistributive taxation. According to the libertarian, people should be free to spend their money however they see fit, provided they don't use it to violate other people's rights; we cannot justify spending their money on their behalf, for example, by using redistributive taxation to help the poor, since this is not a matter of preventing them violating other people's rights. It is a matter of providing positive aid, which is something we cannot legitimately force people to do. The only way of justifying redistributive taxation would be to say, first, that we all have a positive duty towards the poor—a duty to help them, rather than merely not to harm them—and second, that the state has the right to force us to fulfil this duty, rather than simply leaving it up to us. On the libertarian view, positive duties are unenforceable: the only kind of duty that can legitimately be enforced is the negative kind, the duty not to interfere with others or actively cause them harm.[7]

How should we respond to this? If we want to preserve the possibility of intervention, either we could try to argue that although the libertarian is right about redistributive taxation, he is wrong about equal opportunity, because the two are not in fact properly analogous; or we could try to show that he is wrong about both. I favour the second line of response. I have already said that I think the libertarian is right to point out the analogy between the two cases—that private sector employers have property rights over jobs, analogous to the right that any private individual has to spend his money as he sees fit. In particular, I agree that there is no point in insisting that jobs are different simply because they are somehow a 'public' matter. This just begs the question, until we are provided with an account of exactly what this difference is between 'public' and 'private'. (In deciding who to hire, an employer is deciding how to spend his money, and this makes it in one sense a private matter. At the same time, his decision will affect other people, and so is in another sense public; but this is true of almost all decisions, many of which we would regard as definitively 'private', such as decisions about who you spend your time with.) But we can agree with the libertarian that private sector employers have property rights over jobs, without agreeing with him about what *follows* from this; that is, without agreeing that this means we cannot legitimately restrict employers' behaviour in any way, other than to prevent them actively violating the rights of job applicants. Indeed, if we don't accept the analogous implications in the sphere of redistributive taxation—that is, if we don't accept that we cannot tax the rich simply on the basis that they have certain positive duties to the rest of society, duties which we can legitimately force them to fulfil—then there is no reason to accept the same implications in the sphere of employment.

Libertarians tend to react to this move by arguing that if we don't want to accept the *implications* of property rights—if we assert that the state has the right to take people's money off them and spend it on their behalf, or has the right to tell the owners of private sector companies how to make decisions—then we have to admit that what we are really doing is attacking the very idea of private property. But this is wrong in both cases: placing certain restrictions on property rights, like taking a certain proportion of people's money off them, is not the same as attacking the very idea of private property. Consider the following example. At the moment, if you own a house of outstanding beauty or architectural or historical significance, there are restrictions on what you can do with it. You cannot simply build a neo-Victorian conservatory on the back of it. This kind of restriction is clearly not based on the idea that, if you did build a neo-Victorian conservatory on the back of it, you would be violating any particular person's rights. There is no one who *individually* has the right that you not build a neo-Victorian conservatory on the back of your house. Nevertheless, you do not have the right to do so. You have certain duties to society as a whole, and these duties place limitations on your property rights. But we would not naturally say that because of this you don't really *own* your house after all.

Of course, at this point it is possible to run a slippery slope argument: to argue that we can't keep chipping away at property rights without *at some point* threatening to undermine the very idea of private property. Suppose we elected a truly left-wing government, and it decided that people shouldn't be allowed to buy educational advantage for their children, to buy their way to the front of the queue for medical treatment, and so on. If it kept on adding to the list of things we weren't allowed to do, would there not come a point at which we would start to wonder whether there was any point in having money, if we couldn't use it to buy anything that really mattered to us? There are two ways of responding to this kind of argument. The conciliatory way is to say that although there might indeed be a slippery slope somewhere here, we don't need to worry about it just yet, since there is a long way to go before we even come close to threatening the idea of private property. The aggressive way, by contrast, is to say that so long as there is a good reason for each successive restriction on what we can do with our money, then if it should turn out that, taken together, the restrictions ultimately threaten the very idea of private property, so much the worse for private property. Now, the kind of person who worries about slippery slope arguments will probably prefer the aggressive response—

taking a stand while he still can—but in fact this is not ideal for our purposes in the present context. The aggressive response would cause this particular debate, which started as a relatively narrow debate about the way private sector jobs should be allocated, to spill over into a much wider debate about whether there should even *be* a private sector. I have already suggested that tactically speaking this would be a mistake. Moreover, the conciliatory response is in fact more than adequate for our purposes, since the slippery slope argument is especially weak in this particular case. Even if the owner of a private sector company had his freedom to hire *completely* removed, he would remain free to change other things about the company, free to spend the money he made from owning it, and indeed free to sell it if he so wished. In other words, even if he had his freedom to hire completely removed, this wouldn't threaten the point of owning the company. Given that most theories of equal opportunity don't in fact require the complete removal of employers' freedom to hire, but merely that certain restrictions be placed on that freedom, it is doubly hard to present these theories as in effect being a surreptitious attack on the very idea of private enterprise.

It seems that we can dismiss the libertarian objection, that the only legitimate reason for constraining private sector employers' free exercise of their property rights is to prevent them violating the rights of other people. Just as we tax the rich on the basis that they have certain positive duties to society, so we can, if we so decide, regulate the way employers hire, simply on the basis that they have certain positive duties to society. I don't mean to prejudge the issue here: it remains to be seen whether the various different arguments for regulation are in fact any good. It is the libertarian who prejudges the issue, by stipulating that only one particular *kind* of argument for regulation could ever succeed. I have tried to show why this is a mistake. For those who are not satisfied by the attempt, I attempt a fuller treatment of the libertarian position later on in the book, in Part 3.

2.4. *Direct and indirect intervention*

I have been talking about the difficulties of justifying intervening in the way employers make decisions, especially in the private sector. But there is an alternative: we could try to pursue whatever aims we have in this area *indirectly*—that is, without actually intervening in the way employers make decisions. Suppose we wanted to promote equality. Rather than demanding that employers actually allocate jobs in a way that gives every applicant an equal chance, we could try to adjust the background conditions in such a way that there is some *earlier* point in everyone's life at which they have an equal chance. For example, we could look at the types of people (in terms of race, family background, geography, etc.) who currently tend to do well or badly in the competition for jobs, and shift the balance of educational resources towards those types who currently tend to do badly. This would move us closer to equality of prospects—with the proviso that this equality would apply at the point when people entered the education system rather than at the point when they actually applied for a job.

If on the other hand we wanted to promote merit rather than equality, again we could do this indirectly: instead of requiring that the best person always be given the job, we could simply concentrate on creating the background conditions in which merit will thrive, and rely on the fact that employers will generally hire the best person voluntarily.

It is sometimes argued that this kind of indirect approach is in fact the only acceptable approach. Suppose, for example, we believe in equality—specifically, suppose we believe that everyone has the right to an equal 'life chance'. Even if this is true, it is surely not something anyone has a specific claim on *employers* to bring about; it is a claim on society as a whole, rather than on employers in particular. In which case, in responding to such claims, should we not restrict ourselves to measures that place the burden on society as a whole, rather than placing a disproportionate share on employers? Instead of interfering in the way employers make decisions, we should focus on the background conditions—that is, on rectifying the educational and social inequalities that cause some kinds of applicant to have better chances than others. These educational and social initiatives would be paid for out of tax revenue, thereby spreading the burden more evenly across society as a whole.

This, at least, is what employers will try to argue. But it is not, however, a convincing argument. It simply does not follow that, unless applicants have a specific claim against employers, it is wrong or unfair for employers to bear the principal cost of helping them. It is a perfectly general point that the burden of satisfying a given moral claim can fall disproportionately on a particular person or group simply because they happen to be in a position to do something about it. Indeed, consider what the contrary position would mean in certain other contexts. Again, take the example of redistributive taxation. We would have to think, for example, that even though it is a terrible shame that people are starving, that fact alone cannot justify enforced redistribution; we must ask whether they are starving because they have been unjustly treated, and if so, we must find the perpetrators, since they alone can be forced to pay. This is absurd. It is quite proper for the well off to be forced to help the badly off. It may be that the well off are in fact guilty of treating the badly off unfairly—through some kind of economic exploitation, for example—but this is surely irrelevant. The burden falls on the well off simply because they happen to be able to pay, not because independently of that they have any more reason to pay than anyone else does. Similarly, even if we do think the right to equal opportunity is just an abstract right, rather than a right specifically against employers, there is no reason to feel that we cannot intervene directly in the way employers make decisions. (In fact, it should by now be clear that there is something inconsistent in saying we should restrict ourselves to intervening indirectly, if that means restricting ourselves to pursuing our aims through social and educational measures paid for out of tax revenue. The inconsistency lies in the fact that, as we have implicitly seen, any income-based or wealth-based tax would run up against exactly the same objection. The well off pay more, simply because they can afford to pay more, not because independently of that they have any more reason to pay.)

I am not saying that the right to equal opportunity *is* an abstract right; I am merely arguing that even if it were, this would not restrict us in terms of how we can act on it. But equally, on many theories of equal opportunity, it is clearly not just an abstract right: it is a specific right to be treated in a certain way when you apply for a job. This is what I earlier described as a bottom-up theory. The clearest example is the view that people should not be discriminated against, when it comes to getting a job, on the basis of things like race or sex. It is true that even this kind of bottom-up theory could still be implemented in an indirect way, if that was what we wanted to do. If we used education and social policy to try to stamp out racism, so that future generations of employers would be less likely to have the prejudices let alone to act on them, then fewer applicants would end up being discriminated against, without our ever having had to interfere in the way employers made their decisions. But it is fair to say that few anti-discrimination campaigners would think of choosing this kind of indirect approach as an *alternative* to the direct, interventionist approach. They would argue that the two should be pursued in parallel. Since their view is, in the first place, a view about how individual applicants should be treated, they naturally assume that if their view is sound, then of course it will justify intervening directly in the way applicants are treated. It is the top-down theorists who are more likely to be tempted to rely exclusively on the indirect approach. But I have tried to show that even in their case, there is no principled reason why they have to do so.

2.5. *The scope of the debate*

The contrasts I have just outlined—between top-down and bottom-up theories, and direct and indirect approaches—will be useful in keeping track of the various views discussed in the rest of the book. For now, there is one last thing I want to say about the background to the debate, before I move on to give a brief outline of the book as a whole. What I want to say concerns the *scope* of the debate. These days, people talk about equality of opportunity in relation to all sorts of things: not just jobs, but education, health, standards of living, and so on. There are two possibilities here. Either they understand 'equality of opportunity' to refer to a general principle of distributive justice[8] which can be applied to other things besides jobs; or else they take it to apply specifically to jobs, but in a way that has implications for other, related things. For example, when people talk about equality of opportunity in relation to education, the idea might be that places at good schools or universities are sufficiently analogous to jobs for us to expect the same distributive principle to apply; or else the idea might be that since a person's education affects their job prospects, then if we are pursuing a certain ideal in the sphere of jobs, we will need to think about what we can do in related spheres, such as education, to support that pursuit. (For example, if we are trying to ensure that children from different backgrounds have equal job prospects, we will need to think about how children's job prospects are affected by their chances of getting in to a good school or university.) Similarly, when people talk about equality of opportunity in relation to health, the idea might be that we should think about health in the same way we think about jobs, saying that people should have an equal opportunity to live a healthy life;[9] or else the idea might be that equality of opportunity applies specifically to jobs, but that equality of opportunity in relation to jobs requires, among other things, that everyone enjoy a certain level of health.

My position here is the same as on the difference between top-down and bottom-up approaches. I am not interested in getting involved in an argument about which of these two ways of bringing things like education and health into the debate is the *right* way—at least not in the sense of the right way of understanding equality of opportunity. Clearly it is worth thinking about education and health in both ways. That is, we should think about education and health *both* in terms of their impact on job prospects *and* as goods in their own right—and when we consider them as goods in their own right, they do seem to present many of the same problems as jobs. For example, there is exactly the same need to reconcile, on the one hand, the claims to fair treatment on the part of the individuals who are competing for scarce positions or resources, and, on the other, the interests that society has in these positions or resources being allocated in ways that are efficient rather than necessarily fair. Given this similarity in the overall structure of the problem, of course it will be worth asking whether the principles we end up applying to jobs should also be extended to health and education. But equally, given that these other contexts are merely similar rather than identical, we cannot assume, purely because we decide against a certain principle in the sphere of jobs, that this principle can be ruled out in all other spheres as well. For example, we might decide against meritocracy in the sphere of jobs, but persist with it in the sphere of education; or we might decide against equality in the sphere of jobs, but persist with it in the sphere of health; and so on.

In the course of what follows, I return several times to these parallels between jobs and health and education, but without ever attempting anything like a systematic treatment of health and education in their own right. Issues of health and education therefore play an essentially subsidiary role in the discussion, considered more in terms of their effects on job prospects than as interesting subjects in their own right. But I want to make clear that in approaching these subjects in this way, I am not trying to say that work is the most important thing in our lives, and that everything else, including our health and education, should be made subservient to it. In either case this would be a terrible thing to believe. It just so happens that jobs, and not health or education, are the primary subject of this particular book.

3. AN OUTLINE OF THE ARGUMENT

So much for preliminaries. The real argument begins, in Part 1, with the view that the best person should always get the job—the view I call 'meritocracy'. Before I outline the argument of this part of the book, I should deal first with one possible objection to even discussing meritocracy in a book of this kind. The objection is that there is no point in arguing either for or against meritocracy—it is just a fact of life. Any employer who doesn't hire on merit will go out of business, so there is no need to *tell* them to hire on merit. I hope it will be obvious that this is too simplistic. First, because not all employers operate in a competitive market—even if we disregard public sector jobs. And second, because even those employers who do operate in a competitive market wouldn't necessarily be driven out of business if they failed to hire on merit. Not many markets are quite that competitive. So meritocracy is not inevitable: like all the other theories, it is something we can support or impose if that is what we decide to do. The question is whether we should.

I have chosen to treat meritocracy first because it seems to be the default position. People who wouldn't consider themselves remotely political or ideological turn out to believe in meritocracy; indeed, its hold is such that even people whose ultimate values seem to be quite at odds with its basic premise nevertheless seem to accept that their values have to be fitted in around it. For example, we might have expected egalitarians to be opposed to meritocracy, since egalitarianism emphasizes that we are all *equal*, whereas meritocracy is all about finding out who is the *best*. But many egalitarians clearly feel they can only argue for equality as an adjunct to meritocracy. They understand meritocracy to imply some kind of competition, so their egalitarianism takes the form of arguing that everyone should start the competition in an equal position, or should have an equal chance of winning. Or consider the kind of person who doesn't really have any kind of positive view about how jobs ought to be allocated, but who thinks that things like race or sex definitely should not matter when it comes to getting a job. This kind of person often ends up being persuaded, or persuading himself, that if he is so sure that race or sex should *not* matter, this must after all reveal some deeper belief about what *should* matter—in other words, a deeper belief in some kind of meritocracy.

Anyway, for whatever reason, most people seem to assume that meritocracy must be at least part of the answer to the question of how jobs should be allocated. My aim is to loosen this grip that meritocracy has on the debate. I argue, first, that hiring on merit has more to do with efficiency than fairness, and second, that assuming we are conceding that employers have at least some rights in this area, it is difficult to see how these rights could be overridden by considerations of mere efficiency. In the face of this argument, most meritocrats will, I think, choose to stand and fight on the first point rather than the second—that is, they will deny that meritocracy is nothing to do with fairness. In their favour, we certainly don't *feel* it is just a question of efficiency if we are rejected on grounds other than merit—we feel it is unfair. But I argue that this is simply because we have come to have certain expectations, and think we have a right that these expectations not be disappointed; or else it is because we are guilty of confusing one idea that it is unfair to be rejected on any grounds other than merit, with the quite different and much more limited idea of non-discrimination—that is, the idea that it is unfair to be rejected on grounds of something like race or sex. In either case we are making a mistake, since neither expectations nor non-discrimination actually supports meritocracy.

The issue of expectations is a complicated one, but in simple terms my position is as follows. If employers generally hire on merit, then people will come to expect that they will continue to hire on merit, and will be disappointed if this doesn't happen; but it is unclear what moral weight should be given to this sense of disappointment. Given that people's expectations are in part determined simply by how things currently are, if we accord them too much weight, we will just be privileging the status quo. Why not instead go to the other extreme—starting with a blank sheet of paper, asking what the ideal system would look like, and only then thinking about how best to manage people's expectations in getting there? I am not suggesting that this 'blank sheet of paper' approach is always the right one. (I argued earlier that if the equal opportunity debate is to hold people's interest, it needs to stay self-contained, which means making certain assumptions, such as the continued presence of some kind of market economy.) But on the specific issue of expectations, the 'blank sheet of paper' approach does seem to be the right one—especially as there are ways of taking people's expectations into account without simply giving in to them. We could treat expectations not as inputs to first-order questions—questions about how society should be organized—but rather as inputs to second-order questions—questions about when, and how quickly, any necessary changes should be made.

As for the relation between meritocracy and non-discrimination (the second possible explanation of why merit is linked in people's minds with fairness), the situation here is that although meritocracy entails non-discrimination, non-discrimination does not entail meritocracy. And even the fact that meritocracy entails non-discrimination is not all that significant: requiring employers to hire on merit is merely one way of making sure they don't discriminate on the basis of things like race or sex, not the only possible way. Another would be to introduce specific principles forbidding all the different kinds of discrimination we decide are unfair. It is true that, of these two, meritocracy would be the simpler, using a single principle to explain why all these different kinds of discrimination should be ruled out; but to prefer it on that basis alone would suggest a wholly misplaced desire for theoretical neatness.

So I reject the idea that employers should be legally obliged to hire the best person. It is a separate question, as I indicated earlier, whether we should try to further the cause of merit in less direct ways, by creating the background conditions in which merit can thrive, and then leaving it up to employers whether they take advantage of that. Now, there are two ways of understanding this indirect kind of meritocracy. On the first, the promotion of merit should be the sole objective of educational and social policy. According to this view, the *only* reason for making sure, for example, that everyone gets a decent education, is so that we can then be confident that it really is the best people who are getting the jobs. But this must be wrong: indeed, once again it probably rests on a misplaced desire for theoretical simplicity. This leaves the more moderate view, the view that the promotion of merit is merely *one* of the things we should be trying to do in education, social policy, and so on. This is the view I discuss later in Part 1—though I discuss it only briefly. In the end, this just isn't the way most meritocrats understand meritocracy. Like anti-discrimination campaigners, meritocrats tend to advocate the indirect pursuit of their aims, but only in the sense that they think the state should be promoting their aims indirectly *as well as* directly. They tend to think of meritocracy first and foremost as a matter of being fair to applicants at the point when they apply for a job, and therefore as something that should be enforced directly. This is the kind of meritocracy I oppose—and this is one of the main reasons I describe myself as being 'against' equality of opportunity. As I have repeatedly emphasized, most people think meritocracy must be at least part of what is meant by 'equality of opportunity', and they think equality of opportunity is about being fair to applicants; so they conclude that meritocracy is about being fair to applicants—and therefore the kind of thing that warrants direct state intervention. It is this supposed connection, between meritocracy and fairness, and the consequent belief in direct intervention, that I reject.

I turn next, in Part 2, to the second of the two ideas that dominate contemporary thinking in this area: the idea of equality. It is true that equality doesn't have quite the universal appeal that meritocracy enjoys. Indeed, in the UK at least, it almost disappeared from mainstream political debate for the ten years between the mid-1980s and the mid-1990s. But it now appears to be on the way back.[10] And if it is on the way back as far as *politics* is concerned, as far as academic philosophy is concerned it never really went away—in large part because of the continuing influence of John Rawls's egalitarian masterpiece, *A Theory of Justice*.[11] For my part, I have tried to pick the best egalitarian arguments from both politics and academic philosophy. This means, of course, that I cannot claim to offer a truly comprehensive survey. But one of the problems in trying to bring any kind of shape to the discussion is the fact that the idea of equality enters the debate in such a confusing variety of ways and places. For example, there is the question of whether everyone should enjoy the same opportunities, or should start in the same position, or should literally have an equal chance of success. Besides this, there is the fact—which I mentioned earlier—that all three types of egalitarian often seem confused about whether their chosen form of equality is supposed to be desirable in itself, or merely a prerequisite of fair competition (the 'level playing-field').

I begin Part 2 by discussing the latter kind of view—the kind of view that sees equality as subsidiary to the idea of competition. But most of Part 2 is devoted to the kind of egalitarianism that actually *starts* from a belief in equality, rather than bringing it in at a later stage in the argument. Among those views which actually start from a belief in equality, the most promising, at least in the abstract, are those which start not from the idea that we are all equal in terms of some property we each separately possess, but from the idea that our equality consists in our relations with one another; in other words, from the idea that we are all partners in a common enterprise. I argue that this is the kind of argument we have in mind when we say, for example, that everyone should have an equal vote. It turns out, however, that there are two distinct problems with trying to transfer this kind of argument to the sphere of jobs. First, it is not clear that the argument can be transferred from a political context to an economic context. Second, even if we thought it could make this leap, and we took this to mean that everyone had an equal claim on all the benefits of a modern market economy, including the benefits of having a decently paid and minimally satisfying job, we would come up against the further problem that equality in this area just doesn't seem to be possible. That is, it just doesn't seem possible for everyone to have a job—certainly not for everyone to have an equally good job. Of course, this is exactly why egalitarians end up arguing that everyone should have an equal opportunity, or an equal chance. But the problem is that this kind of equality—everyone having an equal opportunity or chance *to become unequal*—doesn't seem like a very good way of expressing the idea that we are all in some sense partners in a common enterprise.

For these reasons, then, I reject the idea of equality. It is worth emphasizing the stark nature of my position here. Many people disagree with egalitarianism only in that they think equality isn't the *only* thing that is important. They think it must sometimes be sacrificed to other aims. My position is much stronger than this: I argue, for the reasons outlined above, that equality just isn't something we should be pursuing *at all* in this area, either on its own or in combination with other values. As I said earlier, it is because I reject both equality and meritocracy that I have called the book *Against Equality of Opportunity*. These two ideas, or some combination of the two, are central to most people's understanding of equality of opportunity. However, it is also true, as I made clear in Section 1, that not everyone shares this understanding. For some, equality of opportunity does seem to mean only that people shouldn't be discriminated against on the basis of things like race or sex. I have already explained that I am not opposed to this more limited idea. But I think it is fair to say that relatively few people think of equality of opportunity as meaning *only* this, which is why I feel justified in calling the book *Against Equality of Opportunity*. It is true that almost everyone associates equality of opportunity with non-discrimination, but they think of non-discrimination as *part* of equality of opportunity, rather than the whole thing. Indeed, for those who believe in equality, or meritocracy, or both, non-discrimination is just a logical entailment of their more fundamental position: discrimination is wrong *because* it fails to treat people equally, or because it prevents the best person getting the job.

This is, I suppose, the main way in which my view of non-discrimination differs from the standard view. The standard view simply subsumes non-discrimination under some more general theory of equal opportunity, whereas I argue that we need to treat it as a separate issue. You might think—of course I am going to say this, given that I oppose meritocracy and equality. But the reason we need to treat non-discrimination separately is not just because the more general theories of equal opportunity happen to be wrong. Consider an employer who refuses to give jobs to black applicants because he thinks they are mentally or morally inferior. Saying that this is wrong because he is failing to treat them equally, or failing to treat them according to their merits, does not capture what is *distinctively* wrong with it. It makes his behaviour look the same as any other way of treating people unequally, or non-meritocratically, when in fact even egalitarians and meritocrats reserve a special anger or distaste for discrimination. It is this idea, that discrimination is somehow especially wrong, which I explore in Part 3.

No doubt some readers will be wondering whether *from a practical point of view* this third part of the book really needed writing. If we all agree that discrimination is wrong, do we really need to ask *why* it is wrong? Isn't this the kind of question that only a philosopher would waste his time asking? I don't think so. Different answers to the question of why discrimination is wrong will imply different things for borderline cases—for example, the kind of case where an employer discriminates against black applicants not because he thinks they are inferior people, but because he thinks they tend to be less good at the job. Similarly, different ways of understanding why discrimination is wrong will imply different things when it comes to extending our account to less familiar *contexts*. For example, even if we all agree that it is wrong for employers to discriminate on grounds of race, what about people who discriminate on grounds of race in their choice of friends? Some think this is just the same; others think that although it is equally wrong from a moral point of view, it is not the kind of thing the state should get involved in; others think it is not the same kind of thing at all. In order to decide which of these attitudes is the right one we need to start by thinking about exactly why we object to discrimination in the more familiar context of jobs.

So although at first discrimination might seem like a fairly tired subject for discussion, in fact there are many questions we still need to address, and Part 3 of the book represents my attempt to address them. First, I offer my own explanation of what makes discrimination wrong (when it is wrong): I argue that it is wrong because it involves treating people with contempt, when that is not deserved. I then explore the implications of this view. For example, there are ways of discriminating between people on grounds of race or sex which do not express contempt; if my first point is right, then we should try to separate these kinds of discrimination from the kinds that do express contempt, and treat them differently. (I realize that, to some people, to suggest that certain kinds of discrimination are not necessarily wrong will seem like a contradiction in terms. But these are probably the same people who don't even see the point of asking why discrimination is wrong in the first place. Given that they don't really want to have the debate, it will be no surprise if they don't like the conclusions either.)

The discussion of this alternative approach to discrimination brings the book to a close. To sum up, then, my overall position is roughly this: meritocracy might be rational, but cannot legitimately be imposed on people; equality just isn't something we should be pursuing in this area; and non-discrimination, though definitely something we should be pursuing, should be interpreted more narrowly than it generally is. Now, I can imagine some readers reaching this point and asking: *is that it?* To which I will say two things. First, even if this was the whole answer, we couldn't assume it was wrong purely because it was so limited. Second, I am not in fact saying that it is the whole answer. There *is* something positive we should be doing, besides non-discrimination—only it has nothing to do with either equality or merit. What we should be doing is trying to make sure that no one is left without hope—or, to put it another way, to make sure that no one is left in a position where there is nothing they can do to change their life for the better. Again, I can imagine an impatient reader wondering—did we really need a philosopher to tell us something as obvious as this? But I am not embarrassed about being reduced to saying the obvious. There are philosophers who would rather say something interesting and wrong than something boring and right, but I am not one of them. I never expected I would need to persuade anyone of the *appeal* of this idea—the idea that no one should be left in a position where there is nothing they can do to change their life for the better. I agree that its appeal is obvious. In fact, trying to explain its appeal, trying to reduce it to something more fundamental, might actually be counter-productive. It might be one of those ideas, like 'eating people is wrong', which is more persuasive than any general principle one might offer in its support. Anyway, I am not going to try to explain its appeal here. All I hope to do is, first, to disentangle it from any associations with meritocracy and equality; and second, to warn that even after it has been disentangled we must be careful not to take it in the wrong direction.

Take meritocracy first. When people say they believe in meritocracy, often it is this idea they really have in mind—that it is a shame for so much talent to go to waste through lack of opportunity—rather than some fully worked-out picture of a society in which every position or reward is decided on the basis of merit. People sign up to meritocracy because they think it follows from thinking that talent should not go to waste, when in fact it does not follow. Meritocracy has much wider implications, and needs a good deal more argument. (It seeks to regulate every hiring decision, whereas the idea that talent should not go to waste does not—at least not so long as 'waste' is understood in an absolute sense.)[12] Something similar happens with equality. People say they are against inequality, but often what really bothers them is simply that people are left without any real hope at all—a thought that concerns people's *absolute* rather than *relative* position. What bothers them is the fact that some people are so *badly* off while others are so *well* off.[13] This is quite different from being upset by the mere fact that some are better off than others: what they object to is not so much the gap between the better and worse off as the absolute position of each.

The first thing, then, is simply to separate all these ideas. Until this separation is achieved, meritocracy and equality will continue to attract support from people who really believe in the less demanding idea that no one should be left without hope. The second thing, as I said, is to make sure that if we decide to go with this less demanding idea, we take it in the right direction. What this idea is saying is that it is a good thing for people to have some control over their lives—to see their lives as stories they help construct, stories whose evolving shape reflects, among other things, the good and bad choices they make along the way. (This is, I think, the basic idea underlying the liberal belief in freedom.) The alternative is for people to see their lives as something that just *happens* to them, which seems hopelessly limiting. Of course, not everyone will agree with this. Some will think there is no point in saying that people ought to take control of their lives, since in fact no one can really be said to control anything—certainly not in the sense of being truly *responsible* for it. The reason people think this is usually because they think that everything that ever happens, including human thoughts and behaviour, is predetermined by prior events, and they take this predetermination to be incompatible with anyone's being responsible for anything. Evidently I disagree with some part of this argument, since I think it does make sense to talk about people being in control of things, and about the moral significance of their being in control. But the issue of moral responsibility is a notoriously intractable one, and I don't pretend to make any significant contribution to it here. I am just concerned to clarify the assumptions behind my view, and to register that not everyone shares them. The first point, then, is that some people will disagree with my view because they disagree with the very idea that people have any real control over their lives, at least in the sense of being responsible for what happens to them. But perhaps the more interesting point of disagreement is with those who *do* believe in the idea of control or responsibility, but who develop this idea in a different direction. The direction I am suggesting is to say that since it is a good thing for people to have some control over their lives, the state should try to make sure that as many people as possible are in this position. The direction that most of contemporary political philosophy takes, by contrast, is to say that the state should try to make sure that people's prospects depend *only* on what they can control. While my view is a fundamentally *positive* view, this other view is fundamentally negative. My view says simply that people's lives should be to some extent under their control. The other view says that people's lives should *not* be affected by anything that is *not* under their control.[14]

What is wrong with this other view? It implies that we should be trying to give people *complete* control over their lives. Perhaps some will think that this is no longer such an absurd thing to hope for. We know more about the world, and ourselves, than ever before. By combining this new-found knowledge with ever-increasing wealth and technological resources, perhaps we will finally succeed in bringing the world to heel. This certainly seems to be what many westerners are trying to do. We live in increasingly controlled environments; we spend vast sums, individually and collectively, on health care, in the hope that we will bring our health entirely under our control; we seek, again through health care and related industries, to control such things as mood, personality, and the having of children; we buy glossy magazines which tell us how to control our careers and relationships. And when something goes wrong, in any area of our lives, instead of simply accepting that sometimes things go wrong, we look around for someone to sue.

However, the underlying assumption—that we should be trying to bring every aspect of our lives entirely under our control—is really no less absurd now than it ever was. For most of us, the most important thing in our lives is the relationships we have with other people, and this is something we could never bring completely under our control, nor would we want to. It is of course a logical impossibility for *everyone* to bring their relationships completely under their control, given that they are having relationships with each other. But there is something more than logical possibility at stake here. If the problem was just one of logical possibility, that would imply that being unlucky in love is *just as unfair* as being unlucky in getting a job, and that the only difference is that nothing can be done about it. This is an implication which I suspect many contemporary political philosophers would be happy to embrace; but it cannot be right. If we really think about the possibility of being unlucky in love, we will realize that we don't even *want* things to be otherwise—we don't want to be unlucky, of course, but equally we don't want it to be *impossible* to be unlucky. We want to be lucky, rather than wanting this kind of bad luck to be removed from the world. Or at least, this is how I feel. Even supposing I could completely control my relationships—supposing, that is, I could completely control the desires and reactions of everyone I was involved with—this would be something I would despise to do, just as I despise the kind of person who only ever allows himself to become involved with people he can completely control, and pity the kind of person who, for the same kind of reason, avoids getting closely involved with anyone.

Of course, at this point anyone who has ever actually argued for the opposing view—that is, who has ever argued that people should not suffer because of things beyond their control—will object that they never intended this principle to be applied to personal life. The fact that it does not apply to every aspect of our lives, they will say, does not undermine its specific claim to apply to this one aspect of our lives, namely, our prospects of getting a job. In a sense this is true, though it strikes me as an advantage of my view (i.e. the positive view that we should try to give everyone some control over their lives) that it *does* seem to apply to every aspect of our lives, to personal life as much as working life. The onus is on the supporters of the negative view to come up with some explanation of why their principle applies in some areas but not others—and in particular, why it does not apply in what for most people is the most important area of their lives.

But even this is not the biggest problem for the negative view. The biggest problem concerns its underlying motivation. What both the positive and negative views aim to do is explain and reinforce the simple intuition I began with—the idea that no one should be left in a position where there is nothing they can do to improve their lives. I think the positive view succeeds in this, elaborating on the liberal idea that people should be able to see their lives as something they help construct, a story whose evolving shape reflects, among other things, the good and bad choices they make along the way. By contrast, the negative view is a failure. The idea that we should be trying to bring every aspect of people's lives under their control is not even *attractive*: far from explaining and reinforcing our initial feelings, it seems to leave us with something far less secure than what we started with.

Nevertheless, this negative view is disturbingly and increasingly common. There is even a growing tendency to combine this negative way of thinking about control with a commitment to equality, resulting in the view that *it is unfair for one person to have less than another through no fault of his own*.[15] In other words, nothing that is beyond my control should affect my life in the sense of making me worse off than anyone else. This view compounds the hubris of thinking we could bring everything under our control with a certain kind of resentment characteristic of egalitarians. It tells us to approach life thinking not just that luck is our enemy, but that other people's good luck is our injustice. This is a cheerless way to think about life, and a terrible thing to bring one's children up to believe.

I suggest that we replace this negative way of thinking with the simple positive idea that we should try to give everyone some control over their life. There is a lot more to say about this idea, especially in terms of drawing out its implications. But this is not the place to start on that large and open-ended project. This book is about ideas, rather than detailed implications, and this particular idea is fairly obvious *as an idea*. This is one reason why it remains in the background for much of what follows, while I spend most of my time criticizing opposing views. In other words, I spend most of the time telling the reader what they ought not to think, rather than what they ought to think. This is probably no bad thing, since philosophy is better at telling people what they ought not to think. It can show people what is wrong with their arguments, whereas getting them to believe the right arguments is probably better done by inspiration than direct instruction. As such, it is something I am unsuited to by temperament, as well as unqualified by training.

NOTES

1. But see e.g. Simon Blackburn, *Ruling Passions* (Oxford: Oxford University Press, 1998), ch. 9.
2. See e.g. R. H. Tawney, *Equality* (London: George Allen and Unwin, 1931), ch. 2: ii.
3. A word about terminology. 'The distribution of jobs' is ambiguous between, on the one hand, employers' actions in 'distributing' jobs, and on the other, the overall pattern which results from those actions. To avoid this ambiguity, I generally use 'distribution' only to refer to the overall pattern, and I avoid using 'distribute' as a verb; when talking about what employers actually do, I use the verb 'allocate' and the noun 'allocation'.
4. Contemporary top-down egalitarians tend to argue that people should 'face up to the costs of their choices'. See e.g. Will Kymlicka, *Contemporary Political*

Philosophy (Oxford: Oxford University Press, 1990), 73–5. I return to this theme at the end of the Introduction.

5. See Robert Nozick, *Anarchy, State, and Utopia* (New York: Basic Books, 1974), 153–64.

6. Though in fact for many libertarians even this would be conceding too much. I take up this point in Part 3, Sect. 3, below.

7. See Nozick, *Anarchy, State, and Utopia*. A good summary of his position can be found on 170.

8. A word about terminology again. So far I have been talking about the *fair* way for jobs to be distributed; now I have started talking about principles of distributive *justice*. Some philosophers have distinguished between justice and fairness, but throughout this book I use them interchangeably. Clearly, though, either or both represent a narrower notion than the notion of what is *right*, or what one *ought* to do. (For example, sometimes it is right to be merciful, even though that involves precisely not doing what justice or fairness demands.)

9. Which might lead us to think, for example, that people with smoking-related illnesses have less of a claim to free treatment than others, given that they had the *opportunity* to live a healthy life, but chose to do something which they knew might damage their health.

10. At the time of writing, for example, I listened to a national radio programme on equality of opportunity, which opened with the question: 'Why this revived and officially sanctioned talk of equality?' ('Equally Different', *Analysis*, Radio 4, 16 Mar. 2000).

11. *A Theory of Justice* (Oxford: Oxford University Press, 1971). For an outline of Rawls's position on equality of opportunity, see 72–4.

12. Of course, if waste is understood in a relative sense—that is, if a given talent's being 'wasted' is taken to cover anything other than its being exploited to the fullest possible extent—then this idea, that talent should not go to waste, *will* have implications for every single decision.

13. G. A. Cohen, who describes himself as an egalitarian, admits as much: see his 'Incentives, Inequality and Community', in the *Tanner Lectures on Human Values*, 1992: 267.

14. Cohen, for example, argues that 'the primary egalitarian impulse is to extinguish the influence on distribution of . . . brute luck' ('On the Currency of Egalitarian Justice', *Ethics* 99 (1989), 908), where by 'brute luck' he means anything that is beyond the person's control (916). See also Stuart White, 'What Do Egalitarians Want?', in Jane Franklin (ed.), *Equality* (London: Institute for Public Policy Research, 1997), 62.

15. See e.g. besides Cohen and White (see previous note), Thomas Nagel, *Equality and Partiality* (Oxford: Oxford University Press, 1991), 71; and Larry Temkin, *Inequality* (Oxford: Oxford University Press, 1993), 13.

PART I

Meritocracy

I. TWO CONCEPTS OF MERITOCRACY

The aim of the next two parts of the book is to loosen the grip that the ideas of merit and equality have on our thinking in this area, in the hope that other ideas and approaches might then find room to breathe. I take the idea of meritocracy first because, as I noted in the Introduction, it seems to be the default position. By 'meritocracy' I mean what most people seem to mean by this word—the view that the best person should always get the job.[1] But this view is not as simple as it appears: there are, as I also noted in the Introduction, at least two different ways of understanding it, and people are often unclear about which version they believe in. Both versions involve the idea of *competition*, but they understand it in different ways. On the first way of understanding it, the point of competition is to give everyone a chance to earn the right to a job. On the second way of understanding it, the point is not to *create* winners and losers, by giving people the chance to earn rewards, but to *reveal* who the best person is. The best person would still have been the best even if there hadn't been a competition.

In the first version, as I have said, the idea is that people should be given jobs as a reward for something they have done. In the second version, people are given jobs not in recognition of anything they have *done*, but in recognition of what they are *like*. Here the competition for jobs is like a beauty contest: you don't have to *do* anything, except enter the competition, and hope that you are the one to catch the employer's eye. On the first version, by contrast, the competition for jobs is more like a sporting competition, in which the competitors actually have to do something in order to win. The point of a sporting competition is not that it is already determined who is the best, and that we bring everyone together only in order to find out who it is. How people perform is not just a *measure* of how good they are. If you perform best on the day, this is not merely evidence that you deserve to win, it follows *by definition* that you deserve to win. (Suppose everyone agrees that one of the other competitors is, in fact, better than you, and just happened to perform badly on the day. That doesn't mean they deserved to win. By contrast, on the first version of meritocracy— the beauty contest version—if everyone agreed that the best person didn't win, that would suggest there was something wrong with the way the competition was run.)

Some might argue that strictly speaking only one of these two kinds of competition—the sporting kind—is really a competition. When it comes to examples of the other kind, like beauty contests, we might *talk* about them as 'competitions', and refer to the entrants as 'contestants' or 'competitors', but this is just a loose way of talking, given that the entrants don't actually have to *do* anything. Now, as a matter of language, I have some sympathy with this argument. But in this particular context, so far from excluding the beauty contest kind of competition, we might think that it is precisely the other, stricter kind of competition which we should be excluding. After all, we only introduced the idea of competition as a way of throwing light on the idea of meritocracy; and if the stricter kind of competition illustrates anything, it is a system based on *desert* rather than merit (that is, it is a system in which people earn rewards through what they *do*, as opposed to meriting recognition on the basis of what they are like).[2] But I don't intend to exclude either kind of competition from the discussion. I am not trying to offer a linguistic analysis of the terms 'meritocracy' and 'competition';[3] I am trying to offer a philosophical analysis of the ideas behind these terms. My point is that when people say they believe in meritocracy, they generally associate that with the idea of competition, and they generally understand competition in one of the two ways I have identified; so for the moment we need to keep both versions in mind.

In fact, in terms of what people actually believe, I suspect that most people operate with some confused mixture of these two ways of thinking. Of course, they might reply that it is I who am confused—that the contrast I have drawn, between two supposedly distinct ways of thinking, is completely artificial. They might argue that beauty contests are just as much about seeing who does best on the day—in terms of posing, deportment, and so on—as about finding out who is the prettiest; or they might argue that *all* games and contests and competitions are partly about finding out who is the best, and partly about seeing who does best on the day. I doubt they are right on either point, but it doesn't really matter. It doesn't matter whether any pure examples of either kind of competition actually exist. What matters is that there are these two distinct ways of understanding the idea that the best person should always get the job. On one way of understanding it, employers should be looking at the past, at what people have done, to find the person who is the best in the sense of morally the most deserving. On the other way of understanding it, employers should be thinking only about which of the applicants is *best for the job*—in which case, whatever the applicants have done in the past is relevant only in terms of what it tells employers about how they might perform if they got the job. We need to assess these two ways of thinking separately, even if most people don't separate them clearly in their own minds. For although people often run them together, or deny that there is any difference between them, they exemplify one of the important contrasts I marked in the Introduction, between *top-down* and *bottom-up* views of equal opportunity. The idea that jobs should be seen as rewards for the morally deserving is probably a top-down view. That is, it starts from some idea about what the overall distribution of jobs, or job prospects, should look like—it should reflect people's deserts—and then derives from that some conclusions about how individual decisions should be made. In contrast, the view that employers should be thinking only about who would be best at the job is almost certainly a bottom-up view: it starts from the thought that this is the only fair or rational way to make any given decision, and whatever implications that has, in terms of how the overall distribution of jobs will look, are purely incidental.

2. MERITOCRACY AS A WAY OF REWARDING DESERT

Having separated these two ways of understanding meritocracy, I hope to show, separately, that neither is compelling. I am going to start with the view that meritocracy is about making sure that everyone gets what they deserve—or, to put it another way, about giving everyone the chance to earn the right to a job. I suspect that deep down this view is really motivated by thoughts about pay. If you asked people, straight out, whether they thought jobs should be allocated on the basis of desert, they would probably say no. But they might well say that once someone has a job, what they get *paid* should be based on what they deserve. And at this point, the kind of meritocrat we are thinking about here will try to force them into the following choice: for pay to be deserved, it must depend either on how hard the job is, or on how hard it was to get the job in the first place. Since it is not obvious how we can answer the first of these questions (which is 'harder work', coal mining or brain surgery?), it is tempting to fall back on the second. That is, it is tempting to think that it doesn't matter how much people are paid for different kinds of job, so long as they deserved to get the job in the first place. If there was an open competition for every job, then assuming more people would try for higher-paying than lower-paying jobs, those who ended up getting them would deserve the extra reward—not because the jobs were harder in themselves, but because they were harder to get in the first place.

If this was the point of having a competition for jobs, then the competition would have to look very different from the way we understand it today. It would have to be a competition in the strict sense, not just in the loose sense, in which when we talk about people competing for a job, we mean only that everyone is free to apply, and then the employer picks the best. As we have seen, in this loose kind of 'competition' there is no suggestion that applicants have to *do* anything, except apply and wait to see if they are picked—which means it is nothing to do with rewarding desert. That said, I am not sure what the competition for jobs would look like if it really was a matter of rewarding desert. But I am going to leave this question aside for the moment, because I want to pursue a more serious objection to the whole underlying view, the view that it doesn't matter how much people are paid, so long as they deserved to get the job in the first place.

The more serious objection is that this view has nothing to say about the *size* of the differences in people's earnings. Suppose two people both apply for the same highly paid job. One of them gets it, and the other ends up with something much less well paid. On the view we are looking at here, the question of whether the first person deserves to be paid more than the second is a simple one: either he deserved the job more than the second person, or he didn't; and if he did, then *any* subsequent difference between their earnings, however large, would seem to be deserved.

Now, if this is what people mean by equality of opportunity, then it does seem right to say that it avoids the difficult question, simply accepting that some jobs pay much better than others, and just asking who should be on which end of this inequality, rather than asking why things have to be so unequal in the first place. Of course, this is an objection which is often levelled at the whole equal opportunity debate. I noted this in the

Introduction, and dismissed it, saying that the debate doesn't try to avoid the difficult question, it merely recognizes that we have to face both questions—one about how jobs should be allocated, and one about how much they should pay. Thinking about the first question isn't an excuse for not thinking about the second. Of course we should also be thinking about why some jobs are so much better paid than others. But there will always be some differences—some jobs will always be more desirable than others, even if it was possible to remove disparities in pay—so the question of allocation will never go away. This is why the objection doesn't undermine the debate as a whole. But if we look at the particular view under discussion here, we can see that it absolutely does try to use the issue of allocation as an excuse for not thinking about the question of how much people should be paid. So even if the objection is not valid when directed at the whole equal opportunity debate, it is valid when directed at this particular version of equal opportunity.

It would, perhaps, be possible to refine this view so that it no longer looked like it was just trying to avoid the difficult question. Rather than merely ensuring that there was competition for each individual job, there would have to be one centrally organized competition for all jobs, with jobs being allocated according to performance in that competition, and with the relative desirability of each job, including how well it paid, being adjusted to match people's relative performances. But this merely brings us back to the practical question of what this kind of competition would actually look like; and once again I am going to put this question on one side, because I want to pursue a more serious objection, an objection to the underlying motivation behind the view rather than the detail of the view itself.

As I said at the start of this section, I think that what really motivates this kind of view is the simple thought that it would be nice to feel that people were getting paid what they deserve. If I am right, then I have a suggestion to make. If all we want is to be able to feel that people are getting paid what they deserve, then we should start thinking about what they deserve to be paid for actually doing whatever kind of work it is they do, never mind whether they deserved to get the job in the first place. After all, the fact that it is a more difficult question is no very good reason for avoiding it. We might start by saying that people deserve a decent wage for a decent day's work. When we say that immigrant construction workers deserve to be paid a decent wage, since their work is hard and often dangerous, this has nothing to do with whether they deserved to get the job in the first place.

The point is that they deserve the money *for doing the work*, never mind whether they deserved to get the job. Perhaps they got the job through a family contact; if so, this would surely not mean that they didn't deserve to be paid a decent wage after all. And 'a decent wage for a decent day's work' is not, I think, a relative idea: that is, it is not fundamentally concerned with the relation between how much one set of people are getting and how much other people are getting. If it is relative to anything, it is to how much money a person needs to live at a decent standard of living in the society in question. There is a difference between this kind of relativity, relativity to context, and the other kind, direct relativity to what other people are getting.

We tend to assume that in asking how much someone deserves to be paid we *must* mean how much they deserve relative to other people. This is certainly what happens in collective wage negotiations or pay reviews. And perhaps it is why, when we come to think about equal opportunity, we end up falling back on the idea of a competition: since in a competition, the question of what one person deserves *is* directly relative to what other people deserve. But the idea of desert is not in itself an inherently relative idea: we don't always think about it in relative terms. Punishment is a good example. I am not suggesting that punishment is the perfect mirror image of reward, but it is analogous in this sense: it involves treating people in a certain way because they are thought to deserve it, on the basis of something they have done. And in thinking about punishment we do not always think about desert in relative terms. It is true that it sometimes seems as if we do. Whenever we want to object to the sentence for a given type of crime, we tend to draw comparisons with the sentences for other types of crime—as when, for example, we comment that it is wrong for crimes against the person to receive shorter sentences than crimes against property. But if we think a little harder, we will see that such comparisons are really meant to suggest that one of the two kinds of sentence must be wrong in itself—that is, disproportionate to the type of crime—rather than to suggest that the relation between sentences is what really matters.

To see why the relation between different sentences cannot be all that really matters, consider the following thought experiment. Imagine we finally arrived at a fair penal system, with everyone generally receiving the right sentence for their crimes. Would we then object if someone suggested that every sentence should be multiplied tenfold? If we thought that the *relation between* sentences was all that really mattered, we wouldn't be able to object, since the relations between different sentences would be preserved. But I suspect that most of us would object—we would think a tenfold increase was unfair to everyone. This implies that we don't in fact think about desert in exclusively relative terms.

This conclusion is reinforced by considering the way we think about retribution on a personal level, when institutions are not involved. In this kind of context, many of us tend to think along the lines of 'an eye for an eye'. This is a classic example of a retributive principle which focuses on the relation between the thing done and the response, not on the relation between this response and other responses. Suppose you insult me, and I reply by punching you in the face. You would probably resent this; but surely what you resent is the disproportion between what you did and what was done to you in return, not (or not merely) that others have done similar things and got away with less. It is only when institutions take on the business of retribution that we start to talk as if the relation between cases is what really matters. I am not denying that it makes a difference when institutions get involved: it does, perhaps, create a new reason for worrying about relativities (or as we might more naturally say, consistency), as well as simply worrying about whether the right decision is made in any given case. But in starting to worry about relativities we should not forget that the institutions were originally brought in to enforce existing principles which were not previously understood in a relative way. If the previous way of understanding these principles simply disappears and is completely replaced by a new, relative way of understanding them, that would have defeated the purpose of bringing in the institutions in the first place.

It might be argued that punishment or retribution is an unhelpful analogy: it is a special case, since it is not a matter of distributing a scarce good. Scarce goods are what we are thinking about in this book, and with scarce goods, if someone is getting more than they deserve, then someone else *must* be getting less than they deserve, since there is only so much to go around. In this particular context we are talking about pay, which is scarce—in the sense that at any given time there is only so much wealth to go round—so people's claims must after all be inherently relative. But this is a fallacious argument. If there is an answer to the question of how much everyone deserves to be paid, this answer surely doesn't specify what is to be done with every last pound of the total available wealth; but that is what would be required for it to follow, from someone getting more than they deserve, that someone else must be getting less than they deserve. The crucial point is not whether a good is scarce in the formal sense, meaning limited, but whether the total amount available is insufficient to cover everyone's claims. This is what makes us start talking about *competing claims*. We talk about claims being 'competing' when they can't all be fully satisfied: they are competing just in that sense, in terms of whether they are going to be satisfied, not necessarily in any deeper sense.

I should emphasize that I am not denying that claims of desert are sometimes relative; I am denying that they are *always* relative. My point is that the idea of 'a decent wage for a decent day's work' doesn't have to be a relative idea, just because it involves desert. Once this point has been granted, the next question is whether we can take desert, in this particular context, beyond this minimal idea that everyone who does a decent day's work should get a decent wage. There seem to me to be three possibilities here. The first is that we should take punishment as our model, and try to think in a non-relative way about what everyone deserves for doing different kinds of work. I confess I have no idea how far we could get with this. If it looks too daunting, the second possibility is to say that questions of desert run out as soon as we go beyond the minimal idea of a decent wage for a decent day's work, leaving only the question of what people are *entitled to* under the rules.[4] The third possibility is that once we go beyond the minimal idea of a decent wage for a decent day's work, questions of desert don't run out, but they do become relative. (They remain, however, questions about what people deserve for actually doing the work, rather than for getting the job in the first place, so it would still be wrong to fall back on our earlier idea that it doesn't matter how much people are paid for different kinds of work, so long as everyone is given the chance to compete for every job.)

If we wanted to pursue this third possibility, we could try arguing—and this is just a suggestion—that people's relative deserts are captured by the market rate for their services. The market rate is the price of labour, and price is a relative idea: it makes no sense to ask the price of one person's labour independently of the price of everyone else's. If we go down this route, we would need to exclude cases where people are able to manipulate what counts as the 'going rate' for their services, and include only those cases where the 'going rate' is genuinely determined by the operations of something approaching a free market. But even then I am sure there will be objections to the idea that the market rate represents what people deserve. The market rate is a function of the interaction of a whole range of complex variables, which means that two people can do exactly the same thing in different contexts and receive quite different rewards; if this was true of punishment, the objectors will say, we would think it grossly unfair.

The two variables which affect the going rate are *supply*—how many other people could do as good a job as you—and *demand*—how many people want what you have to offer, and how much they want it. John Rawls flatly asserts that it is 'perfectly obvious and has long been agreed to' that neither of these factors is morally significant.[5] I disagree: it is far from obvious why we should be trying to filter out these 'external' aspects of 'what you do' in order to arrive at some kind of context-free description of what you do, such as the amount of effort you put in. I think this idea probably springs from the assumption that what someone deserves must be something *internal to them*, rather than merely accidental. But this assumption trades on a confusion. It is true that desert can't be accidental: you can only be said to deserve to be rewarded for something if you did it intentionally. But making desert conditional on intention, which is, in a sense, 'internal' to the person, is not the same as making it into something wholly 'internal'. To suppose that we should try to understand intentional acts in a way that makes them wholly 'internal'—completely independent of their context, and of what other people think of them—is absurd. Consider again the case of punishment. Here, to try to arrive at some context-free description of what someone did, abstracting from how that affected other people, would miss the point of the whole exercise. In civilized societies, we generally punish people precisely because of the effects their actions have on others, not merely because we object to what is going on inside their heads.

I think it is similarly difficult to argue, with regard to how much people deserve to get paid, that the context is 'morally arbitrary'—i.e., that it is irrelevant how many people want what they have to offer, and how much they want it, or how many other people could do as good a job in satisfying those wants. I see no reason why we should be trying to filter out these aspects of what people do and treat them as irrelevant. Why should relevance to others, or rarity value, not be seen as contributory factors in determining the 'social value' of the work someone does, and therefore in determining what they deserve to be paid for doing it?

The only real problem with this suggestion, as I see it, is that we are forced to regard how much people are prepared to pay for something as an indication of how much they want it, when in fact it is a poor indication. The rich will pay more for the satisfaction of their idlest whims than the poor can afford to pay for the satisfaction of their most urgent needs. The question is whether this distortion swamps the extent to which 'revealed preferences' *can* legitimately be seen as having a bearing on what people deserve. If not, then we can still regard the market rate as at least offering an approximation to people's relative deserts. (Some will argue that the mere presence of a distorting factor, however small, *contaminates* the overall result. But, like the liberal philosophers I criticized at the end of the Introduction, they are guilty of taking what started out as a positive idea—that people should be paid what they deserve—and twisting it into something negative, into the idea that no one should get anything they *don't* deserve.)

That is all I am going to say about this idea, that we could regard people's relative deserts as being captured by the market rate for what they do. I do not for a moment claim to have conclusively rescued this idea from the derision it customarily attracts. Indeed, there are further questions I haven't even mentioned, such as whether pay is even the right *kind* of reward—when compared with, say, admiration or status. The reason I am not going to pursue these questions is because it is really no part of my overall position to argue for the idea that people's pay should reflect what they deserve. My point is just that something like this idea is the real motivation behind a certain understanding of meritocracy. On this understanding, jobs should be allocated by means of a competition, purely because then we wouldn't have to worry about how much people are paid, so long as they deserved to get the job in the first place. I have tried to show that we shouldn't feel forced into this view *even if we share the underlying motivation*—i.e., that it would be nice to be able to feel that people were getting paid what they deserve—because we could just as well follow that same motivation in various other directions. These other directions might not be fully worked out, but we should remember that the competitive view is itself not much more than a sketch. It still faces the question of exactly what the competition would look like in practice—remembering that it has to be a competition in the strict sense, not just in the loose sense, in which when we talk about people competing for a job, we mean only that everyone is free to apply and then the employer picks the best. It has to be a competition in which people are required to *do* things, if it is to explain why people *deserve* the reward of a good job. Moreover, if it is to escape the criticism that it is just a way of avoiding the difficult question of why some jobs pay so much better than others, it has to involve setting up a single, centrally organized competition for all jobs, with the relative desirability of each job being adjusted to match people's relative performances in the competition. To achieve this we would need to do more than just rank jobs and match this ranking with people's placing in the competition; we would need to know exactly *how much* better the winner's job has to be than that of the second placed person, and so on all the way down. This would be a very hard question to answer—indeed, it is pretty much the same as asking exactly how much people should be paid for different kinds of work, which was the question we started off trying to avoid.

3. MERITOCRACY AS HIRING THE BEST PERSON FOR THE JOB

I started the discussion of meritocracy by distinguishing two ways in which that idea, and the related idea of competition, might be understood. On the first, the point of competition is to give everyone a chance to earn the right to a job. I have rejected this view, and questioned the motivation behind it. I turn now to the second way of understanding meritocracy and competition, according to which jobs are not rewards for the deserving, but are simply given to those who will be best at them. On this view, whatever people might have done in the past is relevant only in terms of what it tells employers about how good they are likely to be at the job. We might talk about the best person 'deserving' the job, but we are using 'deserving' in a loose sense. In this loose sense, when we talk about what someone 'deserves', we are really just talking in general terms about how they should be treated; we don't necessarily mean that there is anything they have actually done which deserves reward in the strict sense.[6] Similarly, when we talk about people 'competing' for jobs, we mean this in the way that we talk about 'competitors' in a beauty contest: they are competing only in the sense that they are hoping they will be the one to catch the employer's eye. This kind of 'competition' doesn't actually require them to *do* anything; accordingly, if they are successful, this should not be seen as a reward for anything they have done. Of course, once they get the job, what they get paid for doing it can be seen as a reward. But as far as getting the job in the first place is concerned, anything they might do beforehand in trying to get it—gaining qualifications, experience, or whatever—is relevant not in itself, but only to the extent that it will make them better at the job.

If this is what we mean by 'merit'—simply whether someone would be good at the job—can we really demand that employers hire on merit? The obvious problem is that while hiring on any other basis might be unreasonable, or even irrational, if this is all we can say, it doesn't seem to give the state grounds to intervene. If equal opportunity means meritocracy, but meritocracy just means efficiency, then it is hard to see how equal opportunity is supposed to justify intervening in employers' decisions and telling them what to do. The mere fact that the state could organize your affairs more efficiently than you can does not give it the right to do so.

This remains true despite the fact that meritocracy would actually be far less restrictive than other conceptions of equal opportunity, for example, than most egalitarian conceptions. It would be less restrictive in that although employers would be obliged to hire the best person for the job, they would enjoy a certain amount of licence in terms of how they interpreted this principle. It doesn't really make sense to suppose there could be some centrally formulated, universal measure of 'merit', which could be applied in a purely mechanical way to every job. Most jobs call for a wide range of qualities. Imposing a central system of meritocracy would mean stipulating, for each job, and for each of the many qualities which are relevant to that job, exactly what counts as having the quality, and exactly how the different qualities stack up against each other in terms of relative importance. This is hopelessly unrealistic. Both aspects of the problem call for judgement in each particular case, and the only sensible way of policing meritocracy would be to require an employer to show, on demand, how his decision represented a reasonable interpretation of the merit principle. This would still constitute a limitation on his freedom, but it would be much less restrictive than, for example, saying that he had to give every applicant literally an equal chance of getting the job.

Nevertheless, *any* restriction on employers' freedom requires justification. It requires justification for the two reasons that I set out in the Introduction: first, because any interference with anyone's freedom, however limited, requires justification; and second, because in the specific case of employers, at least if we are talking about private sector employers, they also have *property rights* over the decision of whom they employ. They are the ones who are going to pay the wages, and as a default position we should at least start by assuming that they have the right to spend that money as they see fit. When we think about meritocracy against this background, the problem is that mere efficiency doesn't even seem to be the right *kind* of basis on which to start talking about intervention. The problem is not that the argument for intervention might not be strong enough; it is that there is no way it could ever be strong enough. Mere efficiency could never outweigh an employer's right to carry on his business without interference.

Perhaps at this point a meritocrat will complain that I have got completely the wrong end of the stick: I am talking about forcing employers to hire on merit because this is efficient or rational, when in fact I should be talking about things from the point of view of the *applicants*. Of course the point is not merely that it is inefficient or irrational for an employer to hire someone who is no good at the job: the point is that in doing so he is treating the other applicants unfairly. This, however, just begs the question, until we are told exactly how he is supposed to be treating them unfairly. The problem for the meritocrat is that being the best person for the job doesn't give you a moral claim on it. This statement calls for some explanation. Having a moral claim on something usually means that if you don't get it, you have grounds for complaint. In fact, this is not quite right: your claim might be outweighed by other moral claims, or by other kinds of moral consideration, in which case you wouldn't have grounds for complaint after all. But the essential point is that if you have a moral claim on something, that means there is *some* sort of moral presumption in favour of your getting it. This is exactly what seems to be missing in the argument for hiring on merit, when merit just means being good at the job. There is a good *reason* to give the job to the best person, but that isn't the same as their having a moral claim on it.

One way a meritocrat might try to get round this problem is by explicitly linking the idea of fairness to that of reason or rationality. He might argue that if the only *reasonable* thing to do is to give the job to the best person, then this is also what fairness demands, since it is unfair to treat people unreasonably. This would be a neat argument, if it worked. But does it work? Let us start with the final step. Is it unfair to treat people unreasonably? Not always. Suppose someone stops me in the street to ask the time. Clearly the only reasonable thing for me to do, assuming I have a watch, is to tell him. But there are any number of things I might do instead. Suppose I am in a bad mood, and I just pull a face and walk on past. This would be unreasonable, yes; rude, certainly; but I don't think it would be *unfair*. However, perhaps this is not a very charitable interpretation of the meritocrat's argument here. If we interpret him as saying that it is unfair to treat people unreasonably *when they have serious interests at stake*, then perhaps the argument seems plausible enough after all. If we grant the meritocrat this much, we end up with the following position: being the best person for the job might not give you a moral claim on it, but you have some sort of moral claim to be treated reasonably, in virtue of how important it is to you that you get the job. It is because of how important it is to you, not because of your merits, that the employer is obliged to treat you fairly; but treating you fairly means treating you reasonably, which means treating you on your merits.

Again, this is a neat argument, but there is also something slightly odd about it. It implies that if it *wasn't* important to you whether you got the job, then it wouldn't be unfair for the employer not to treat you on your merits; but that since it *is* important to you, it is unfair—even though in both cases your application is based solely on your merits, rather than on how important it is to you. I am merely going to register this odd implication: first, because I admit I don't know exactly what to make of it; and second, because I intend to pursue a different line of attack. There is a more serious problem with the meritocrat's position here, concerning the underlying principle itself, the principle that it is wrong or unfair to treat people unreasonably. Now, it is certainly wrong to harm others without good reason. But an employer can't be said to *harm* people when he doesn't give them a job: he is merely omitting to give them something. True, we might still think it wrong even to omit to give someone something, where that is done for no reason at all. For example, if I have something that would make you very happy but is worthless to me, and out of spite or simple thoughtlessness I don't give it to you, perhaps that is wrong of me. But this still doesn't really capture what is going on in the present case. We shouldn't think of an employer as looking at each applicant in turn and deciding whether to give them a job. He has a limited number of jobs at his disposal, and has to choose who is going to get one and who is not; some are going to miss out whatever happens. The question is whether it is wrong to make the *choice*, of who is going to miss out, for no reason at all. In order to think so, we would have to interpret the underlying principle in something like the following way: it is wrong to act without reason in an area where people have serious interests at stake. This is by no means a crazy principle. It is, however, quite a strong principle, and has very wide-ranging implications. But I am going to let this pass. First, because a proper discussion of a general principle like this would take me beyond the scope of this book (though it is useful to have clarified exactly what the merito-crat has to believe, for his position to make sense). And second and more importantly, because even if we accept this principle, there is still a further question about whether it really applies in the present case.

The question is whether we can equate acting non-meritocratically with acting without reason. In so far as we are tempted to condemn people for acting 'without reason', that is because we have in mind someone acting thoughtlessly or even capriciously or wilfully; there does seem to be something offensive about behaving like this when serious interests are at stake. But is it really true that if an employer makes a choice on any basis other than merit, this necessarily counts as acting without reason in this strong sense? Well, there is a way of understanding 'merit' which makes this true by definition. This is the sense in which a person's 'merits' just means any fact about them that might constitute grounds for a reasonable decision.[7] But this is precisely the problem with this way of understanding 'merit': that it is so wide as to be almost empty. It turns the principle that 'jobs should be allocated on merit' into a purely formal principle: it just means that jobs should be allocated on reasonable grounds. If you define merit in this way, then you don't need to *argue* that hiring on merit is the only reasonable thing to do, since this becomes true by definition. But you do face the problem that you haven't actually got any closer to telling us how jobs should be allocated. Your definition means that almost everything an employer might do—including, for example, giving jobs to members of his family—will count as an interpretation of 'meritocracy'. This is certainly not how 'merit' and 'meritocracy' are generally understood: they are usually understood in much narrower terms.

It is a good question, however, exactly how narrowly they should be understood. Consider the following example. A few years ago, the more progressive American medical schools decided that since there was a relative shortage of doctors prepared to practise in the poorer parts of the community, and a relative surplus of doctors keen to practise in the richer parts, the schools should favour applicants who were more likely to go on to practise in the poorer parts.[8] Many people objected to this policy, on the grounds that it was not meritocratic. They weren't prepared to accept that being the kind of person who was more likely to practise in areas of great need makes you a *better candidate*; they insisted that the medical schools should stick to asking only which candidates were likely to go on to make the best doctors, and leave it at that. In this particular case, I think the objectors were operating with too narrow an understanding of 'merit'. They had lost sight of the purpose of medical schools, which is not to create the best doctors just for the sake of it, but to train doctors on the explicit understanding that they will go on to make themselves useful in society. It clearly then makes sense to speculate on exactly how useful any given applicant will turn out to be, not just in terms of how good they will be at the job in some narrow sense, but also in terms of wider factors such as how likely they are to practise in areas of great need.

Of course, even if we include this kind of factor in the definition of 'merit', it will remain a fairly narrow notion. It is still tied in some way to the job itself. This is much narrower than taking 'merit' to cover any reasonable grounds for a decision, as was suggested initially. That suggestion would mean including things like, for example, which applicants *needed* the job most, as well as things like whether they are a friend, or a member of the family. If I ask myself which of these successively wider readings of 'merit' best reflects ordinary usage, the answer has to be one of the narrower readings: either the narrowest reading, which is restricted to qualities directly related to doing the job, or a slightly wider one that also includes usefulness in some wider sense, as in the medical school example. But in the end, the question of which of these different readings of 'merit' best captures ordinary usage is not an especially interesting one. The interesting question is whether it is irrational to hire on any basis other than 'merit'—or rather, whether it is unfair, because irrational, which means first deciding whether it is irrational. On the widest reading of 'merit', it is indeed irrational to hire on any other basis, but this is true by definition. On any other reading it is false. This should be clearest in the case of the narrowest reading, on which 'merit' is understood to cover only those qualities that relate to tasks directly involved in the job. If 'merit' is understood in this way, then clearly it will not be *irrational* to hire on any other basis. In the medical school case, even those who opposed the policy of preferring applicants who are more likely to practise in poorer areas would have conceded that this policy was perfectly *rational*. They thought it unfair rather than irrational. However, this meant they could not argue that it was unfair *because* irrational. The same is true of the kind of case where an enlightened employer considers whether applicants really *need* the job—whether they are currently unemployed, whether they have dependants, and so on. Again, many would say that such factors should be excluded from the decision, and they would probably put this by saying that the choice should be made 'on merit alone'. But they would be hard put to argue that there is anything *irrational* about considering, when thinking about whether to give someone a job, whether they really need it. It is worth remembering here that when we were first tempted to condemn employers for acting irrationally, or 'without reason', that was because we had in mind someone acting thoughtlessly, or even capriciously or wilfully. To give someone a job because they really need it hardly counts as acting irrationally in this absolute sense.

4. ARE EMPLOYERS OBLIGED TO HIRE THE *BEST* PEOPLE?

It is not clear, then, that an employer acts irrationally whenever he makes a decision on any basis other than merit. But anyway meritocracy is generally thought to go beyond making sure that nothing except merit enters the decision: it is generally understood to mean that the *best* person should always get the job. These two ideas are related but different: the idea that the best person should always get the job entails that nothing else except merit should enter the decision, but the reverse does not hold. An employer might agree that he should think about nothing else than whether applicants will be good at the job, but still show no interest in trying to find the *best* applicant.

Suppose we come across an employer who behaves in the following way. When looking to fill a vacant job, he doesn't think about anything other than merit, but he simply takes the first acceptable candidate who comes through the door. Moreover, he doesn't bother to ensure that he attracts the widest or best pool of applicants in the first place. This suggests that he isn't particularly interested in trying to find the best candidate. The possibility of this kind of case suggests that even if we could prove that it was irrational, and therefore unfair, to hire on any basis other than merit, we would still not have established meritocracy as it is generally understood —that is, as requiring that employers always hire the *best* person for the job. We need to ask, separately, whether it is irrational not to maximize.

Before I tackle this question, I need first to ward off a possible objection from the rational choice theorists, who will accuse me of having falsely described what is going on in the kind of case I have just outlined. What this employer's behaviour really shows, they will say, is that it is too costly to try to find the 'best' candidate in the traditional, narrow sense. That doesn't mean he is not maximizing; he is merely maximizing with respect to a wider set of values. At the point when the first acceptable candidate comes through the door, that candidate just is the best candidate for him, in the sense of being, at that point, the cheapest acceptable candidate. It is true that some of the candidates he has yet to see might be better, in the narrow sense, but they are worse in the sense that it would cost him time and money to see them.

Now, we would not normally say that this kind of fact—whether someone happened to be the first acceptable candidate through the door—could make them the 'best' candidate. But this is because, as I explained in the last section, we tend to operate with a traditional, narrow idea of merit. We need to go beyond this narrow way of thinking if we want to get to grips with the question of maximization. If we stick to talking about merit in the narrow sense, then as soon as we try to discuss a case in which it doesn't seem irrational not to maximize, the rational choice theorists will be able to object that this case doesn't tell us anything about whether it is irrational not to maximize—it just tells us that in this particular case it is rational to maximize with respect to a wider notion of 'merit'. To pre-empt this move, we need to confront the question of whether rationality really requires employers to try to find the best person even in the widest possible sense of 'best'. Then if we end up concluding that it does not, we will know that it really is the requirement to maximize we are objecting to, not just some overly narrow conception of what should be on the list of things to be maximized.

The rational choice theorists are not finished yet, however. They will argue that it doesn't even make sense to ask whether employers *ought* to be trying to hire the best person in the widest possible sense of 'best'. According-ing to rational choice theory, it is just a brute fact about human nature that people are always trying to maximize *something*. Indeed, it is this assumption which led the rational choice theorists to insist, in the face of my original example, that the employer was maximizing even though he explicitly denied it. What we are faced with here is an example of pseudo-science: a theory which provides a framework for interpreting human behaviour which is supposed to stand or fall by its explanatory usefulness, but which turns out to be impossible to falsify, because its adherents have already decided that they are going to redescribe every apparent counter-example so that it no longer looks like a counter-example. For a rational choice theor-ist, whenever anyone does anything, almost by definition that means they think it the best course of action with respect to some weighted set of values. Any instance of behaviour which looks as if it might not be maximizing must be redescribed as maximizing with respect to some further value— even if that further value has to be spuriously constructed from the behaviour it is supposed to explain. (Consider, for example, the fact that people often stick with what they have, even when something better comes along. This is described by rational choice theorists as an example of people maximizing with respect to the value of an easy life.)

That is all I am going to say about rational choice theory. The maximiz-ing view is anyway far more interesting when it is understood not as a descriptive theory of human behaviour, held true by definition, but as a normative theory which tells us how we *ought* to behave. However, although it is more interesting when understood this way, it fairly quickly runs into difficulties. First, there are good reasons for doubting that truly global maximization—finding the course of action which is the best relative to every possible consideration which might be relevant—is even possible. When many distinct considerations are at stake, finding the best course of action would mean arriving at a complete answer as to how all the different considerations stack up against each other; and there are reasons for doubting that such an answer will always be available.[9] But I am going to leave this problem on one side, because I want to consider whether we *ought* to maximize, never mind whether we can. Let us then go back to the case of the employer who simply takes the first acceptable candidate who comes through the door. Let us assume that he is not doing this because he is especially busy: he simply wants to hire someone acceptable, and as soon as he sees someone acceptable, he takes them. Is he doing anything wrong? Remember the shape of the overall argument: the idea was that if he is behaving irrationally, that entitles us to intervene, because it is wrong to treat people irrationally where serious interests are at stake. So the question is whether it is right to describe this kind of behaviour, where an employer simply takes the first acceptable candidate who comes through the door, as *irrational*. And I am not sure that it is right. There is a perfectly clear sense in which the employer has good reason for doing what he does: he is taking on this person because he deems them acceptable. What he lacks is any reason for choosing them *rather than any other acceptable candidate*. But if this is all we can say—that he is not doing what he has *most* reason to do, indeed, that he is not even *trying* to do what he has most reason to do—can we really present this as irrational?

Many people assume that not even *trying* to do what you have most reason to do must be irrational. But this is because they simply assume that rationality is inherently maximizing, which is precisely what is at issue. Perhaps it will help to bring the question into focus if we move to an example from a different context, the context of personal life. In personal life, the problem with believing that rationality is inherently maximizing is that it prevents you treating those close to you as they would like to be treated. They would like, at least sometimes, for you to take the fact that they want or need something to be sufficient reason to act, without first stopping to ask yourself what else you might be doing. In other words, they would like you to act without first stopping to ask yourself whether the thing you are about to do is what you have *most* reason to do. Of course, it might well be what you have most reason to do; but that isn't necessarily what they want you to be thinking while you are doing it.

We need to be careful about how we put this point. The supporters of maximization will say that if the point is merely that those close to you would rather you didn't always think in a maximizing way, then they can concede it: of course, if you want the people close to you to be happy, then you should allow them to believe that you are thinking in a non-maximizing way. And if you can't succeed in deceiving them, perhaps you should even try to stop thinking in a maximizing way. There is nothing non-maximizing about this—their happiness is one of the things you are trying to maximize, and there is nothing paradoxical in thinking about how you can achieve this, and ending up concluding that you should stop thinking. Nevertheless, this whole line of response surely gets things backwards. It may well be true that thinking in a non-maximizing way when you deal with people close to you is the way to make them happy, but this is surely a *consequence* of their realizing that this is the right way for you to think, rather than what *makes* it the right way for you to think. Needless to say, the supporters of maximization have an answer to this too. (It is one of their defining characteristics that they have an answer to everything. This is because even though they claim to believe in maximization as a normative rather than a descriptive theory, they tend to fall back on the descriptive theory when the normative theory comes under threat. That is, if they are having trouble convincing us that we *ought* to maximize, they will shrug their shoulders and say: you just *are* maximizing, whether you like it or not.) Their answer will be that if this kind of spontaneity is indeed a good thing, then it should be included in the list of goods to be maximized. This shows how far they are from grasping what is really at issue in this argument. For the charge against them is not that they have too narrow a view of what matters (though this is true enough of many maximizing theories, such as utilitarianism), but that they have too narrow a view about how you are supposed to think about the things that matter. True, not all supporters of maximization make the mistake of saying that until you are sure what you have most reason to do, you should keep trying to figure it out. To think *that* is to make a separate mistake about means rather than ends: to fail to see that trying to figure out what you have most reason to do is not necessarily the best way of bringing it about that you do what you have most reason to do. Sophisticated supporters of maximization realize this. But they still have to face the more profound question of whether it is irrational not even to *want* to do whatever it is you have most reason to do. Suppose you take your reason for following a given course of action to be solely based on a particular value. If you should become aware of an alternative course of action which is superior with respect to that value and at least equal in all other respects, would it be irrational not to switch? This at least doesn't imply that you should always be on the lookout for something better: it just tells you that if something better presents itself, whether you were looking for it or not, it would be irrational not to take it. However, this still seems to be incompatible with the way most of us think about, for example, our relationships with other people. If I think about all the things I like about my girlfriend, and then someone comes along who has all these qualities and more, or who possesses all these qualities to a greater degree, would it really be *irrational* for me not even to try to switch? I don't think so—and not just because the potential gains are offset by the expected cost of switching.[10]

As will be clear from the way I have been arguing, I take this kind of example to demonstrate that sometimes it is not irrational not even to want to do what you have most reason to do. However, at this point the kind of person who thinks that rationality is inherently maximizing might jump the other way, saying that if maximizing turns out to be incompatible with certain kinds of personal relations, then the only thing this tells us is that those kinds of personal relations must be irrational. Now, this should strike us as a deeply suspect move—after all, what counts as rational behaviour in any given context is surely dependent on, rather than prior to, what we know about how reasonable people actually behave in that context. But it also isn't a particularly good move from a dialectical point of view in terms of the present argument. Remember the overall shape of the argument: that if a certain way of treating people can be shown to be irrational, then it is also shown to be unfair, since it is unfair to treat people irrationally. The problem is that even if we do decide that it would be irrational for me not even to try to switch from my existing girlfriend to some new and better alternative, we surely wouldn't think I was treating anyone unfairly. And since the way I am behaving is obviously not unfair, the example seems to present us with a choice: either we preserve the link between fairness and rationality but give up on the link between rationality and maximization, or else we give up on the link between fairness and rationality. Either way, this spells trouble for the argument we have been considering here—the argument that employers are obliged to maximize because any other way of behaving is unfair because irrational.

However, perhaps I have underestimated my opponent. Perhaps a truly desperate supporter of maximization would insist, even in the girlfriend example, that if I didn't even try to switch, I would be treating the alternative girl unfairly—after all, we have agreed that her claims are the stronger. My behaviour could be unfair while at the same time being admirably loyal, and this could mean that overall it was not wrong. Or else, it could be wrong overall but not the kind of thing anyone should do anything about. These are possible positions—just barely—and they would allow a desperate supporter of maximization to persist in arguing, along the lines I have set out, that employers are obliged to hire the best person for the job. But I doubt that the argument will have many takers, as soon as people realize the kind of implications it has in other areas.

That is all I am going to say about maximization. I have tried to show that rationality is not inherently maximizing, which means that employers who don't even try to find the best candidate aren't necessarily being irrational—and therefore aren't necessarily treating anyone unfairly. But in terms of the overall relation between the ideas of meritocracy and rationality, we should also remember that in discussing maximization we have been talking about whether employers are obliged to hire the best applicant in the widest possible sense of 'best'. When it comes to thinking about merit in the more usual, narrow sense—where being the best person for the job means being the one who would make the most widgets per hour, say—we should remember that there are *two* reasons why, if an employer isn't even trying to find the best applicant, he isn't necessarily being unfair. First, because he might have decided that he just needed to find someone who was *good enough* at making widgets, never mind whether the *best*— this is what I have been arguing in the present section. But also, second, because he might be acting for some reason which falls outside the scope of merit in this narrow sense, but which remains a perfectly respectable reason—which is what I tried to show in the last section.

5. WHEN BEING GOOD AT THE JOB IS NOT JUST A MEANS TO AN END

'Merit' in the narrow sense, as I have said, is a matter of being good at the job, and so far I have been assuming that being good at the job is merely a means to an end. This is true enough of many jobs: employers hire people who are good at the job merely because that is the way to make money. But sometimes being good at the job is not merely a means to an end. There are two ways in which it might amount to more than that. First, the activity itself might have non-instrumental value. This is true, for example, of professional sport, or professional music—or indeed professional philosophy. Second, even if the activity itself does not have non-instrumental value, the qualities required to do it well might be admirable in themselves, rather than merely useful. Certain types of manual work, for example, might not have non-instrumental value in themselves, but might call for courage, or dexterity, or some other kind of physical prowess. These qualities are merit-worthy in a sense which is not purely instrumental: they are useful, of course, but they are not *merely* useful.

How many jobs exemplify one or other of these two kinds of non-instrumental value? It might be thought that while the first—the kind where the activity itself has non-instrumental value—is quite rare, the second—the kind where the qualities required to do the job well are admirable rather than merely useful—is almost universal. Don't *all* jobs require at least *some* qualities which are admirable in themselves? Well, we can certainly imagine a job where none of the qualities required were admirable in themselves. Consider a job whose sole requirement was to be as tall as possible. Being tall is often useful, but it is not admirable in itself. However, I don't intend to get bogged down in a debate over how many jobs are really like this. I am going to take a different approach, arguing that even if every job *did* have non-instrumental value, or required admirable qualities to do it well, it still would not follow that employers should always hire the best person for the job.

Let us start by considering the second way in which being good at the job can be more than just a means to an end. Why might anyone think it would follow, from the fact that the qualities required to do the job are admirable rather than merely useful, that employers were obliged to recognize those qualities in deciding who should get the job? Well, remember that if we understand 'merit' in purely commercial terms, there is a problem with trying to argue that it is unfair of employers not to hire on merit: that being the best person for the job in this sense doesn't give you any kind of moral claim on it. If you are the best person for the job in a purely commercial sense, that is a good *reason* for the employer to give you the job, but it doesn't give you any sort of moral claim. However, if the qualities required by the job are admirable in themselves, rather than merely useful, being the best person for the job *does* seem to give you some sort of moral claim on it. After all, don't qualities that are admirable in themselves *demand recognition*? If you possess certain qualities which are valuable in a purely commercial sense, there is no obvious sense in which anyone else is obliged to recognize them. But if you are a good sportsman, or musician, or philosopher, then if people fail to recognize this, are they not doing you an injustice?

There is a sense in which they are. If by 'merits' we mean qualities that are admirable in themselves, rather than merely useful, there is indeed a sense in which such qualities demand recognition. They don't necessarily demand recognition from everyone, but they demand recognition from anyone who is involved in the same kind of activity. If you care nothing for cricket, you are not obliged to recognize my merits as a cricketer (assuming I had any). But if you see yourself as a cricketer too, then you are obliged to recognize my merits. This might seem enough to rescue a limited kind of meritocracy. That is, where a given job requires admirable qualities, it might seem that the employer is obliged to recognize those qualities in the applicants. However, it is one thing to say that these qualities must be recognized, quite another to say that they must be recognized *in the way the job is allocated*. Suppose you apply for a job as a philosopher in some university philosophy department. Suppose you are in fact the best philosopher who applies, and yet the job goes to someone else. Can you complain that your merits were not recognized? The selection committee could reply that they recognized your merits, they just decided to give the job to someone else—someone less good at philosophy, but who needed the job more, or deserved it more, in the sense that he had worked harder for his success. They *recognized* your merits, they just decided not to express that recognition in their decision. Now, you could argue that they have missed an opportunity here, but this is a different argument. The point is that there is a gap between thinking that your merits constitute some sort of general moral claim to recognition, and thinking you have a specific moral claim on the department to promote merit—and to promote it the greatest possible extent. The second idea does not obviously follow from the first.

But is it not an *insult* to be passed over in favour of someone who is in fact worse than you? Well, it is a good question, given that we are looking for an argument for meritocracy which could support state intervention, whether the state should even concern itself with insults. But I am going to leave this to one side. There are other, more serious problems with this idea, that it is an insult to be passed over in favour of someone worse than you. The first problem is that this doesn't really amount to an argument for thinking employers should be obliged to hire on merit: it *presupposes* that they already are hiring on merit. Only if they already are hiring on merit can their decision be interpreted as expressing a judgement about your merits—and therefore as an insult, if the judgement is incorrect. So all this idea really implies is that *if* employers generally hire on merit, it is important for them to be consistent. If on the other hand they don't always hire on merit—and especially if they make that clear to all concerned—then it won't be reasonable to take it as an insult if they pass you over in favour of someone worse than you. Moreover, even if employers *are* hiring on merit, there is a second problem. The idea that it is an insult to be passed over in favour of someone worse than you trades on a confusion between absolute and comparative judgements. Being passed over doesn't necessarily imply that you aren't up to the job, merely that you aren't the *best* person for the job. Unless the successful applicant is truly awful, this judgement can hardly be described as insulting, even if it is incorrect.

At this point, a meritocrat might try falling back on the other way in which being good at the job can be more than just a means to an end: namely, through the activity itself having non-instrumental value. Of course, activities that have non-instrumental value will tend also to require admirable qualities. This is true of all three examples I gave earlier—sport, music, and philosophy. But let us now forget about the debate over admirable qualities, and focus on what is supposed to follow simply from the activity itself having non-instrumental value. The argument might go something like this. Certain jobs have 'internal' goals and values—goals and values that can only be pursued within the job—and in such cases, the decision of who gets the job should depend on these 'internal' criteria, rather than on 'external', commercial criteria. Selection for a football team, for example, should be based on footballing criteria, not on questions such as who would enable the club to sell the most sponsorship.

Might this kind of argument rescue a kind of meritocracy, albeit one that was severely limited in scope? The problem is that on this interpretation, meritocracy is no longer obviously an argument about being fair to applicants. And if the charge is no longer that hiring non-meritocratically is unfair, but simply a betrayal of certain impersonal goals and values, it is doubtful whether the state should get involved. Consider the variety of other ways, besides hiring decisions, in which the 'internal goals' of activities like professional sport or music or philosophy might be betrayed. A sports team might adopt tactics which, though successful, were against the spirit of the game; an orchestra might adopt a philistine, populist repertoire; a philosophy department might adopt a shallow, trendy syllabus. All these things would represent a betrayal of the relevant internal goals and values, and yet we would be unlikely to think the state should get involved. Hiring seems somehow different. But the reason it seems different is precisely because we think it is about being fair to applicants; if we did come to think of it as simply a question of respecting the relevant internal goals and values, we would probably view it in the same way that we view the tactics of a sports team, or the repertoire of an orchestra, or the syllabus of a philosophy department. That is, we would think that although it is undoubtedly a shame if these things are done in a way that compromises the relevant internal values, nevertheless the state should respect the autonomy of these professions, and refuse to get involved.

It is true that there is one profession which seems like an obvious exception to this: namely, the medical profession. I will discuss public sector jobs separately later, but even in private medicine most of us would probably assume that the state is entitled to get involved. However, this is not because we think private medical practitioners have a duty to respect the internal goals and values of medicine; it is because we think they have certain duties to their *patients*. Accordingly, the state's role in making sure they fulfil these duties warrants intervening in all sorts of other areas of private medicine besides hiring. So while the medical profession is indeed an example of a profession where the state is legitimately involved in regulating private sector hiring, this example cannot vindicate our tendency to believe that hiring is *special*: that is, it cannot explain why the state should intervene in hiring while leaving other things alone. Moreover, it cannot vindicate our initial sense of *why* the state should intervene: once again, the idea that the best person should get the job turns out to have nothing to do with being fair to applicants. It has more to do with looking after the interests of patients.

It seems, then, that this second idea—that jobs can have 'internal' values—is no better placed to rescue meritocracy than was the first idea, the idea that sometimes the qualities required to do a job are admirable in themselves. Certainly neither of these ideas can vindicate our sense that meritocracy is a matter of being fair to applicants. However, perhaps we need to abandon the assumption that meritocracy is anything to do with being fair to applicants, and consider other kinds of reason why we might think employers ought to hire on merit. This is the direction I intend to take now. In the remainder of the present section, I explore other possible arguments related to the idea of internal values. In the next section, I then consider whether there might be a more straightforward argument for meritocracy based on efficiency.

Suppose we argued that where a job has internal goals and values, the employer has a duty to respect them, not because he owes this to the applicants, but because he owes it to the goals and values themselves. So, for example, the idea would be that the manager of a sports team has a duty *to the game* to pick the best team, that the people who run an orchestra have a duty *to music* to pick the best players, that the members of a philosophy department have a duty *to the subject* to pick the best philosophers, and so on. The first question is whether this is really supposed to apply to every job which could be said to have internal goals and values. Now, perhaps this is not very many jobs: the set of jobs which have internal goals and values is probably smaller than the set of jobs which merely require admirable qualities. But internal goals and values aren't restricted to professions like sport or music or philosophy. Consider, for example, the business of lawnmower manufacture. Our first thought here might be that unlike sport or music or philosophy, lawnmower manufacture is essentially a commercial business. Nevertheless, it is possible to imagine a lawnmower manufacturer who wasn't motivated solely by commercial considerations, but who really wanted to carry on the tradition of making good lawnmowers. This tradition meets the test of being an 'internal' goal or value. It has some non-instrumental value, and this value cannot be realized anywhere else: if it is to thrive, that will have to be through people like this employer pursuing it. So even lawnmower manufacture turns out to have internal goals and values. What would it mean for an employer to respect these goals and values in his hiring policy? It might mean, for example, hiring engineers or craftsmen who are, in a commercial sense, unnecessarily good at their job. Now, I am not saying there would be anything wrong or irrational in doing this; but we surely wouldn't dream of suggesting that a lawnmower manufacturer is *obliged* to see his business in this way. If he happily churns out lawnmowers that are merely passable, or even downright shoddy, but continue to sell, would we really say that he has failed to grasp the 'inner logic' of lawnmower manufacture?

The point I am trying to make here is not that there *is* no 'inner logic' to lawnmower manufacture. We have seen that it is easy to imagine how a lawnmower manufacturer could think there was such an inner logic, and how he might act on that; and we have conceded that there would be nothing wrong or irrational in this. But it does seem to be up to him whether he chooses to see his business in this way. The question is why we cannot accept the same kind of conclusion in other areas. Why do we think that some internal goals and values are somehow *not* optional? Perhaps even in professional sport or music or philosophy we should concede that pursuing excellence to the greatest possible extent is just one of the many different ways in which a sports team or an orchestra or a philosophy department can choose to understand what they are doing. If instead they choose to understand what they are doing as running a business, there is not obviously anything immoral or irrational in that.

However, perhaps the argument is supposed to be that the people who run sports teams, and orchestras, and philosophy departments, have a duty not directly to the internal values themselves, but to *society*, in their capacity as the custodians of those values. But if so, it is a good question how far we are supposed to generalize this point. Of how many businesses or professions are we really prepared to say that society has a genuine interest in their internal values, such that we are prepared to override employers' right to hire as they see fit? On this way of looking at things, it starts to look as if the difference between sport or music or philosophy on the one hand, and something like lawnmower manufacture on the other, is not that the former have genuine internal values while the latter does not, but merely that society has a more profound interest in the internal values of the former, with the result that we are not prepared to leave the maintenance of those values to the operations of the free market. By contrast, in the case of lawnmower manufacture, we are more likely to say that if its internal values are not commercially viable—that is, if individual consumers are not prepared to pay for them—then by itself that shows that society can't really have that much of an interest in them.

I don't know whether this really is the right way to look at things, but for the sake of argument, I am going to concede that, for this or some other reason, at least some employers are under some kind of obligation to respect the internal goals and values of their business or profession. This is because I want to try to show that *even when this is true*, it does not follow that employers are obliged to hire the best person for the job. Again, I first need to understand why anyone might think it did follow. One possibility is if they believed that rationality was inherently maximizing. It might then seem to follow that, if a given business or profession had some kind of internal goal, it would be irrational for anyone involved not to want to pursue that goal to the greatest possible extent. However, I have already rejected the idea that rationality is inherently maximizing. It is therefore not possible to come up with a *general* argument for a maximizing meritocracy based on the idea of internal goals. We need to look at each case individually, and ask ourselves whether the particular goals at stake are the kind of goals that have to be conceived of in a maximizing way. This does seem to be true of some internal goals. For example, the internal goal of medicine is to save lives and relieve suffering, and it would be peculiar to set out to save lives or relieve suffering without thinking you ought to be trying to save as many lives, or relieve as much suffering, as possible. Other internal goals also seem to demand maximization, but incidentally rather than inherently. Sport is an example. At least part of the point of playing sport is to win; it is this competitive element which implies that whoever selects the team ought to be trying to pick not just a *good* team, but the *best*. But not all professions which have internal goals or values fall into one or other of these two categories. For example, it is difficult to argue that the internal goals of the other two professions I have mentioned—music and philosophy—demand maximization in either of these two ways. I do not mean to deny that many who are involved with orchestras or philosophy departments do conceive of their aims in maximizing terms, since clearly they do. Many of them conceive of their aims along exactly the same lines as a sports team: they think they should always be striving to be better than other orchestras or departments, and they think of this as an end in itself, not merely as a means of securing funding. But this is just another example of the old mistake of seeing life as a competition. If you see life as a competition, then of course you will think the same way about your job. We need to forget about competition—about the fact that orchestras or philosophy departments are competing against other orchestras or philosophy departments, whether for money or people or anything else—and just think about a single orchestra or a single philosophy department in isolation. Is there any *inherent* reason why it should be trying to be as good as possible at whatever it is trying to be good at? The question, note, is not whether this is a *reasonable* thing for an orchestra or a philosophy department to try to do. The question is whether it is the *only* reasonable thing for them to try to do—whether, if they aren't trying to be as good as possible at whatever it is they are trying to be good at, we can conclude that they have no respect for the goals and values of their profession. I think we would draw this conclusion about a doctor, or a football manager: if a doctor didn't see why he should be trying to save as many lives as possible, or if a football manager didn't see why he ought to be trying to pick the best team, we would probably say that they didn't understand their job. I am not so sure we can really say the same of the selection committee for a job in music or philosophy.

Let us put the idea of maximization to one side, and think about a different, weaker suggestion: that employers should be obliged to make the decision of who gets a job on 'internal' criteria alone. This is one of the two aspects of meritocracy—first, the idea that hiring decisions should be based on merit *and nothing else*, and second, the idea that the *best* person should always get the job—which I distinguished at the start of Section 4. I noted that the second entails the first, but not the other way around. Now I want to see, in relation to this one particular way of arguing for meritocracy, whether the first aspect has any independent appeal when it is no longer supported by the second. It does seem as if it might have independent appeal. We might think, for example, that when the pursuit of profit starts to influence the way decisions get made in areas like sport or music or philosophy, that must be a bad thing, not just because it indicates that the relevant internal goals and values aren't being pursued to the maximum possible extent, but because it shows that those internal goals and values have been in some deeper way *contaminated* by the sordid pursuit of profit. This idea of contamination looks like the germ of a quite different argument for meritocracy. However, the first thing to say here is that even if commerce is a contaminating influence, the same might not be true of every 'external' factor. Remember that in this context, factors such as how much applicants need or deserve a job would also be deemed 'external'. If it is specifically commercialization that we are concerned about, it is a mistake to try to use the distinction between 'internal' and 'external' to attack it.[11] Moreover, even commerce is not as powerful a contaminant as is sometimes thought. It is often suggested that as soon as a football club or a university tries to make money (or at least more money than it needs to survive), it becomes a business *rather than* a football club or a university. But, to take football first, it is surely possible for a football club to be *both* a business *and* a football club. So long as when the team is actually playing football it does so in a way that remains true to the internal values of football, the club's pursuit of these values can survive the fact that it is also motivated by other reasons. The same is true of a university. Provided the actual process of education and scholarship is carried out in a way that remains true to the relevant internal values, the university's pursuit of those values can survive the fact that it is also motivated by other reasons—with, for example, academics being hired at least in part on the basis of their ability to bring in money or raise profile, and students admitted at least in part on the basis of ability to pay.

It is time to sum up where we have got to in this section. First, even if being good at the job isn't just a means to an end—indeed, even if the job both has non-instrumental value in itself *and* requires admirable qualities to do it well—applicants still don't have the right that employers should hire the best person. Nor do employers have any independent, impersonal duty to hire the best person, or even to exclude all factors other than merit from their deliberations. So in terms of what we can legitimately demand of employers, the situation is after all the same as when 'merit' is understood in purely commercial terms. We can only forbid employers to act *without reason*, in the strong sense, where that means acting thoughtlessly or capriciously or wilfully. If by contrast all we can say about them is that they are failing to pursue the internal goals or values of their business to the greatest possible extent, that doesn't necessarily count as acting without reason, and therefore doesn't count as treating anyone unfairly.

6. ARGUMENTS FOR MERITOCRACY THAT APPEAL TO EFFICIENCY RATHER THAN FAIRNESS

I suspect that the idea I discussed in the last section, that hiring decisions should reflect businesses' or professions' 'internal values', was never very central to most people's understanding of meritocracy. Most people think employers should be obliged to hire the best person for the job regardless of whether the job or the qualities required to do it well have any inherent value. But we have seen the problem with this kind of position: that once meritocracy starts to look as if it is purely a matter of efficiency, and nothing to do with being fair to applicants, it is hard to see how it can justify intervening and telling employers how they ought to make decisions. One way a meritocrat might try to get around this, as we saw in Sections 3 and 4, is by linking efficiency to the idea of rationality, and then linking rationality to fairness. So we find meritocrats arguing that if rationality requires employers to hire the best person, then this must also be what fairness demands, since it is unfair to treat people irrationally. But we have also seen the problem with this line of argument, namely, that it is difficult to equate acting non-meritocratically with acting irrationally.

I want now to consider a different kind of argument, one that appeals directly to efficiency without trying to link efficiency with fairness. The reader might be wondering why it has taken me so long to get around to considering this argument for meritocracy. Is it not the most obvious? Well, it cannot be the version most people believe in. Two things make me say this. First, people seem to think of meritocracy as being at least part of equality of opportunity, and they think of equality of opportunity as being about fairness to applicants, rather than simply making the economy more efficient. Second, most meritocrats seem to think that meritocracy justifies intervention, and we might expect that employers' rights against intervention could only be overridden by an argument based on fairness, rather than on efficiency alone. However, I made clear in the Introduction that I was not going to place any artificial limits on the discussion by restricting myself to considering only those views which could be thought of as possible interpretations of equal opportunity. The fact that a purely efficiency-based meritocracy doesn't seem as if it could count as an interpretation of equal opportunity doesn't make it any less interesting as an answer to the question of how jobs should be allocated.

The first thing to note about the argument from efficiency is that what we are looking for is an argument for *maximizing* efficiency, if the view it is supposed to support is the view that the *best* person should always get the job. It would be easy enough to argue that employers shouldn't be allowed to hire people who are downright incompetent, on the grounds that this might result in the economy completely breaking down. But that wouldn't support a maximizing meritocracy, the view that the best person should always get the job. It would support a much weaker version—one which required only that employers not hire people who are downright incompetent. This is a very minimal kind of meritocracy—and unlike the maximizing kind, is something we probably could leave to the operations of the free market.

What reason might we have, then, for requiring employers to *maximize* efficiency? Clearly any answer to this question is going to depart radically from the way the discussion has gone up to this point. It will have to appeal not to the claims of applicants, but to the claims of the consumers of the goods or services which it would be their job to produce or provide. The question is whether consumers have a claim that efficiency be *maximized*, and if so, whether this claim is strong enough to justify intervening in the way employers make decisions. Well, don't we all have an interest in the things we want being provided as cheaply or competently as possible?

Yes, but the problem is that our merely *wanting* things to be provided more cheaply or competently doesn't obviously amount to a *moral* claim; and if it doesn't amount to a moral claim, it doesn't look as if it will be able to justify overriding employers' rights to hire as they see fit. We might all *want* employers to hire as efficiently as possible, but we do not have the *right* that they do so.

At this point a meritocrat might try to come up with a counter-example —a case where appealing to consumer interests does seem to justify imposing meritocracy. The most obvious such case, as I suggested in the last section, is medicine. In this case, 'consumer' interests, in the shape of patients' interests, do seem important enough to justify overriding employers' rights to hire as they see fit. However, it is not clear that this example really helps the meritocrat in his attempt to base a perfectly general argument for meritocracy on consumer interests, since medicine is self-evidently a special case: it involves needs rather than mere wants. There is no problem understanding how consumer *needs* might justify placing certain constraints on the way employers can behave. But any general argument for meritocracy will have to be based on consumer wants rather than needs.

There is also a second respect in which the medical example might be misleading. When we say that the medical profession should be meritocratic, are we thinking here about public or private medicine? If we are thinking about public medicine, then once again this is no help to the meritocrat in his attempt to come up with a general argument for meritocracy. There are special reasons why meritocracy is easier to justify in the public sector (I explore these reasons in the next section). The interesting question for present purposes is whether patients' needs are weighty enough to justify imposing meritocracy even in private medicine. I am not sure whether they are—at least, not if we are talking about the strong, maximizing version of meritocracy. I cannot see why, if the state was already providing a parallel system of public medicine for everyone who needed it, it would also be duty-bound to ensure that those who chose to go private were getting the best possible value for money. Of course, in practice, if the public medical system is failing to provide treatment to everyone who needs it, or is failing to provide treatment of an acceptable standard, then those who end up going private cannot really be said to have had any *choice*. But even then, the way to react to these public sector failings is surely to try to put them right, instead of trying to compensate by interfering in private medicine.

I am not suggesting that the state should simply keep out of private medicine. Certainly there should be minimum standards: no one should be allowed to perform operations unless they have some minimum level of medical training. What I am contesting is whether the state should go so far as to demand that private medicine be run *as efficiently as possible*. If I am right, then even in the medical case, where the 'consumer interests' at stake are vital needs rather than mere wants, those interests still cannot justify meritocracy as it is generally understood—as demanding that the *best* person always get the job.

It seems that the meritocrat has to abandon the idea that efficiency is good because of what it does for the immediate satisfaction of consumer interests. He could argue instead that the reason we should maximize efficiency is not because of anything this would do for anyone directly, but because of its *long-term effects*. For example, he could argue that maximizing efficiency is good because it increases long-term economic prosperity. Now, I am going to leave to one side the empirical question of whether state-regulated meritocracy could really succeed in increasing long-term economic prosperity. This is not a question for a philosopher to try to answer. The question for our purposes is: assuming state-regulated meritocracy could increase long-term prosperity, what is supposed to be the *value* of doing so? It has to be a moral argument, since it has to justify overriding employers' rights to hire as they see fit. And long-term economic prosperity does have all sorts of morally desirable effects. For example, it enables the state to do more for the poor and needy without getting into the political difficulties of putting up taxes. It also increases the total number of jobs there are to go round.

There is nothing wrong with trying to base the argument for meritocracy on these morally desirable long-term effects of maximizing efficiency —apart from the fact that the argument ends up looking pretty contrived. It begins to look like an argument constructed to fit a conclusion that has already been decided. As I have noted, there is a certain kind of person who is unshakably convinced that meritocracy is the answer, and who, if you persuade him that his current arguments for meritocracy are flawed, will simply start looking for more. However, although this is not a very respectable way to conduct a debate, it doesn't mean we can assume the end result is necessarily wrong. It could still be a good argument. But it does generate problems of consistency. For example, why, if the aim of maximizing efficiency is thought important enough to override employers' freedom to hire, isn't it also thought important enough to override applicants' freedom to choose which jobs to apply for—or, for that matter, their security of tenure once they have got a job? If we really took the drive for efficiency seriously, it seems we would end up not with meritocracy in the way it is usually understood—that is, with employers being obliged to hire the best applicants, but with applicants remaining free to choose what jobs to apply for, and workers, once they are in a job, being granted some kind of security of tenure—but with the freedoms of employers and workers and applicants alike being sacrificed to the idol of efficiency.

On the standard view, where meritocracy is understood as a matter of being fair to applicants, it is clear enough why applicants' freedoms are not in question: the concern for applicants' interests that makes us argue for fair treatment also makes us support, first, their freedom of choice, and second, their security of tenure once they get a job. The apparent inconsistency only surfaces when meritocracy is separated from the claims of applicants and is understood as being motivated purely by thoughts about efficiency. Efficiency does seem to tell in favour of a more single-minded kind of meritocracy, in which people can be drafted into jobs for which they are well suited, whether they want to do them or not, and in which they have no claim to staying in a job if someone better should come along. After all, if the aim is simply to get the best person for the job, why should we restrict ourselves to selecting from those who actually apply? And if you have to be the best person to get the job in the first place, why should you not also have to *stay* the best in order to keep it?

But perhaps these questions are not all that difficult for even an efficiency-based meritocrat to answer. Both freedom of occupational choice and security of tenure can be presented not as external constraints imposed on the pursuit of efficiency, but as deriving from efficiency itself. Take security of tenure first. It can be argued that if people were always worrying about whether someone better might come along and put them out of a job, this would be so bad for morale as to result in a net loss in efficiency, even after allowing for the admitted inefficiency of leaving people in jobs when they are no longer the best people available. There is little point in striving to find the best people unless you also try to get the best out of them when they are actually in the job. Similarly, freedom of occupational choice can be thought of as an essential part of efficiency rather than as an external constraint on it. First, because people will work harder if they are doing something they have freely chosen. Second, because freedom of occupational choice is a necessary condition of the free market in labour, and the free market in labour is the only proven mechanism for efficiently matching qualified people with vacant positions. Greater gains might *in theory* be available to a centrally planned system which forces talented but reluctant workers out of sub-optimal jobs they have freely chosen, but in practice the inability of such a system to acquire the necessary information, about people's talents and about the social value of work, ensures that this advantage will remain purely theoretical.

It seems, then, that even an efficiency-based meritocrat can after all explain why we should limit ourselves to intervening in the way employers make decisions, and not in the choices of applicants or the security of workers. It is, however, an interesting implication of the efficiency-based position that the state would be perfectly *entitled* to intervene in the way applicants make their decisions, and perfectly entitled to require employers to fire workers as soon as anyone better becomes available. The only reason it should not intervene is because intervention might do more harm than good, not because it would be unfair. Besides this slightly disturbing implication, there is also a further problem of consistency, only this time in a different direction. Even if we stick to intervening against employers, rather than workers or applicants, why should we restrict ourselves to intervening only in *hiring*? If meritocracy is based on efficiency, and if this is deemed important enough to justify intervening in employers' decisions, why not just say that the state is entitled to intervene every time it sees an employer using resources inefficiently? Once again, the special focus on hiring seems to be left over from the assumption that meritocracy is all about being fair to applicants. As soon as we accept that meritocracy is based on efficiency alone, and nothing to do with being fair to applicants, we should be equally prepared to intervene in other aspects of the way employers do business—for example, in the way they make their investments. This really does start to look like an attack on the very idea of private enterprise. I argued in the Introduction that it is dangerous to allow the debate about equal opportunity to spill over into a broader debate about private enterprise. If I am right, then the efficiency-based meritocrat has to explain what it is about hiring decisions which makes them a special target for intervention. He can't just say that the reason we shouldn't intervene in investment decisions is because it is more efficient to leave these decisions up to the market, unless he can explain why the same doesn't also apply to hiring decisions.

Of course, as with any issue of consistency, there are two ways the efficiency-based meritocrat can jump at this point. He could admit defeat; or he could embrace the implication that his argument supports pursuing efficiency in a more aggressive way than perhaps even he had realized. That is, he could embrace the implication that the state should intervene every time it sees an employer using resources in a sub-optimal way—provided it can be sure that intervention wouldn't do more harm than good. Similarly, he could embrace the implication that the state is entitled to intervene in the choices of applicants, and to require employers to fire workers as soon as anyone better becomes available—the only question being whether that intervention would actually increase long-term economic efficiency. Now, if any reader is tempted to jump this way, I am not sure what I can say to stop them. Perhaps there is nothing wrong with our choosing, as a society, to attach more weight to long-term economic prosperity than we attach to certain individual freedoms. In the end, it comes down to a choice between fundamental values—a choice about what kind of society we want to be. I don't believe that philosophy can always provide a definitive answer to questions of this kind, so I shall restrict myself to making one observation. This is that in making the choice, we should be careful about thinking of the demand for increased long-term economic prosperity as insatiable. This is precisely what is implied in arguing that we need to *maximize* efficiency—which is what is required to support meritocracy as it is generally understood, as the view that employers should always hire the *best* person for the job. Even if we base the argument for increased long-term economic prosperity on its morally desirable effects, such as reducing poverty or increasing overall employment, it is still a good question whether we should conceive of these in an insatiable, maximizing way. Equally, if we do decide to conceive of them in this way, it is then a good question whether we should carry on thinking of them as overriding all other social aims, all the way down.

7. MERITOCRACY IN THE PUBLIC SECTOR

In considering the case of medicine in the last section, I remarked that it is easier to justify imposing meritocracy in public medicine than in private medicine. My point there was that we should focus on the private sector if we want to test whether a given argument for meritocracy might apply universally, since if the argument succeeds in the private sector it will probably succeed in the public sector as well. This has been my approach throughout the discussion; the result so far has been that none of the various arguments has looked as if it might apply in the private sector. I want now to consider whether there might be a case for meritocracy within the public sector alone.

Even when I was still considering meritocracy in relation to the private sector, I made the point (in Sect. 3) that although meritocracy can appear very demanding, it is in fact easier to justify, in many respects, than some other conceptions of equality of opportunity. It leaves employers with a considerable amount of licence in terms of how they apply it, and is therefore difficult to oppose on freedom-based grounds. But, as I made clear in the Introduction, freedom-based grounds are not the only grounds for opposing intervention. There is also the idea that employers have property rights over jobs: since they are the ones who are going to pay the wages, their freedom to hire is just an example of their general right to spend their money as they see fit. It is this second ground for opposing intervention that differentiates between the private and public sectors. The wages of public sector employees are paid out of public funds, so if we are to talk about property rights in this context, those rights must belong to society, and the jobs can be thought of as being at society's disposal. So neither of the two arguments against intervention—the freedom-based argument nor the property rights argument—tells against meritocracy in the public sector. This means we don't even have to pretend that the efficiency argument is somehow also a moral argument, either by linking efficiency to fairness through the idea of rationality, or by appealing to its morally desirable long-term effects. We simply point out that public sector jobs should be allocated on merit, since anything else would be inefficient, and leave it at that.

Or so the meritocrat would have us believe. But can things really be so simple? It might seem that for public sector jobs to be allocated on anything other than merit would represent an intolerable waste of public money. Consider again the example of a university. I argued in Section 5 that there is no reason why a university should be *required* to understand itself as being dedicated to promoting excellence to the exclusion of all else; it can choose to understand itself in this way if it so wishes, but equally it should be free to choose to understand itself in a variety of different ways. But now we might be tempted to qualify this position: perhaps it applies to privately funded universities, but publicly funded universities surely *are* obliged to understand themselves as being dedicated to promoting excellence to the exclusion of all else—and therefore *are* obliged always to hire on merit alone.

Before we accept this conclusion, however, we should recall exactly what meritocracy, in this narrow sense, excludes. It excludes, for example, thinking about which of the applicants really *needs* the job. Now, this probably should be excluded if we are talking about appointing a surgeon. But suppose we are talking instead about hiring an unskilled park labourer. In this kind of case I can't see that there would be anything wrong with taking the needs of the different applicants into account. Certainly it would be misleading to describe this as 'wasting' public money. These two cases, the surgeon and the park labourer, represent the two extremes. University appointments fall somewhere between the two, and accordingly it is genuinely difficult to know what to say about them. Suppose a university department decided that the balance of its appointments, in terms of sex or race or cultural grouping, should reflect the balance of the society of which it is a part—even if that sometimes meant hiring someone other than the person who would be best at the job. Could we really describe this as a waste of public money? I am not sure we could. But note that I am not suggesting that every university department ought to behave like this. Even at the extreme where the claims of meritocracy seem least compelling—where we are talking about hiring an unskilled park labourer—there is nothing to stop people *choosing* to be ruthless meritocrats. The point is just that we, and they, shouldn't pretend they have no choice. The same is true of university appointments. It would be perfectly reasonable for society to decide that publicly funded universities are there only to recognize and promote excellence. But we don't have to. We could decide to give them a certain amount of autonomy, and this means accepting that they might decide to take into account other things about applicants than their ability to do the job.

So far in this section I have been talking about the exclusionary aspect of meritocracy—the idea that hiring decisions should be based on merit *and nothing else*. But I think that what I have said applies equally to the separate aspect of maximization—the idea that the *best* person should always get the job. Whatever values we decide the public sector ought to be pursuing, it would be perfectly *reasonable* to decide that they ought to pursue them to the maximum extent, but it is not obviously rationally *required*. Of course we don't want public sector institutions to waste money (in an absolute sense),[12] but nor perhaps should we want them always to be obsessed with making the most efficient use of it. True, sometimes it is only right that they be obsessed with efficiency: when it comes to saving lives or relieving suffering, as I said earlier, we would think there was something wrong if they weren't trying to be as efficient as possible. But perhaps they should not be quite so obsessed with efficiency, or value for money, when it comes to providing the good things in life: parks, for example, but also the arts, and maybe even education.

8. LEGITIMATE EXPECTATIONS

The argument for meritocracy looks to be in poor shape. None of the various approaches discussed so far, even those that only purported to cover a narrow range of jobs, have looked as if they could support meritocracy as it is usually understood, that is, as the view that the *best* person should always get the job. Perhaps the least bad argument is the one that bases meritocracy on efficiency alone. But even here it is difficult to argue that we really need to *maximize* efficiency; moreover, if we do argue for maximization, this will probably turn out to have implications far beyond hiring, and I suspect that it will come as a surprise to most of meritocracy's supporters that this is where the debate ends up. Its supporters clearly think of meritocracy as being essentially about hiring—specifically, about being fair to applicants at the point when they apply for a job.

I think this leaves the meritocrat with one last throw, namely, to argue that meritocracy is justified by the idea that people have certain *expectations*, and that it is unfair to disappoint them. However, I intend to argue, first, that this isn't a particularly good argument; second, that even if it was, it wouldn't apply in the present case; and third, that even if it was, and even if it did apply in the present case, it would not be clear exactly what it was supposed to imply. But before I start, I should perhaps try to clarify exactly what the argument is trying to say. Clearly it cannot just be saying that if an employer explicitly stated that he was going to hire on merit (e.g. when advertising the job) then this is what he now ought to do. *That* idea—that if you said you were going to do something, then you should do it—is something we can understand perfectly well without having to bring in the idea of expectations. What introducing expectations is supposed to do is show how you can incur certain obligations purely because of patterns in the way you behave, regardless of whether you have done anything that could be interpreted as making a promise or contract.

In the present case, the idea is that, *despite* the fact that not all employers make any explicit undertaking to hire on merit, and *despite* the fact that even those who do hire on merit are motivated by considerations of efficiency rather than fairness, the mere fact that employers generally do hire on merit, and therefore that everyone expects them to hire on merit, nevertheless means that it would now be unfair of them to do anything else. Now, for this argument to stand any chance of being successful, we need to add a couple of qualifications. First, the expectations in question have to be *reasonable*: that is, they have to be a reasonable thing to expect in the circumstances. For example, if my father, and his father before him, and his father before that, all went to the same Oxford college, that might cause me to have certain expectations for myself, but those expectations would not necessarily be reasonable. My forebears might all have been clever, articulate, and industrious young men; this, rather than any family connection, might be the most reasonable explanation of why they got in. The second qualification is that the expectations must also be 'legitimate'. What this means is that they must have been formed against a background that is not unjust.[13] For example, if I have always lived in idle luxury, but I have been living off the exploitation of others, it would not be legitimate for me to expect that lifestyle to continue.

These two qualifications are sensible enough, but they cannot make the basic principle sound if it isn't sound already. The real question is whether the bare fact of giving rise to expectations, even if they are reasonable and legitimate, can generate an obligation not to disappoint them. It is important to emphasize that the argument is about *obligation*: the point is not just that people would *prefer* you to behave predictably, so that if you don't want to upset them, you should try not to disappoint their expectations. That might be true, and it might give you a *reason* to conform to their expectations, but it wouldn't make it *unfair* not to; so it cannot help the meritocrat. The meritocrat needs to show that it is *unfair* to disappoint people's expectations.

It is easy enough to come up with examples that tell against this. Suppose you run a small firm, and for many years you have contracted out the cleaning of your office to the same company. You have been perfectly satisfied with the service, but then one day a friend of yours tells you he has set up a cleaning company, and so when your cleaning contract comes up for renewal, you switch it to your friend's company. Now, the owner of the other company might be surprised and disappointed—he might reasonably have expected you to continue using his company—but does he have any grounds for *complaint*? Have you treated him unfairly? I don't think so.

No doubt a believer in expectations will dismiss this as a bad analogy, on the grounds that failing to get a job is much more serious than losing a customer. Expectations only create obligations, he will say, in cases where serious interests are at stake. I'm not sure that this is a good reply, since I'm not sure that failing to get a job will *always* be more serious than losing a customer. In either case, how serious it is would seem to depend on how many other options you have. But anyhow, even if introducing the idea of seriousness could succeed in rescuing the general principle—the principle that merely giving rise to expectations can bring certain obligations—we would still have to confront the second question, of whether this general principle really applies in the present case. Now, the good news for the meritocrat is that there is no problem with either reasonableness or legitimacy. It does seem to be reasonable for people to expect employers to hire on merit, given that this is what employers have generally done in the past; and it also seems to be legitimate, provided we believe that the practice of hiring on merit is not itself unjust.[14] But there is another problem: it is employers *as a class* who generate the expectations, and yet the obligation to satisfy those expectations is supposed to be binding on them *as individuals*. The question, to put it in general terms, is whether simply being a member of a group of people who tend to behave in a certain way, such that other people come to expect that this is the way members of this group will behave, can really place you under an obligation to satisfy those expectations, even if you personally were not one of those who encouraged them. I think the answer to this question has to be no.

But again, even if I am wrong on this point, and the answer is yes, this is not the end of the argument. We still have to confront the third question: assuming the expectations principle is sound and actually applies in the present case, what exactly does it imply? One reason for being cautious about what it implies is that it is a purely procedural, rather than substantive, principle. Invoking the idea of expectations to support meritocracy presupposes that meritocracy is already the norm. Indeed, it only makes sense to talk about people's expectations against some fixed background. If, instead of asking how employers should behave given this fixed background, we were to see ourselves as starting with a blank sheet of paper, and asking what the ideal system would look like, then the idea of expectations couldn't support meritocracy—any more than it could support *any* position. It would imply only that whatever system we came up with, it should be phased in gradually and with fair warning.

But perhaps I have misunderstood the idea of expectations. It is not just about people being *disappointed*, its supporters might say: the point is that people have built their whole lives around their expectations of what will happen when they enter the job market. They have seen that employers tend to hire on merit, and consequently they have invested time and effort in making themselves into stronger candidates. Those efforts now deserve to be rewarded. There are two things to say about this. The first is that, while it seems to strengthen the intuitive force of the appeal to expectations,

I don't think it can get around one of the problems I have already raised: that the way employers behave *as a class* cannot give rise to obligations binding on individual employers. Perhaps people do deserve to be rewarded for the effort they have put in to making themselves into stronger candidates, but even if they do, this doesn't mean that every single employer is obliged to reward them. If a given employer can truthfully say that *he* has never done anything that could be interpreted as encouraging people to invest time and effort in making themselves into stronger candidates, it will be difficult to argue that he is obliged to reward those efforts now.

The second, more fundamental point is that it is a mistake to see this new argument as simply strengthening the intuitive force of the appeal to expectations. Unlike the way in which I first interpreted the appeal to expectations, this new way of interpreting it changes the whole nature of the argument for meritocracy. It uses the idea of expectations to turn what started out as an argument about *merit* into an argument about *desert*. When it started out, the argument was that the best person should get the job. This has now turned into the argument that since people have made an effort to become stronger candidates, they deserve to be rewarded. It seems we are back with the version of meritocracy outlined in Section 2: the idea of meritocracy as a way of rewarding people for their efforts. I have already raised some general questions about this version of meritocracy. But there is the further problem that this *particular* attempt to turn meritocracy from a forward-looking view into a backward-looking view actually winds up stuck uneasily between the two. We are being asked to see meritocracy *as it currently exists* as a way of rewarding people's efforts, but it is not a very accurate way of rewarding them. It rewards people for where they have ended up, rather than rewarding them for how much effort they expended to get there. This is what I meant when at the very start of the discussion I said that people are sometimes confused over whether meritocracy is about merit or desert. If they want to see people being rewarded for their efforts, they really shouldn't be supporting meritocracy at all, since meritocracy as generally understood isn't interested in asking what proportion of someone's current merits is down to effort and what proportion is down to things like environment or natural talent. They could object that an exclusively desert-based system—the kind of system I discussed in Section 2—would be unworkable. But even if they were right, that would not imply, contrary to what they seem to think, that we have to make do with meritocracy because it is at least partly desert-based. Virtually every possible system or pattern of allocation would be *partly* desert-based: whatever employers tended to look for, or were required to look for, people would have the chance to try to adapt to that, and their efforts would gain partial reward.

There is, however, an alternative way of interpreting the argument that people should be rewarded for their efforts at self-improvement. On this alternative reading, the argument is not really backward-looking at all, but forward-looking: it is not about rewarding people's deserts, but about encouraging people to invest in their future. If we want the next generation to invest in their future, we should make sure the present generation are seen to be getting a return on their investments. The first thing to say here is that if this is the way we are supposed to understand the appeal to expectations—as looking forward rather than back—then this negates the objection I raised above, to the effect that since an individual employer might personally have done nothing to encourage people to make an effort to become better candidates, he is not obliged to reward those efforts. It also negates another of my criticisms of the expectations argument: namely, that the idea of expectations is purely procedural, and has no necessary connection with the substantive ideal of meritocracy. I argued that whatever system was in place, provided it was in place for long enough, people would come to build certain expectations around it, and this would constitute an argument in favour of preserving it. The implication was that since this could be true of any system whatever, it cannot be a very strong argument in favour of any particular system. But the forward-looking way of understanding the appeal to expectations— i.e., that fulfilling people's expectations is just a way of encouraging the next generation to invest in their future—*is* necessarily tied to meritocracy. It is a logical supplement to the argument from efficiency. But by the same token, this also means that the appeal to expectations is not, on this way of understanding it, a *new* argument: it is, precisely, just another appeal to efficiency. And it certainly means that the expectations argument is no longer anything to do with *fairness*—which will, I think, defeat the object for many meritocrats. They saw in the idea of expectations a way of vindicating their feeling that meritocracy is all about being fair to applicants, without actually having to abandon the hard-nosed underlying view that meritocracy is all about efficiency. But it turns out that the only version of the expectations argument which actually supports meritocracy cannot after all justify their sense that there must be some connection between meritocracy and fairness.

9. SHOULD WE BE TRYING TO PROMOTE MERIT INDIRECTLY?

I have argued, first, that we cannot obviously demand that employers always hire the best person for the job, and second, that *fairness* certainly doesn't demand that they do so. But I made the point in the Introduction that even if we decide we cannot directly require employers to promote merit, we still have the option of promoting merit *indirectly*. We can concentrate on creating the background conditions in which merit can thrive, and simply rely on private sector employers voluntarily taking advantage of that. In these terms, there are all sorts of things we could be doing to promote merit, without having to intervene in the way employers make decisions. The most obvious route is through state-funded education; there is also the more subtle possibility of trying to create a public culture in which merit is valued.

The first thing to say here, as I said in the Introduction, is that this can't be the *only* thing we should be doing in education, social policy, and so on. It is true that some meritocrats do seem to imply that the only reason for making sure, for example, that everyone gets a decent education is so that we can be confident later on that it really is the best people who are getting the jobs. But this cannot be the *only* reason for making sure that everyone gets a decent education. This leaves the more moderate view, the view that *one* of the things we should be trying to do in education, social policy, and so on is to create the conditions under which merit can thrive. But even this moderate view raises some interesting questions. If 'merit' is a matter of being good at the job, and being good at the job is just a means to an end—that is, if merit is understood in a purely commercial sense—why should it be the state's business to promote merit, even indirectly? Presumably for the kinds of reasons outlined in Section 6: because if employers make money, that is thought to be good for everyone in the long run, in terms of creating more jobs, more money to spend on public services, and so on. But I also pointed out, in Section 6, two things we should bear in mind before we decide to sacrifice everything in pursuit of increased long-term economic prosperity and the advantages that might bring. First, we need to think about whether the demand for increased prosperity and its advantages should really be thought of as insatiable. And, relatedly, we need to think about whether there might not be other things we could be doing with our time and money. Both these points apply just as much to pursuing prosperity indirectly, through using state education to promote economic merit, as to pursuing it directly, by intervening in the way employers make decisions. The state education system is surely not there simply to increase long-term economic prosperity—even if that would have morally desirable effects. Otherwise education becomes mere *training*. (This seems to be, increasingly, the orthodox view. But we would be well advised before it is too late to recall the alternative view of education espoused by Aristotle: that we educate ourselves not in order to make ourselves into better workers, but in order that we might make better use of our leisure. Of course, I am aware that most of those who are now in their last few years at school, or at university, think exactly the opposite: they think the point of being there is precisely to get a better job than they would otherwise have got. But they are making a mistake, and it is one that society should not encourage them in making.

10. CONCLUSIONS

Much more remains to be said about the question of whether we should be promoting merit indirectly, but I make no apology for the fact that I have spent most of my time discussing the direct version of meritocracy, the view that employers should be required to hire the best person for the job. This direct approach seems to be the way meritocrats think—which means it is the way most of us think, if I am right in suggesting that most of us have meritocratic thoughts at least some of the time. Of course we think the state should be promoting merit indirectly *as well*; but we tend to think of meritocracy first and foremost as a matter of being fair to applicants at the point when they apply for a job. And this is the really fundamental thing about the suggestion that we might switch to promoting merit indirectly: it can't change the fact that promoting merit has nothing to do with being *fair*. In terms of the structure of the meritocratic argument, the idea that we might switch to promoting merit indirectly only came in because of the worry that if merit really is nothing to do with fairness, then it can't obviously support direct intervention. Switching to promoting merit indirectly does away with the problem of having to support intervention, but it cannot change the fact that the feeling we started out with, that it is somehow *unfair* for employers not to hire on merit, has turned out to be utterly without foundation. It simply avoids the question of whether this feeling is justified or not. And yet it is precisely this feeling, which seems to be almost universal, which dominates the debate. It is this feeling which explains why meritocracy is something like a default position—why even egalitarians, whose ultimate values we might expect to be completely at odds with meritocracy, nevertheless seem to think they can only argue for equality as an adjunct to meritocracy. Like everyone else, they have accepted that meritocracy must be at least part of the answer to the question of how jobs should be allocated, and so are left to try to fit in their own ideals around it.

I hope that I have at least put some pressure on this modern orthodoxy. True, I have conceded that if we understand 'merit' in the wide sense, where it just means anything that might constitute grounds for a reasonable decision, then by definition it is unreasonable to decide on any other grounds; and if it is unreasonable, then perhaps it is also unfair, if we decide that it is unfair to treat people unreasonably when serious interests are at stake. But this wide sense of 'merit' is not the way the word is usually understood. It turns the principle that 'jobs should be allocated on merit' into a purely formal principle. If we understand 'merit' in the more usual narrow sense, where 'the best candidate' means the one who would be best *at the job*, it is not necessarily unreasonable to decide on other grounds, and therefore not necessarily unfair. Understanding 'merit' in this narrow sense, we cannot avoid concluding that meritocracy is not what people think it is. They think it is about being fair to applicants at the point when they apply for a job, but in fact it turns out to be based on efficiency rather than fairness.

I have tried to illustrate how meritocracy's supporters, when confronted with this unpalatable fact, react by trying to explain that although the argument might start off appealing to efficiency, it somehow turns into an argument about fairness—or at least into an argument with some kind of moral force. So we find them appealing to the morally significant long-term benefits of efficiency, or else to the unfairness of disappointing people's expectations. But these appeals are unsuccessful. I showed in Section 8 that the appeal to legitimate expectations is both questionable in general terms, and not obviously applicable in this case. Earlier, in Section 6, I explained the two main problems with appealing to the long-term benefits of efficiency. First, there is a problem of consistency: of explaining why, if efficiency defeats the presumption against interfering in the way employers make decisions, it doesn't also defeat the presumption against interfering in other aspects of private enterprise. Second, like every other argument for meritocracy, the appeal to the long-term benefits of efficiency finds it difficult to explain why we have to *maximize* efficiency—which is necessary to justify meritocracy as it is usually understood, that is, as the principle that the *best* person should always get the job.

It seems we have to conclude that while hiring the best person for the job is a perfectly *reasonable* thing to do, it is neither rationally nor morally *required*. Of course, this conclusion leaves us with something to explain, namely, why we all have this feeling that meritocracy is morally required. Why do we have this strong sense that it is unfair for anyone other than the best person to get the job? I think there are two possible explanations of this. The first is that we are guilty of over-extending the idea of procedural justice. Procedural justice states that if a certain law is in force, then justice demands that it be applied consistently—whether or not the law was itself motivated by considerations of substantive justice in the first place. So, for example, we think it is only fair that the rich and famous should be subject to the same laws as the rest of us. Now, why do I say we are guilty of over-extending this idea when we bring it into the present debate? It is a procedural argument, and so relies on meritocracy already being in force, when strictly speaking this is not the case. Employers might generally hire on merit, but they are not following any explicit rule. So we cannot argue that since some people are clearly being treated on merit, everyone must be. The mere existence of a general *tendency* can't support a claim of procedural justice. Moreover, because procedural justice is a purely procedural idea, it cannot anyhow pull any weight in this kind of debate—a debate about what the law should be. Procedural justice has nothing to say about what the law should be: it says only that, whatever it is, it should be implemented consistently.

The second possible explanation of why we associate meritocracy with fairness is because we confuse it with the idea of discrimination. We might think we are outraged whenever the best person doesn't get the job, but in fact what really outrages us is when we see people being discriminated against on the basis of things like race or sex. These are quite separate ideas. It is true that requiring employers to hire on merit would be one way of making sure they didn't discriminate on the basis of things like race or sex. But it is only one way of doing this: we could instead just introduce specific principles forbidding discrimination. Of course, that would mean facing up to the difficult question of exactly which kinds of discrimination we think are unfair. But only a misplaced desire for theoretical simplicity could prevent us from seeing that this approach actually has an important advantage. By keeping the idea of non-discrimination conceptually separate from the idea of meritocracy, it enables us to maintain our conviction that discrimination is wrong because it wrongs those who are discriminated against, rather than because it is inefficient. It also means picking up some loose ends—principally, explaining exactly why discrimination is wrong if not because it is anti-meritocratic. However, this will have to wait until Part 3. Before that, in Part 2, we need to get to grips with the second idea which dominates the contemporary debate, the idea of equality.

NOTES

1. The '-cracy' part of 'meritocracy' suggests that the word should be reserved for the idea of *rule* by the best. But Michael Young, who introduced the word into general usage in his satire *The Rise of the Meritocracy: 1870–2033* (London: Thames and Hudson, 1958), extended it to jobs in general, and these days the word seems to have lost any specific association with power.

2. I should admit that in contrasting desert and merit, I am using 'desert' itself in a strict sense—the sense in which we would say of someone who was guilty of a crime (and was responsible for their actions, etc.) that they deserved to be punished. It is true that sometimes when we talk about 'what someone deserves' we mean 'deserves' in a much looser sense: we mean, roughly, how they should be treated, and that might take into account their merits (and needs etc.) as well as their strict deserts. But when I use 'deserve' or 'desert' in this book, I always mean in the strict, narrow sense, unless I indicate otherwise.

3. See again n. 1.

4. This distinction, between what people deserve and what they are entitled to under the rules (where the rules themselves are based on some notion other than desert), comes from Rawls (*A Theory of Justice*, 312–13). The difference is that Rawls takes this view all the way down, that is, he doesn't think we can even talk about people deserving a decent wage (as distinct from being entitled to it under the rules).

5. *A Theory of Justice*, 311.

6. See n. 2.

7. See e.g. J. R. Lucas, *Responsibility* (Oxford: Oxford University Press, 1993), 124.

8. See Allan Sindler, *Bakke, DeFunis, and Minority Admissions: The Quest for Equal Opportunity* (New York: Longman, 1978), 149–50.

9. See e.g. David Wiggins, *Needs, Values, Truth*, 3rd edn. (Oxford: Blackwell, 1998), essay X.

10. Compare e.g. Ruth Chang, *Incommensurability, Incomparability and Practical Reason* (Cambridge, Mass.: Harvard University Press, 1997), 12–13.

11. Michael Walzer is an example of someone who argues that jobs (and many other things besides) should be allocated according to 'internal' criteria, but whose arguments and examples really only illustrate the corrupting influence of one particular 'external' criterion, namely, money. See his *Spheres of Justice* (New York: Basic Books, 1983).

12. See n. 12 to the Introduction.

13. See Rawls, *A Theory of Justice*, 313.

14. I have argued that justice neither forbids nor requires it. But some of the arguments I discuss (and reject) in Parts 2 and 3 (e.g. the argument that people's prospects should not depend on anything that is beyond their control) would imply that it is unjust.

PART 2

Equality

I. EQUALITY AND MERITOCRACY

I remarked in the Introduction how the idea of equality crops up in a bewildering variety of demands in this debate. For example, some people demand that everyone should have an 'equal opportunity in the competition for jobs'; others talk about people having 'equal life chances'; others urge us to be altogether more radical, to try to make sure that everyone actually gets a job (and an equally good job) instead of accepting that there will always be inequalities and merely trying to introduce some kind of equality into the way these inequalities are distributed. It is true that the third kind of view can't really be said to have much to do with 'equality of opportunity', at least not in the way most people understand that idea. But I made clear in the Introduction that this book is not just about analysing the concept of equality of opportunity—and therefore that I am not going to restrict myself to discussing only those views which can be thought of as rival interpretations of that idea. The aim of the book is to ask what is the fair way for jobs to be allocated, and all three kinds of view outlined above are genuine attempts to answer that question, whether or not they can be thought of as rival interpretations of equality of opportunity.

In what follows I will be trying to do my best on egalitarianism's behalf, trying to see if somewhere among the many different arguments there is one that might succeed. There are two reasons for taking this approach. First, because the best views are the only ones worth attacking. There is no point wasting time and words in knocking down straw men. Second, because if it seems *too* easy to dismiss equality, we have probably missed something. Egalitarians may be wrong, but they are not stupid.

However, I think it is important in the end to understand that they *are* wrong, and this is what I hope to show. I make no apology for this essentially negative approach, since if it succeeds, it will have shown something important: that whatever other values might bear on the question of how jobs should be allocated, equality isn't one of them. This alone, if it were to be widely accepted, would change the debate forever. It is true that equality doesn't enjoy quite the same status as meritocracy. Almost everybody thinks that some form of meritocracy must be at least part of what we should be aiming for, and this is not quite true of equality. Yet there is still a majority—at least of those who talk and write about these matters— who seem to think that equality too must be at least part of what we should be aiming for. They accept that equality is not the only thing that matters, that it must be combined with, sometimes even sacrificed to, other values —most notably meritocracy. But if I am right, we need to go much further than this. The point about equality is not that it should come far down the list of our priorities, or that it is impractical or unhelpfully confrontational. The point is that it just isn't something we should be aiming for *at all* in this area.

Or so I hope to show. But before I start, it is worth trying to give the debate some structure. I have already noted that there is a wide range of egalitarian arguments in this area. The first thing is to separate them into two broad types. In the first, equality is put forward as the sole or main principle for governing the way jobs are allocated; in the second, it is combined with meritocracy. Examples of the combined type include the classical view, that the best person should get the job but that everyone should have an equal opportunity to apply, and the modern view which has developed out of this, that the best person should get the job but that everyone should have an equal opportunity or chance of becoming the best. There are two ways to understand these combined views. On one way, they involve a genuine commitment to two distinct values, equality and meritocracy. On the other, the egalitarian part is not really a separate principle at all. Consider again the classical view that the best person should get the job but that everyone should have an equal opportunity to apply. If this means simply that anyone should be able to apply for any job and be judged on their merits, then it does not involve equality as a distinct principle: it is just another way of describing meritocracy. It appeals to equality only in a purely procedural sense. It says that since these are the rules—that jobs should be allocated on merit—they should be applied equally to everyone. To say that rules should be applied equally to everyone doesn't really add anything to saying that they are rules. It is part of the very notion of a rule that it should be applied equally to everyone.

For a view to count as properly egalitarian it must say that people should be treated equally in some more substantial sense than this. What about the more modern combined view, that the best person should get the job but that everyone should have an equal opportunity or chance of becoming the best? The first question is what exactly is meant by saying that everyone should have an equal *opportunity* or *chance* of becoming the best. It might mean that everyone should start in an equal position; or it might mean that everyone should have access to an equal amount of resources. Now, either of these is a more substantial kind of equality than everyone simply being subject to the same rules; but neither appeals to equality as a distinct value. In each case the argument starts from the belief in competition, and the kind of equality it recommends just derives from the idea of competition itself. The argument is like the idea that all the runners in a race should start at the same point, or be given the same equipment.

It is worth examining this race metaphor more closely, since it crops up so often in discussions of equal opportunity. There are, I think, two different reasons why people might decide to see the process of getting a job as being like a race. These two reasons correspond to the two concepts of meritocracy outlined at the start of Part 1. The first concept of meritocracy sees the point of a competition or race as being the only way we can think of those who are successful as *deserving* their success. If we start thinking along these lines, it is a short step to thinking that everyone should start the race *equal*, for it is natural to think that unless everyone starts equal, no one can be said to deserve their success. The second concept of meritocracy sees a competition or race not as a medium in which people earn their success, but simply as a way of identifying talent. On this view, the point of a race is not that the result is morally significant in itself, but merely that it serves to sort the talented from the less talented. Here too there is a role for initial equality. Even if the race is just about sorting the talented from the less talented, we might think that in order to draw our the *right* differences between people, we need to remove any other differences that might get in the way; in which case this too might tell in favour of a kind of initial equality. The idea would be that starting everyone off in the same environment is the only way to identify their natural potential.

But again, neither of these ways of understanding the race metaphor involves appealing to equality as a distinct value. In both cases the argument doesn't *start* with an appeal to equality: it starts with an appeal to competition, and only brings in equality as a means to an end—as a way of identifying people's potential, or of making sure they get what they deserve. Moreover, in each case, this further end is itself fundamentally *anti*-egalitarian: it is about promoting or recognizing *differences* between people, rather than emphasizing their equality. Clearly this kind of position is very different from pure egalitarianism. But it is also very different from the kind of position in which a genuine egalitarianism is combined with meritocracy—in which the pursuit of meritocracy is tempered by some kind of equality, rather than supported by it. This involves arguing for initial equality not because it is the only way of making sure that we are really getting the best people, or the only way of making sure that the winners deserve their success, but because getting the best people or making sure the winners deserve their success are not the only things we care about. According to this kind of view, people must be owed something more than simply a chance to apply for jobs in a meritocratic competition. They must be owed some kind of positive assistance before they reach that point; and the reason for thinking they are owed this positive assistance has nothing to do with making the competition more efficient, or making the winner more deserving. Of course, in determining what kind of positive assistance to give them, we should think about what will be useful to them in the competition—but only because this will be useful to them, not because it will be useful from the point of view of the competition.

If you hold this kind of view, it should still be an open question exactly what principle should govern the way the positive assistance is handed out: whether it should indeed be some principle of equality, or whether, for example, it should be something closer to the more minimal idea I outlined at the end of the Introduction, the idea that no one should be left without hope. However, for the moment I am going to ignore this question. The point I want to make here concerns the overall shape of the position—since it seems to me that one of the biggest problems with the equal opportunity debate is precisely that people aren't clear about the overall shape of their position, let alone the detail. They find themselves with certain beliefs about what should happen to people *in* the competition, and certain beliefs about what should happen to people *before* the competition, but they aren't clear whether these beliefs are derived from the same source, or whether they genuinely reflect a commitment to two distinct principles or values.

In part this is because they try to have it all ways, depending on who they are talking to. If they are faced with opponents who complain about the *cost* of giving people assistance before the competition, they tend to reply in the style of ruthless meritocrats, arguing that the real cost lies in *not* spending the money, since so much potential would then be wasted, for want of a little money being spent on developing it at an early stage. This way of arguing definitely gives the impression that the two parts of the view are derived from the same principle. Similarly, if they are faced with the kind of opponent who objects on principle to giving people *equal* assistance, on the basis that people simply aren't equally deserving, they reply that of course people aren't equally deserving *in the end*, but nevertheless unless they *start* equal, we can't say anything about what they deserve in the end. Those who claim to believe in desert but resist equality even as an initial requirement, they will say, are simply undermining their own position. Once again, this creates the impression that the two parts of the view, the belief in competition and the belief in initial equality, are derived from the same principle. The picture is very different, however, if we look at the way people who hold this view tend to argue if they are faced with a different kind of opponent, one who comes from the opposite end of the political spectrum, and who objects to meritocracy on principle as being simply unfair. When faced with this kind of opponent they tend to present the commitment to equality as if it does come from a distinct principle. It becomes a way of *civilizing* meritocracy, of combining the procedural fairness that meritocracy embodies with a quite distinct and more substantial kind of fairness embodied by initial equality.

Can they really argue all three ways at once? That depends on their aims. Clearly a philosopher cannot argue all three ways at once; but if we are talking about a politician trying to build consensus, perhaps he can. However, even a politician cannot *believe* all three arguments at once; and I think some contemporary politicians are in danger of doing just that, becoming the victims of their own rhetoric. They genuinely don't seem to know whether they believe in equality for its own sake, or whether their commitment to initial equality simply derives from some prior commitment to competition. Even if I am wrong, and they are clear in their own minds, they have certainly not contributed to a transparent public debate. If their aim was simply to build consensus then perhaps they have succeeded, but the consensus they have built is a confused and incoherent one, in which too many debates end up going round in circles.

Suppose however we could clear up this mess, and separate the kind of egalitarianism which appeals to equality as a distinct value from the kind in which some kind of initial equality is merely derived from a prior commitment to competition. What is actually *wrong* with the latter kind of view, apart from the fact that people are not always clear what it is? I have already said what I think is wrong with the prior commitment to competition, and

I am not going to repeat that here; I want to focus on what is wrong with the view as a whole. On the first way of understanding it—where a regime of initial equality is seen as a way of identifying people's potential—the problem is an empirical one. The view implies that we can only identify people's natural potential by starting them off in the same environment and letting their natural differences reveal themselves. The problem is that if all we really want to do is identify natural potential, there are probably easier ways of doing it. We could devise tests which control for environmental differences without having to go through the laborious and socially problematic process of actually placing everyone in the same environment. For example, it seems possible that genetic tests will be able to identify natural potential. (I should clarify my position here. I am not saying I am in favour of using genetic tests to identify natural potential. I am not even necessarily in favour of trying to identify natural potential by any means. I am merely saying that *if* we want to identify natural potential, it is not clear that this requires us to impose any kind of initial equality.)

On the second way of understanding the view, where a regime of initial equality is seen as a way of making sure the eventual winners deserve their success, the problems are deeper. The first question is why we are supposed to think of jobs as rewards for the deserving. I first raised this question in Part 1. I argued that even if we grant that desert has to come into the story somewhere, there are ways of being able to think of people deserving what they get paid without having to think they deserved to get the job in the first place. And if we don't have to think they deserved to get the job in the first place, then we don't have to worry about whether everyone started the competition for that job in the same position. An example might help to clarify this point. Suppose a violinist makes a fine recording of a piece of music. The fact that it is a fine recording is surely an impeccable reason for him to get paid for it: he has done something good, and deserves to be rewarded. It is absurd to suggest that this idea must somehow be tempered by the thought that as far as getting the job in the first place is concerned, he was no more deserving than a number of other candidates. If the question is simply whether he deserves to be paid for what he has done, then it is irrelevant whether he deserved to get the job in the first place. And if this is right, we certainly don't have to go further back and ask whether everyone *started* in the same position in terms of their chances of getting that kind of job—whether they all had an equally supportive upbringing, or an equal amount of talent, or whatever. I am sure this is how we would approach what I would argue is an analogous question, that of whether the violinist deserves to enjoy the feeling of pride or accomplishment the recording gives him. This feeling is similar to the financial reward in that it is one of the good things that come to him as a result of what he has done. We wouldn't be tempted to say he didn't deserve this feeling, just because other people weren't in the same position to experience it; so why don't we think about money in the same way?

I have dwelt on this point long enough already, here and in Part 1. For the sake of argument, I am now going to concede that despite everything I have said so far, we might still decide to think of jobs as rewards for the deserving. I am going to concede this because I want to make the point that *even then*, it remains a further question whether we should think of the kind of deservingness that is at issue as being the comparative or competitive kind. It has to be this kind, for it to follow that unless everyone starts equal, no one can be said to deserve their success. And to remind ourselves that there are other kinds, it is instructive once again to compare the way we think about desert in relation to jobs with the way we think about desert in relation to punishment. When we are talking about criminal justice, we don't tend to think that unless everyone starts equal in life, no one can be said to deserve to be punished for anything they do. This is because punishment is obviously not a *game*, so we don't feel the need to talk about a level playing-field (except in the purely formal sense that everyone should be subject to the same rules). I would argue that we should take the same attitude to jobs. We don't *have* to think of the job market as a game, even if we do decide to think of jobs as rewards for the deserving. If we don't think of it as a game, we don't have to assume that the kind of deservingness at issue is the comparative or competitive kind; so we don't have to think that unless everyone starts equal, no one can be said to deserve their success. We can say of someone that they deserved their success because of the effort they put in, without having to say anything about how deserving everyone else is, and therefore without having to say anything about their relative starting-points.

The opposing view, that we *always* have to say something about relative starting-points, might be mixed up with the separate idea, discussed at the end of the Introduction, *that it is unfair for people's lives to be affected by factors beyond their control.* Those who believe in this idea might well think that having a good or bad starting-point in life is precisely the kind of factor which is beyond anyone's control; in which case, this would be another reason for thinking that everyone should start equal. But I showed at the end of the Introduction that the idea itself is unrealistic—and, when we really think about its implications, deeply unappealing. I argued that we should replace it with the simpler, positive aim of trying to give everyone some control over their lives. This positive idea satisfies many of the same intuitions without having such wide and troubling implications.

So much for the derivative kind of egalitarianism—the kind which presents initial equality as a way of identifying people's natural potential, or a way of making sure they get what they deserve, or a way of making sure that their lives are only affected by things that are within their control. For what it is worth, I think that this derivative kind of egalitarianism is anyway not the most interesting way to understand the modern tendency to combine equality with meritocracy. I think that if we are trying to understand the appeal of such views, like the view that the best person should get the job but that everyone should have an equal opportunity or chance of becoming the best, we would do better to see the egalitarian part as distinct, as a way of tempering the excesses of meritocracy. There *is* something unattractive about unrestrained meritocracy, and it is a sign of strength for its supporters to admit this. Of course, the fact that meritocracy is unattractive is far from its only problem: I argued in Part 1 that it just isn't the kind of ideal which could ever justify direct intervention. But for now I am more interested in how it is combined with other values, rather than in whether it is valid in itself. The point I want to make here is that there seem to be independent reasons for thinking that the most interesting kinds of egalitarianism are not those which present equality as subsidiary to meritocracy. Instead, they either combine equality with meritocracy but as a distinct value, or they do not combine equality with meritocracy at all. It is these kinds of egalitarianism which concern me for the remainder of Part 2. I hope to show that equality is not good in itself, which would tell against these and any other views which appeal to equality as a distinct value. If I am right, equality just isn't something we should be striving for at all in this area, either on its own or in combination with other values.

2. SOME COMMON BUT UNSUCCESSFUL ARGUMENTS FOR EQUAL TREATMENT

Those arguments which do appeal to equality as a distinct value can be broken down into three parts. They must begin by trying to show that everyone has an equal claim. Next, they must move from the premise that everyone has an equal claim to the conclusion that everyone should be treated in some way equally. And finally, they must specify in exactly what way people should be treated equally—whether they should be given an equal chance, an equal amount of help, or whatever.

Not everyone will agree with this way of breaking the argument down. Ultimately, I hope it will prove its usefulness in the discussion that follows. However, I want to say a couple of things in its defence before we start. The first concerns the role of the second step in the argument. Some might think that if people's claims are equal, we don't need a further argument to establish that they should be treated in some way equally: the only question is what form of equal treatment is required. In other words, it seems we can move straight from the first step to the third. Why then do I think it worth separating the second step, which tries to establish the abstract argument for equal treatment, in advance of saying exactly what form of equal treatment is required? Well, for one thing because some arguments for equal treatment turn out to rely on the idea that treating people unequally is *irrational*, whereas others argue directly for equality as a distinctively *moral* requirement, without going via the idea of rationality. These two kinds of egalitarian argument are clearly worth distinguishing, and the point where they diverge is the second of the three steps as I have set them out here.

The other thing I want to say in defence of my initial analysis concerns the whole idea that egalitarian arguments can be broken down into separate steps—whether two, or three, or any other number. I am not suggesting that egalitarian arguments fall into distinct steps in the sense that any version of one step could be combined with any version of any other step. For example, the exact respect in which people's claims are thought to be equal (step one) must be connected *in some way* to the exact form of equal treatment which is ultimately supposed to follow (step three). So I am certainly not suggesting that the three steps of any given egalitarian argument should be assessed in complete isolation; and indeed the discussion that follows doesn't fall neatly into three sections corresponding to the three steps. That was never the point of setting out this initial analysis. It is not meant as a framework around which the discussion can be neatly organized. The point is simply that it might help to keep the different parts of the argument separate in our minds, in the sense of always being clear which step we are talking about at any given time.

So much for preliminaries. Let us start, then, with what I have suggested must be the first step in any egalitarian argument, the attempt to establish that everyone has an equal claim—in this case, an equal claim on a job. What *kind* of claim are we talking about here? We could be talking about the same kind of claim we were talking about in Part 1, claims of merit or desert. But egalitarians tend to talk more often in terms of *needs*. People certainly need jobs, and not just because they need the money. There is a second kind of need here which would not be satisfied simply by paying people to do nothing. This is the psychological need to pay your own way, to be responsible for sorting yourself out, rather than simply being a burden on others. For most people, not being able to pay their own way is psychologically damaging—and not just in the obvious sense of how it makes them feel. It also makes it difficult for them to see their lives in the way they ought, as stories they help construct. Being dependent on others encourages a more passive attitude, in which life is seen as something that simply happens to you, as opposed to something that is at least partly under your control. This helps explain why work is so central to self-respect even at the lower end of the income scale. The reason is not that people define themselves by their job, but that unemployment brings with it the shame of having failed to protect yourself and your family from poverty.[1]

How might an egalitarian try to turn this talk about needs into an argument for equality? He will probably start by trying to get us to agree that everyone needs a job—and that in an ideal world, everyone who needed a job would be able to get one. He will then take this to imply that there is at least a *sense* in which everyone has an equal claim on a job. But this is already too quick. When we say that in an ideal world, everyone who needed a job would be able to get one, we are just expressing a general sympathy for our fellow men, the kind of minimal impartial sympathy that most of us take to be the mark of a civilized person. This kind of expression of general sympathy does not imply that we are egalitarians, in any substantial sense. Indeed, when we agree that in an ideal world everyone who needed a job would be able to get one, we probably don't think we are committing ourselves to anything substantial. But to the extent that we are committing ourselves to something, that must be in the context of an altogether different debate, a debate about how many jobs there should be, not about how jobs should be distributed. I have already conceded that the two debates are not completely unrelated: the reason why we care about jobs being fairly distributed is because we recognize that they are important to people, and this also tells in favour of trying to make sure there are more jobs to go round. But although the two questions are related, they are still separate questions; and only one of them, the question of fair distribution, is the subject of this book. This question of fair distribution is only interesting under conditions of scarcity. Where a good is scarce, if we want to argue for equality, we must argue not just that everyone has *a* claim, but that they have *equal* claims. It is true that even if everyone merely has *a* claim, then in an ideal world they would all have a job. But in order to justify treating everyone equally in the actual world, where jobs are scarce, and where there seem to be good reasons for favouring some kinds of people over others, we need to start from the much stronger premise that everyone has an *equal* claim. The problem is that this stronger premise is just as implausible when applied to needs as when applied to merit or desert. People differ in how much they need a job, just as they differ in how good they would be at it, or how much they deserve it. It might be true that everyone (or almost everyone) needs a job to *some* extent; but when it comes to assessing how strong those needs are, clearly some people's needs are going to be stronger than others'.

In the face of this problem, egalitarians might be tempted to look again at the initially less promising idea of desert. Desert-based arguments are not naturally associated with egalitarianism, because the kind of person who believes in desert tends also to think that desert differentiates people, as opposed to making them seem equal. Indeed, in terms of desert, people aren't even equal in the universal sense—that is, it doesn't even seem to be true that everyone deserves a job to *some* extent. However, egalitarians might try to use the idea of desert in a different, negative way. They might argue that *nobody* deserves a job, and take that as a basis for saying that everyone should be treated equally.

This apparently simple argument is in fact quite difficult to assess, because it contains multiple ambiguities. The first ambiguity is whether 'deserves' is being used in a strict or a loose sense.[2] To say that someone deserves a job in a strict sense is to say that they have *earned* it. To say that they deserve a job in a loose sense, on the other hand, is simply to say something about whether they ought to have one. One aspect of this is whether they deserve a job in a strict sense, but there are other aspects, including, for example, whether they need one. In other words, on the strict reading, to argue that nobody deserves a job is to say something about one aspect among many possible aspects of their claims, while on the loose reading, it is to say something about the strength of their claims overall. Besides this, there is a second, separate ambiguity: whether we should take the argument that nobody deserves a job at face value, to mean that nobody has any claim *at all*, or whether it might really mean that nobody has any *more* of a claim than anyone else—which covers the case where people's claims are positive and equal as well as the case where they are equal only in the sense of being equally void.

These two ambiguities are not completely independent of each other. If we are talking about people's *overall* claims, the argument surely cannot be that no one has any claim at all. This would imply not only that nobody strictly deserves a job, but also that nobody merits one, or needs one—which is absurd. With this interpretation of the argument ruled out, we are left with three other possible interpretations. First, that people's overall claims are positive and equal; second, that their claims of strict desert are positive and equal; and third, that their claims of strict desert are equally void. The first and second of these interpretations, each of which involves arguing that claims are positive and equal, face the same problem as the kind of egalitarianism which is based on the idea of need: namely, it is difficult to believe that people's claims just happen to be equal. We might be prepared to believe that everyone is equal in the sense of having *some* claim, but not in the sense of having *equal* claims. With the third interpretation, there is at least a possible argument for thinking people's claims are equal, in the sense of equally void. The argument runs something like this. We might be tempted to think that someone deserves a job if, say, they worked hard at school to get decent qualifications. But the problem is that whether they got decent qualifications doesn't depend *only* on how hard they worked: it also depends on other factors, some of which aren't the kind of thing they can be held responsible for. Indeed, how hard they worked might itself have depended on things they couldn't be held responsible for, such as their genetic predisposition to work hard, or their family background. The same goes for any other plausible basis for a claim of strict desert: when we look more closely, it too will turn out to be influenced by factors people can't be held responsible for, which invalidates it as a basis for a claim of desert. Or so the argument goes.

The very fact that this argument turns out to invalidate every possible basis for a claim of desert suggests that it represents an attack on the idea of desert itself, rather than a specific attack on the relevance of desert to the allocation of jobs. This alone might be enough to make us suspicious: we might wonder whether an idea like desert, which is so central to our everyday dealings with one another, could really turn out to be meaningless.[3] However, let us grant that the egalitarian can establish, either by this general argument or by some argument tied more specifically to the case of jobs, that as far as strict desert is concerned, no one has any claim at all. This just brings us to the next problem, which concerns the route the argument will have to take through the second of the three steps I separated at the start of the section. The second step moves from the premise that everyone has an equal claim to the conclusion that they should be treated in some way equally. The problem is that people's claims being equal in the sense of equally void doesn't obviously have any positive implications for how they should be treated. If no one has any claim at all, why should we care what they get?

This is perhaps the best illustration of why it is necessary to break the egalitarian argument down into three steps rather than just two. As I said at the start of the section, it is tempting to think that if people's claims are equal, then we don't need a further argument for equal treatment; the only question is what form that equal treatment should take. But if people's claims are equal only in the sense of being equally void, then it just *isn't* obvious that this has any positive implications for how they should be treated. We do need a further argument for treating this kind of case as if it was the same as the case where people's claims are positive and equal.

What might such an argument look like? In other times and places, it has sometimes been thought appropriate, where two people each claim something (a horse, a kingdom, a woman), that they should fight for it. This idea can seem alien to us. But it has clear affinities with some versions of equality of opportunity—for example, with the kind of view, discussed in Part 1 and in Section 1 above, which sees the process of getting a job along the lines of a competition or a race. Indeed, this might be the best way of understanding that kind of view: as offering a solution to the problem that, until we allow people to fight to stake a claim, none of them can be said to deserve anything. The terrible weakness in this view, however, is that the proposed solution is quite incompatible with the argument which is used to establish that there is a problem in the first place. The problem is supposed to be that no one deserves a job; and the argument which is used to establish this actually implies that it is impossible for anyone ever to deserve anything. But if this is is true, then it is no solution to have people fight it out, since we wouldn't be able to say that the winners deserved to win.

The other thing to remember about this kind of view, as I suggested in Section 1, is that it does not appeal to equality as a distinct value. It arises when someone who believes in the idea of desert comes across a case where this idea doesn't seem to apply. He reacts by trying to put in place the background conditions which are necessary for desert to come into play—which, depending on his view of desert, might or might not involve some kind of initial equality. This is a quite different kind of argument from the kind which *starts* with a belief in equality. It is the latter kind which I want to focus on in the remainder of Part 2. The first question, then, is whether any argument of this kind applies in the case where people's claims are equally void as well as in the case where their claims are positive and equal.

There is one possible candidate: the argument *that it is unfair for some people to be worse off than others through no fault of their own*. I take this to be the same as saying that it is unfair for some people to be worse off than others unless they *deserve* to be worse off. This argument does succeed in making the kind of case where no one has any claim look like the kind of case where people's claims are positive and equal. If *either* no one deserves a job, *or* everyone is equally deserving, then those who end up without a job (or with a worse than average job) will be worse off than others without deserving to be worse off. Perhaps this really is what lies behind the view that since no one can really be said to deserve anything, everyone should be treated equally. The proponents of this view might have started by thinking that it is unfair for some people to be worse off than others without deserving to, only then to conclude that in fact this rules out all inequality, since no one can really be said to deserve anything. I have already said what I think of this last, additional claim. What I want to focus on now is the kind of egalitarianism which shares the same starting-point, but accepts that some inequalities can be deserved. This seems to be the position of many influential egalitarians, including G. A. Cohen, Ronald Dworkin, and Thomas Nagel.[4]

It is because these egalitarians want to find a role for desert within their theory, and because they understand desert in a distinctive kind of way, that they actually end up invoking equality at two distinct points in the argument. Equality—or rather inequality—plays its first role as a trigger for questions of justice to begin: if there is inequality, then we must first ask whether it is deserved. Equality then plays its second role in determining when an inequality can be said to be deserved: only if everyone started equal can any subsequent inequalities be said to be deserved. I have already contested this second part of the argument. (I argued in Section 1 that initial equality is not necessary for desert—and I also pointed out that this is anyway not a fundamentally egalitarian argument, since the kind of equality it recommends just derives from some prior commitment to the notion of fair competition.) I want to focus now on the first role which equality plays in the argument: as a trigger for questions of justice to begin. If there is inequality, the argument goes, we need to know whether it is deserved— because if it is not deserved, it must be eradicated. It is worth discussing this part of the argument separately, since while it is *normally* combined with an egalitarian view of the conditions which have to be in place for people to come to deserve things, it *could* be combined with a different, non-egalitarian view of those conditions.

Why then do Cohen and Nagel and Dworkin argue that it is unfair for some people to be worse off than others unless they *deserve* to be worse off? The way their argument works is by conflating two quite different ideas: something's being *undeserved*, and its being *unfair*. To see how different these two ideas really are, consider the following example. Two people go for a walk; they are caught in a storm; one is struck dead by lightning. Clearly this is a dreadful shame, and the fate of the one who is struck dead is certainly undeserved—he doesn't deserve to be struck by lightning, and he doesn't deserve to end up worse off than the other person. But this isn't the same thing at all as its being *unfair*. Indeed, this strikes me as the kind of thing which is neither fair nor unfair. It is true that people often say that 'life is unfair', and what they have in mind is exactly this kind of thing, that bad things happen to people without them having done anything to deserve them. But this is surely just a loose way of talking—as I think can be seen if we look at the opposite kind of luck, good luck. From the point of view of Cohen, Nagel, and Dworkin it makes no difference whether we are talking about good luck or bad luck, since their view is a relative one. Their view says that it is unfair for me to have worse luck than you; it doesn't matter whether this is because I have a piece of bad luck or you have a piece of good luck. But what about, for example, the fact that the sun shone every day on your summer holiday, but not on mine? The idea of deservingness just seems inapplicable here; and it surely does not follow, from the fact that the idea of desert is *inapplicable* in a certain kind of case, that something must be done to rectify any inequalities that might arise.

To think that this did follow, we would have to believe that justice demands not only that people get what they deserve, but also that they not get anything they *don't* deserve—or at least that they not get any more of what they don't deserve than anyone else does. And some people—maybe even Cohen and Nagel and Dworkin—clearly do believe this. Again, this position is unable to distinguish one person's good luck from another person's bad luck; but if we think about good luck and bad luck separately, we are far more likely to think that undeserved bad luck should be corrected upwards than we are to think that undeserved good luck should be corrected downwards. Good luck in itself is surely unobjectionable. Consider what we might call 'windfalls'—good things that come to people by sheer good luck. We might decide to confiscate windfalls in order to pay for the correction of other people's bad luck, but there is surely no reason for confiscating them *in themselves*.

Of course, on the egalitarian way of thinking it is impossible to pull apart our intuitions about good luck and bad luck. It makes no sense, for an egalitarian, to ask whether a given change in our relative circumstances should be seen as a stroke of good luck for me or a stroke of bad luck for you. A stroke of good luck for me *just is* a stroke of bad luck for you, since what it does from your point of view is leave you worse off than me through no fault of your own. But reiterating this aspect of the egalitarian position doesn't really answer the point that there is an intuitive asymmetry between good and bad luck, it simply stipulates that any talk of asymmetry is meaningless; which is hardly likely to satisfy anyone who had the intuition in the first place.

Another way to think about this problem is that if the egalitarian way of thinking is right, we might just as well say that the reason we correct for undeserved bad luck is to give us something to do with the resources we get from confiscating windfalls. On the egalitarian way of thinking, this makes just as much sense as putting it the other way round—saying that the reason we confiscate windfalls is so that we can afford to correct for undeserved bad luck. But to put things the first way round is surely crazy. The egalitarian cannot see this: for him it makes no sense to talk about asymmetry between good luck and bad luck, so it can't make sense to talk about priority either.

These are not the only problems with this view, the view that justice demands not only that people get what they deserve but also that they not get anything they don't deserve. The other problems are essentially the same as those I raised at the end of the Introduction, in discussing the view that people's prospects should depend solely on things for which they can be held responsible. I suggested there that this view only makes sense if we see our overall aim as being that of trying to bring everyone's lives completely under their control; I argued that as an aim, this is not just impossible, but undesirable. In place of this impossibly demanding and entirely negative aim I suggested a less demanding and positive aim: that we should help people to see their life as a story over which they have *some* control, never mind complete control. This alternative would itself explain why it is desirable to correct for bad luck—at least if we are talking about really bad luck—since an excessive vulnerability to bad luck is just the sort of thing that leaves people feeling that their life is completely out of their control. This alternative would not, however, tell in favour of rectifying all undeserved differences, since it does not recommend correcting good luck downwards for the sake of it.

So much for the argument that no one should be worse off than anyone else through no fault of their own. But there is a second argument which also has the effect of making the kind of case where claims are equally void look like the kind of case where claims are positive and equal. This is the argument that it is unfair to treat some people worse than others *for no good reason*.[5] Another way of putting this is to say that it is unfair to treat people differently unless you have good reason to treat them differently. Of course, in the context of the debate about how jobs should be allocated, if the only thing we accept as a good reason is how good they are at the job, then this kind of egalitarianism effectively becomes a version of meritocracy. In which case, my objections to it would be the same as my objections to meritocracy: I would contest that the only thing we should accept as a good reason is how good people are at the job. But suppose we take a more relaxed view of what counts as a good reason—what does the argument then imply? Even then it doesn't obviously imply equality. It doesn't necessarily imply equality if people are merely equally deserving, since even if they are equal in this sense, there could still be other good reasons for treating them differently. They might have different needs, or capacities, or whatever. Indeed, it doesn't necessarily imply equality even if people's *overall* claims are equal, because there can be good reasons for treating people differently which are no part of their claims. Suppose, for example, there are a number of patients in a state hospital awaiting treatment for the same illness. Suppose they are all equally needy, and equally deserving, but some are just more expensive to treat than others. If resources are scarce, this is a good reason for giving priority to those who are cheaper to treat, thereby enabling more to be treated overall. We wouldn't naturally say that those who were cheaper to treat had a stronger *claim* to treatment. But nor would we say they were being treated differently *for no good reason*. So we cannot equate people having equal claims with there being no good reason to treat them differently.

If this is right, then it isn't clear that this argument, that it is unfair to treat some people worse than others for no good reason, is going to be any help at all to the egalitarian. It is an argument about what should happen when *reasons* are equal, not about what should happen when *claims* are equal, and overall reasons, being an even wider notion than overall claims, will hardly ever be absolutely equal. However, perhaps there might be some contexts, where there are very strict rules about what could count as a relevant reason, in which overall reasons might sometimes be equal. Let us assume that there are, so that we can pursue the argument a little further. After all, this argument—that it is unfair to treat some people worse than others for no good reason—is made so often by egalitarians that they must believe it has some application. The next question, then, is whether, if overall reasons are equal, that would imply that people should be treated equally. The way the argument tries to establish this is by linking fairness to rationality. The basic idea is that it is irrational to treat people differently without good reason, and that it is unfair to treat people irrationally, at least when serious interests are at stake. This is an idea which meritocrats have separately tried to exploit, as we saw in Part 1. The fact that it involves presenting equal treatment as fair *because rational* again illustrates why it is useful to break down egalitarian arguments into three steps rather than just two. There is a great difference, as I said at the start of this section, between this kind of argument, that equal treatment for equal claims is fair *because rational*, and arguments which argue directly for equality as a distinctively moral requirement, without going via the idea of rationality.

Now, I don't dispute the basic idea here, that it is unfair to behave irrationally when serious interests are at stake. I am going to take the same approach as in Part 1, which is to point out that in this kind of argument, everything depends on exactly what counts as behaving irrationally. Specifically, the question is whether it really is irrational to treat people differently without good reason. The way I am going to test this is to look first at choices that do not involve people. Since the argument is supposed to be that treating people differently without good reason is unfair *because irrational*, it should follow that treating impersonal choices differently without good reason is also irrational. Suppose you are faced with a number of choices, none of which is better than the others. Does it really follow that treating them equally is the only rational thing to do? Suppose, to make the example more concrete, you have to choose between two ways of spending the afternoon, and have no more reason to do one than the other. Would there really be anything *irrational* in simply plumping for one, rather than treating them in some way equally (either by dividing your time between them, or tossing a coin)? I can't see that there would. The argument relies on the fallacious move from the premise that there is insufficient reason to treat two things differently to the conclusion that there is sufficient reason to treat them alike. True, if you simply plump for one, that choice will not be *rationally justified*; but to think that makes it *irrational* is to make the same mistake as Buridan's Ass, the mythical creature that found itself midway between two equally attractive haystacks and starved to death because it could not decide which to head for. We would do better to think of such choices, choices that are underdetermined by reason, as neither rational nor irrational. They are like spontaneous choices, which I discussed in Section 4 of Part 1, and which are similarly not based on any belief that what you are doing is what you have *most* reason to do. That alone cannot make them irrational.

It seems that the argument from insufficient reason cannot help the egalitarian. This brings me to the third and final argument I am going to consider in this section. This argument is very similar to the argument from insufficient reason, but perhaps not exactly the same. It is the idea that there is such a thing as a 'requirement of ethical consistency'—a requirement to 'treat like cases alike'. This too has the effect of making the case where no one has any claim look the same as the case where people's claims are positive and equal. It might just be a different way of putting exactly the same point as the argument from insufficient reason, the point that you should treat every case alike unless you have good reason not to. But it is worth thinking about the notion of consistency separately for a moment, to see whether it might be of any independent use to the egalitarian.

People do sometimes talk about consistency as if it were a separate ethical principle, a virtue in itself. But consider the case where everyone's claim is positive and equal, and you don't satisfy any of them. There is nothing obviously virtuous about that: you are just making the same mistake consistently. Admittedly, it makes a difference if we are talking about a public official who is implementing a rule, since consistency *is* a virtue when it comes to applying rules. I mentioned this—the idea of procedural justice—at the end of Part 1. But I also made the point there that the idea of procedural justice, being purely procedural, cannot pull any weight in a debate about what the rules should be. Procedural justice says only that, whatever the rules are, they should be implemented consistently. The debate we are having here, by contrast, is not about how the rules should be implemented—to which of course the answer is consistently—but about what rules there should be in the first place. Should the rules themselves be egalitarian? Should the law require like cases to be treated alike—in some more substantial sense than simply that the same rule be applied to all? The question is whether the *content* of our laws, rather than their mere *application*, should reflect the idea that people are in some sense equal. This is not the kind of question that can be answered by an appeal to procedural justice.[6]

Once we have separated the idea of consistency from the idea of procedural justice, we can see that consistency plays a purely diagnostic role, rather than being a virtue in itself. Unless we are talking about implementing rules, inconsistency merely indicates that there might have been a mistake; it has no inherent moral significance. Nevertheless, an egalitarian might think he could use this diagnostic role as the basis of an argument for equality. As with the argument from insufficient reason, the idea would be that we can establish a conclusion about unfairness by invoking the prior idea of rationality. Rationality tells us that inconsistency between similar cases suggests that there must have been a mistake in at least one of them. Of course, because this is a point about rationality, it applies to impersonal choices as well as to choices that involve people. It just follows from there being something you are trying to get right across a number of cases. But when this point is applied to choices that involve people, perhaps it can support the idea that inconsistency or inequality is unfair—because it is thought to be unfair to treat people irrationally.

The problem with this argument is that it takes inconsistency beyond its proper diagnostic role, implying that inconsistency is irrational *in itself*, when in fact it does no more than indicate the possibility of error. We cannot argue that unequal/inconsistent treatment is unfair because irrational, until we have actually established that the inconsistency does in fact reveal a mistake in the particular case. Moreover, a further weakness in the argument is that in certain kinds of case, inconsistency cannot even play this limited, diagnostic role. It can only play this role where it is at least *possible* to satisfy every claim. Suppose, again, that you have to choose between two ways of spending the afternoon, and have no more reason to do one than the other; but this time you definitely can't divide your time equally, you have to do one *or* the other. Suppose you simply plumped for one, rather than tossing a coin. It would be a mistake to infer from this that you must have wrongly thought you had more reason to do the thing you plumped for. The same applies when a choice involves people's claims. If you satisfy some people's claims and not others, that can only be taken to indicate that you didn't think their claims were equal if you could in fact have satisfied them all. If it was impossible to satisfy them all, for example because it was impossible to share whatever it was they had claims on, we cannot infer that you must have wrongly thought some had stronger claims than others. So in this kind of case, inequality doesn't even *indicate* irrationality, let alone constitute it.

It seems that neither the argument from insufficient reason nor the so-called requirement of ethical consistency can show that it is irrational, and therefore unfair, to treat equal claims unequally. But even this is perhaps not the biggest problem with these arguments. Suppose it was always irrational to treat people unequally/inconsistently for no good reason. The real problem is that if this was our *only* reason for condemning unequal treatment, we would not have explained what was *distinctively* wrong with it. We would be left with the troubling implication that treating people unequally is neither better nor worse than treating them irrationally in other ways. Treating people unequally would be no worse, for example, than treating them stupidly, or on the basis of faulty reasoning. Yet we would not naturally describe these ways of treating people as unfair. This throws doubt on the whole project of trying to use the idea of rationality to explain why certain ways of treating applicants are unfair. If this is right, then many meritocrats, as well as egalitarians, must go back to the drawing-board.

3. ARGUMENTS FOR EQUALITY IN THE FACE OF DIFFERENCE

Where have we got to? In the last section I looked at those egalitarian arguments which have the effect of making the case where no one has any claim look like the case where claims are positive and equal. With each of these arguments it seemed that the price of making the argument so broad— covering these very different kinds of case, the case where no one has any claim and the case where claims are positive and equal—was that the argument itself had to be quite thin and formal. From now on, I am going to focus only on the kind of case where people's claims are positive and equal. This is where we might expect to find the more substantial arguments for equal treatment.

The problem with this kind of case, as we saw earlier, is that it is difficult to believe that people's claims *are* ever both positive and equal. This is why I quickly passed over the standard egalitarian starting-point, the idea that everyone is equal in that they all need a job. It was simply too difficult to believe that everyone needs a job to exactly the same extent—this being what we have to believe, if we are to argue for genuine equality, as distinct from merely thinking that in an ideal world everyone who needed a job would be able to get one. Now, I think I was right to abandon the idea that any interesting egalitarianism could ever be built on an appeal to people's needs. Where I perhaps went wrong was in simultaneously abandoning the search for any kind of argument for thinking that people's claims are positive and equal, and going off into the dead end of arguing that claims are equal only in the sense of being equally void. Perhaps the real problem with the standard egalitarian argument is the type of claim it is based on. The problem with appealing to people's needs, as with merit and desert, is precisely that these kinds of claim admit of degrees; this leaves the egalitarian with the impossible task of trying to explain why a kind of claim which one might expect to vary in strength just happens to be universally equal. If we want to build a more plausible and satisfying egalitarianism, we should be looking at types of claim which don't admit of degrees— claims which people either have or they don't, and everyone in fact does. An egalitarianism based on this type of claim would be more plausible in that it would no longer have to explain why people's claims just happen to be equal; and it would be more satisfying in that it would rest on some more substantial argument for equality rather than on something thin and formal like the argument from insufficient reason.

We could argue, for example, that everyone has an equal claim on a job because we are all equally human. This is the right kind of idea, since being human does not admit of degrees. Moreover, we could combine this new starting-point with a new way of moving from the premise of equal claims to the conclusion that people must be treated in some way equally. We could argue that everyone must be treated equally because that is the only way to *express* the fact that we are all equally human. (Clearly this particular way of arguing from equal claims to equal treatment can only apply where claims are positive and equal: if instead people's claims were equal in the sense of being equally void, it would be entirely unclear why anyone would feel any need to *express* this.)

This already seems like a much more promising line of argument. It is, however, open to one obvious objection. Even if we agree that being human is a morally significant fact, it is at most one aspect of anyone's claim on anything. The full list of factors relevant to the distribution of any given good will also include some factors—like need, merit, or desert— which do admit of degrees. An opponent of egalitarianism will argue that although our claims might be equal in the sense that we are all equally human, nevertheless, precisely because our claims are *equal* in this respect, no one could really complain if we chose to fall back on some other relevant factor, like merit, as a tie-breaker. However, this objection fails to take account of the other new aspect of this line of argument, the way in which it moves from the premise of equal claims to the conclusion that people must be treated in some way equally. It does this by arguing that treating everyone equally is a way of expressing their equality. If we fell back on a tie-breaker like merit, we would no longer be expressing the fact that people's claims are equal.

This reply—that it would be wrong to fall back on a tie-breaker because of what that would express—is better than trying to argue that there is no factor which could act as a tie-breaker, because no other factor could possibly be thought relevant. It is more persuasive to argue that there *are* important respects in which we differ, but that the one respect in which we are equal is so important that our equality in this respect must be expressed in the way we are treated. A supporter of the tie-breaker approach might reply in turn by asking why we can't think of this equality as being expressed in the fact that we are all given equal consideration under the tie-breaking criteria. But this misses the egalitarian's point. The egalitarian's point, that our fundamental equality must somehow be expressed in the way we are treated, cannot be met by the requirement that everyone's case be given equal consideration under the relevant criteria, since if we think about it we will realize that this requirement would apply even if we *weren't* equal in any fundamental respect. It is nothing more than the requirement of procedural justice; it would apply, for example, within a meritocratic system, regardless of whether that system accepted that underneath people's differing merits they were all fundamentally equal. Egalitarianism has to amount to something more than this.

With the tie-breaker objection out of the way, it seems we have at last found the beginnings of a promising egalitarian argument. In bare outline, the argument is as follows. People are equal in virtue of having a certain kind of claim, which is the kind of claim you either have or you don't, and it so happens that everyone does; and this equality is so much more important than the other respects in which people differ that it must be expressed in the way they are treated. The problem, of course, is actually coming up with a claim which will make the argument work. The first suggestion I considered was the bare fact of being human; but this idea cannot make the second part of the argument work. What the second part of the argument requires is a kind of equality that is so fundamental as to make all other differences pale into insignificance. The fact of our common humanity cannot do this. In fact, the appeal to our common humanity really just *pre-supposes* that there is something especially significant about being human, rather than explaining what that is, and why it is so significant.

One possibility is the idea that people don't just need a job, they have a *right* to a job. It is a good question what this right is supposed to be based on, but leaving that aside for the moment, having a right to something seems like just the kind of claim we are looking for. Rights don't admit of degrees: you either have a right to something or you don't. Everyone who has a right to something therefore deserves to be treated equally, we might think. Moreover, rights are seen by many precisely as being a particularly weighty kind of claim. So, where everyone has a right to something, their equality in that respect might well be thought so much more important than the respects in which they differ as to require that they all be treated equally.

Of course, one question is whether people do in fact have a right to a job—and whether, if they do, it is the right *kind* of right. When we talk about the 'right to work' we might not mean that everyone should be provided with a job, merely that they shouldn't be unfairly prevented from getting one. We might just mean, for example, that no one should be discriminated against on the basis of things like race or sex. But only the 'positive' kind of right, the right to be provided with a job, could generate the kind of argument we are looking for: an argument for treating people equally in some more substantial sense than merely applying the same rules to everyone.

But suppose we did believe that everyone had a positive right to a job. This just brings us to the next problem. To think this could form the basis for a truly egalitarian view is to misunderstand the nature of rights. To say that someone has a positive right to something is to say that he has a claim on it which is sufficient to ground a duty on someone else's part to give it to him.[7] But it is a mistake to think of a duty as a kind of reason which outweighs all other kinds. A duty is indeed a special kind of reason, but the role it plays is *exclusionary* rather than overriding. An exclusionary reason (as Joseph Raz puts it) 'replaces rather than competes with some of the other reasons which apply in the circumstances'.[8] For example, promises generate exclusionary reasons: if you have promised someone that you will help them move house, you shouldn't think of this as *outweighing* any desire you might later have to do something more enjoyable; rather, the fact that you promised *excludes* your now thinking about whether or not you feel like doing it. It does not, however, exclude your thinking about every possible kind of reason which might come up. Presumably there are some possible circumstances which might justifiably absolve you from your promise to help your friend move house. This is the important point for our purposes: that while everyone's having a positive right to a job might exclude *some* otherwise good reasons for treating them differently, it won't necessarily exclude *all* such reasons, and therefore won't necessarily dictate that everyone should be treated equally. To illustrate this point, consider another example, involving a different kind of right in a different kind of context: the right to life-saving medical treatment. To assert that people have a right to life-saving medical treatment is to assert, among other things, that certain ways of choosing between people that might be acceptable in other contexts—ability to pay, for example—should be excluded here. But even in this case the exclusionary force of the right only extends so far. It doesn't extend to excluding consideration of the fact that where resources are limited, we would save more lives if we gave priority to those who are likely to respond better to treatment. The fact that we have a duty to save each person, considered as an individual, doesn't mean we should ignore the fact that some ways of choosing between people would enable us to fulfil our duty to more people overall. Analogously, to return to the case of jobs, even if we did think there was a positive right to work, that might not exclude every possible reason for treating people differently. It might not exclude the thought that, where jobs are scarce, allowing employers to treat applicants differently might actually result in more of them getting a job. We saw in Part 1 that allowing or even requiring employers to choose on merit might have this result—it might be more efficient and so, ultimately, might result in there being more jobs to go round. If so, then even if we did think that everyone had a positive right to work, this wouldn't necessarily justify replacing or combining meritocracy with some form of equality.

These, then, are the first two problems with appealing to the idea of equal rights. First, that when we talk about people having a right to a job, we might not really have the *positive* kind of right in mind; and second, that even if we do, this positive right might not exclude every possible reason for treating people differently. However, there is also a third problem, which is that even where equal rights do seem to require equal treatment, it is possible to argue that the *kind* of equal treatment they require is not really motivated by a concern for equality for its own sake. Truly egalitarian arguments contain the idea that claims are essentially relative, and equal rights are not essentially relative claims. Consider the kind of case where everyone's claim has been satisfied, but there is something left over. If claims are truly relative, then any excess should also be distributed equally. This does not necessarily happen with positive rights. Positive rights are rights to some specified amount of something, and while everyone's having a positive right to a specified amount of something might justify giving everyone an equal share up to that amount, if there was any left over, there would not necessarily be any requirement to divide it equally. It might be the case that no one had any further claim on it at all.

It seems, then, that what we should be looking for is the following: the kind of claim which people either have or they don't, which everyone does in fact have, *and* which is truly relative. According to religious egalitarians, there is such a claim: the fact that we are all God's children. They argue that while there are, of course, other important respects in which we differ, nevertheless the fact that we are all God's children is paramount, and must be expressed in the way we are treated. Now, I happen not to believe that we are all God's children, but I am more interested here in the general shape of the argument. I am using it as an illustration of what an egalitarian argument has to look like, if it is to work. The question is whether there is any secular analogue which could be substituted for the idea that we are all God's children. We have already considered and dismissed one suggestion, which was that we are all equally human. Another common suggestion is that we are all equally conscious beings. One thing to note about this suggestion is that if it did generate a kind of egalitarianism, that would be an egalitarianism that extended beyond the boundaries of the human race, to include all conscious animals. Of course, there is not necessarily anything wrong with that. The more serious problem is that the fact of being conscious, like the fact of being human, is a poor substitute for the supposed fact of being one of God's children in terms of how significant it seems—and therefore how likely it is to silence the other respects in which people differ. It is true that, occasionally, something does seem to follow from the bare fact of being conscious. We ask about the lower animals—lobsters, for example, when thinking about whether it is all right to boil them alive—whether they are conscious, and we tend to think that certain restrictions on the way they can be treated would follow from that fact alone. But this is because we are talking about extending restrictions, rather than about the distribution of some scarce good. When we are talking about extending restrictions, we need only ask who or what has a claim to be covered by these restrictions; whereas when we are talking about distributing some scarce good, as I said earlier, if we want to argue for equality, we must ask not just whether everyone has *a* claim, but whether they have *equal* claims. Can we really argue that all conscious beings have *equal* claims, purely in virtue of being conscious? In particular, can we really argue that the bare fact of being conscious is sufficiently important to silence all other differences? I can't think of a single context in which this idea would be taken seriously—that is, in which we would really think that some scarce good should be distributed equally among all conscious beings purely in virtue of the fact that they are all conscious, and despite their other differences.

Another possibility is to look at human *capacities*. Capacities certainly seem like the kind of thing you either have or you don't; and if we concentrate on those capacities which are distinctively human, this avoids the awkwardness of ending up with an egalitarianism which is dangerously wide. And indeed, we do find many egalitarians basing their views on the fact that, for example, we all have the capacity to be held responsible for our actions, or on the fact that we all have the capacity to form and pursue a rational plan of life. But once again this kind of argument for equal treatment is at its most plausible when we are talking about extending some non-competing right or restriction, rather than when we are talking about distributing some scarce good. It is plausible enough to think that certain non-competing rights—rights to certain kinds of freedom, for example—should be extended to everyone who is capable of pursuing a rational plan of life; and if we are charitable enough to think that almost everyone is capable of pursuing a rational plan of life, we might describe this as a kind of egalitarianism. But what makes it plausible is precisely the fact that the rights which are at stake are not competing: there is no limit to the number of people we can give these freedoms to. It is far more difficult to believe that when we are allocating scarce resources we need only ask who would benefit from them, and ignore the fact that some would benefit from them much more than others. In this case the problem is not, as it was with the argument based on consciousness, that the claim we have chosen to focus on does not seem significant enough to silence other differences. The problem is that it isn't really the kind of claim which you either have or you don't. The capacity to pursue a rational plan of life admits of differences in quality, if not quantity; and the mere fact that we are all equal in terms of having this capacity to *some* extent doesn't seem significant enough to silence these differences.[9]

However, an egalitarian might try to refine this argument. Suppose we are considering whether educational resources should be distributed equally. He might try arguing that the truly striking similarity is not so much the fact that we all have the capacity to pursue a rational plan of life, as the fact that for each and every one of us, there is such a big difference between what we can achieve with our lives if we are given help, and what we can achieve if left alone.[10] It is this similarity, the egalitarian might say, that justifies ignoring our other differences and treating everyone equally in the distribution of educational resources. This argument has a certain appeal; but in the end it doesn't really escape from the problems I have been discussing. Again, the supposed similarity is not detached enough from other differences to make a convincing case for focusing on the similarity and ignoring the differences. It might be true that for each and every one of us, there is this big gap between what we can achieve with and without help. But it is also true that this gap, a measure of potential, is even bigger for some of us than it is for others; and given that, it is unclear why we are supposed to focus only on the similarity, and ignore the differences. It is instructive here to contrast this egalitarian argument with those which start from the premise that we are all God's children. It is easy to understand why the supposed fact of being one of God's children is thought to silence other differences: it is after all a rather unique kind of consideration. By contrast, in this egalitarian argument, the similarity (the fact that there is this big gap between what we can achieve with and without help) and the difference (the fact that this gap is even bigger for some people than for others) are really two aspects of the same phenomenon, and as a result it is not at all clear why we should think that one of them could silence the other.

That is not the end of egalitarianism's problems. Even if the appeal to shared capacities could succeed in motivating equality in the face of difference, it would face the same problem as the argument based on equal rights: it would still not be a *truly* egalitarian argument. We saw when talking about equal rights that the way to test whether an argument is truly egalitarian—in the sense of implying that people's claims are essentially relative—is to vary the degree of scarcity, and see whether the argument continues to support equality. Consider the argument just discussed, the argument that we should think only about the gap between what people can achieve with and without help, and ignore the fact that the gap is bigger for some people than others. This would certainly have less force in a context where everyone already had access to whatever was agreed to be an *adequate* level of help, and where we were just arguing about what, if anything, should be done beyond that. The same might apply even to those arguments which start from the premise that we are all God's children. I was ready to concede earlier that the overall shape of these arguments was sound, even if I had little time for the premise itself. But perhaps these arguments too would lose what force they had if we considered them in a context where everyone already had an adequate amount of whatever was at stake. Consider, for example, the argument that since we are all God's children, we should all be accorded equal respect. Perhaps this only ever seemed plausible because we tend to interpret it to mean that everyone should be treated with some *minimum* degree of respect, not that they should literally be accorded *equal* respect. I suspect the argument would seem far less compelling if it was considered in a context where everyone was already treating each other with some minimum degree of respect— and where, therefore, it was clear that the argument really was demanding *equal* respect. Taken literally, the idea of equal respect is absurd: it is absurd to think that no matter what people are like, or how they conduct them- selves, we should accord them exactly the same degree of respect.

The claims of this 'minimalist' interpretation of seemingly egalitarian arguments are supported by observing that many of these arguments only justify equality in the kind of context where people are clearly short of any acceptable 'minimum'. For example, suppose we are talking about life-and-death decisions—in health care, say, or in the kind of case where a number of people are threatened by some catastrophe and can't all be rescued. Many religious people would argue that since we are all God's children, then regardless of whether some of us are more deserving than others, our fundamental equality must be reflected in the way we are treated; so in a situation where it is impossible to save everyone, everyone must at least be given an equal chance. But to the extent that this seems true, this is probably because saving people's lives is part of the bare min- imum we feel we owe them; it does not imply that people's claims are truly relative beyond that point. If we are indeed all God's children, then surely what this means is that each of us has a non-relative claim, in virtue of being one of God's children, on whatever is necessary to keep us alive. This non-relative claim is like a right: it means that certain ways of choosing between people, ways that might be acceptable in other contexts, are not acceptable when it comes to choosing who lives and who dies. It does not, however, give people an equal claim on all medical resources—including contexts where lives are not at stake.

I think the picture is basically the same when we turn to look at the allocation of jobs. Some views in this area might seem on first glance as if they are truly egalitarian, but really they are interested not in whether people are in an *equal* position, but in whether they are in an *adequate* position. One such example is the view I set out at the end of the Introduction. This view focused on whether people have enough opportunities, and enough help in pursuing those opportunities, such that they can be said to have some control over their lives. We might sometimes use the language of equality in describing this kind of view—we might talk about it as a version of 'equal opportunity'—but the view itself is not really egalitarian. It might justify treating people equally up to the point where everyone is deemed to be in an adequate position, but it does not demand equal treatment beyond that point.

4. EGALITARIAN ARGUMENTS THAT APPEAL NOT TO SOME CLAIM WE ARE EACH SEPARATELY THOUGHT TO POSSESS, BUT TO OUR RELATIONS WITH EACH OTHER

There is one more kind of egalitarian argument we have to consider—one which does seem as if it might actually imply that people's claims are truly relative. Instead of appealing to some claim we are each separately supposed to possess, this kind of argument appeals to the idea that our most fundamental equality consists in our relations with each other. Consider the case of a small and closeknit group who have to divide among themselves the spoils of some collective enterprise. They might decide to divide them equally as a way of expressing their *fraternity*: that is, as a way of expressing that even though they didn't all make the same contribution, they are nevertheless equal in the most important respect, in being equal members of the group. Any other way of dividing the spoils would seem, precisely, divisive, and would not reflect the way they see their relations with each other.

As I said, this kind of argument does seem to imply that claims are truly relative. We saw in the last section that the way to test whether claims are truly relative is to imagine that everyone already has more than they have any claim on in any non-relative sense—and then ask whether, if there is anything left over, this too should be distributed equally. Let us imagine, then, that this small and closeknit group has been collectively over-rewarded, such that all of them are bound to get far more than they could be said to have any claim on in any non-relative sense (for example, as compensation for the work they put in). I suspect that if they are a truly fraternal group, they would still think the rewards should be divided equally, however large they might be.

We seem, at last, to have found an argument which is both fundamentally and truly egalitarian. That is, it actually starts from the idea of equality, rather than simply bringing it in at some later stage; and it implies that people's claims are truly relative. The question is whether the argument can be extended from the kind of case I have just described, the case of a small and closeknit group involved in some common enterprise, to a wider context. It certainly can't be applied to sets of individuals who don't form a 'group' in any substantial sense—who have no shared history or future and who form a 'group' just in the sense that they are the subject of a particular distributive decision. It would be absurd to suggest that such a disparate set of individuals should see their formal membership of this 'group' as more important than their differences. For the same kind of reason, this argument also can't be applied to humanity as a whole. Humanity has never been a collective enterprise in any substantial sense—and is unlikely to become so, unless science fiction becomes reality and we end up battling aliens for our survival. (Perhaps things will seem different to those who believe in God; they might argue that we *should* see every fellow human being as engaged in the same common project, a project laid down by God. But at the same time, this argument perhaps explains why the previous religious argument I considered, the argument that we are all God's children, seemed unable to support egalitarianism just as it stood. Simply saying that we are all God's children emphasizes our similarity in the relationship we each separately have with God, whereas it seems that what an egalitarian needs to do is emphasize the relationship we have with each other. Anyway, as I indicated earlier, I am not going to spend much time discussing religious views. For non-believers, the main point here is that the brotherhood of man is by itself too thin and formal an idea, whatever its source, to sustain a belief in equality in the face of difference.)[11]

So the idea of fraternity does not apply to the human race as a whole, nor to random groups of individuals. But does it at least apply to our fellow *citizens*? Should we think of society as a collective enterprise, such that we can then argue that every citizen has an equal claim on its benefits? If so, these equal claims might extend to the *economic* benefits of society, such as having a decently paid and at least minimally satisfying job. In other words, it might support a genuinely egalitarian conception of equal opportunity. The basic idea here—that society is a collective enterprise, in which our common membership is sometimes more important than our differences —is not all that outlandish. It seems outlandish against the background of contemporary politics, but in fact there are certain contexts in which we already think this way. Most of us, for example, think that all citizens should have an equal vote. This is an example of our thinking that our common membership of society is more important than our differences.

Someone might object at this point that in using this as an example of true egalitarianism, I am contradicting my earlier argument that *scarcity* is what creates the need for egalitarian principles (or indeed any other kind of distributive principle). When it comes to asking who should have a vote, they will say, are we not once again talking about a non-competing right, rather than about the distribution of some scarce good? Well, votes certainly aren't scarce in the way jobs are—we can simply decide to give the vote to as many people as we want. There is, however, a different kind of scarcity involved. To have the vote is to have power; and part of the point of this kind of power is how much you have relative to other people. We couldn't simply decide to give everyone two votes, without the very idea of having two votes becoming meaningless. It is this relativity we have in mind when we insist that not only should all citizens have a vote, they should have an *equal* vote. We aren't just saying that everyone should be equal in having *some* power to determine how they are governed; we are saying that everyone should have the *same* power to determine how they are governed (even if we don't always take this idea to its logical conclusion —in terms of the influence of money in politics, for example).

I am going to assume, then, that the argument for equal votes is a truly egalitarian argument. But what exactly is the argument? Presumably no one would argue that all the reasons which might possibly bear on whether someone should be given a vote are the kind of reasons which don't vary in strength from person to person. The idea must be that although many of the reasons for giving someone a vote *do* vary from person to person, and therefore do imply that some people have a stronger claim than others, nevertheless there is one reason which does not vary and which applies to all adult members of society equally. Moreover, this one respect in which everyone is equal must be thought so much more important than the other respects in which we differ that it must be reflected in everyone having an equal vote.

So what exactly is this fundamental equality? It seems to me that the options are as follows. We could argue that giving people the vote represents a recognition of some universal property, such as the capacity for rational thought or self-direction, a property the mere possession of which we think is significant enough to silence the other, undoubtedly relevant respects in which we are not one another's equals. However, we have already seen the problems with this kind of approach. The alternative is to argue that the really fundamental thing is that we are all equally members of society, where this is not to be understood as saying something about a property we each separately possess, but as saying something about our relations with each other. We interact with each other on the understanding that, as citizens, we are all bound by the law of the land. We take this to imply that the law should treat us equally—and by this we mean something more than that we should be subject to the same laws. We mean something like that the *process* of making law should treat us equally, by giving each of us an equal vote.

This digression into the argument for equal votes has not been entirely incidental; the point is that I am interested in a certain type of egalitarian argument, of which this happens to be a particularly clear example. It is, as I have said, a type of argument which claims not that citizens are equal in terms of some property they each separately possess, but that they are equal in terms of how they relate to each other. This seems the most promising way yet of moving through the first two steps of any egalitarian argument: first establishing that people's claims are equal, and then moving from the premise of equal claims to the conclusion that everyone should be treated in some way equally. But however promising this type of argument might be in general outline, we still have two things to consider. First, we need to know whether this general outline can really be applied to the case of jobs. Second, even if it can, we still need to consider the third step in the argument—the question of exactly what form of equal treatment it would imply. The remainder of the present section addresses the first of these questions; the next section addresses the second.

So can this general outline be filled out to provide an egalitarian argument in the particular case of jobs? I have already shown, through the example of equal votes, that the argument can be translated from small groups to whole societies. The question now is whether it can also be translated, at the level of whole societies, from the political to the economic sphere. Can we really think of society as a collective enterprise in economic as well as political terms? That is what is required if we are to believe that every citizen has an equal claim on all the economic benefits of society, including the benefits of having a decently paid and at least minimally satisfying job.

It is perhaps worth noting before we go any further that if this argument did work, then the limited nature of the egalitarianism it would entail— an egalitarianism extending only to every member of society, not to the human race as a whole—might come as less of a disappointment in this particular context than in certain others. I'm not sure how many people ever thought of equality of opportunity as an ideal that could or should be applied across the whole world (whereas plenty of egalitarians would be disappointed if the argument for equalizing wealth, say, turned out to apply only within borders, rather than across them). But anyway, we have yet to confront the question of why we are supposed to see society as a collective enterprise in economic as well as political terms. Many egalitarians clearly think that economic equality is in some sense a natural extension, if not quite a logical extension, of political equality.[12] But if I was right in my earlier interpretation of the argument for political equality, the extension is not at all natural. The argument for political equality rests on our thinking of ourselves as one another's equals before the law. It is far from clear exactly which aspect of our *economic* dealings with each other is supposed to play the same role. True, there is the fact that in economic affairs, as elsewhere, we are all subject to the same laws; but this is already expressed in our political equality. To the extent that the economic aspect of society is *different* from other aspects, it hardly lends itself to a distinctively economic egalitarianism. The mechanism which drives the success of most modern economies is the market; and the market encourages us to think of our dealings with one another in precisely the opposite way to that which would be required by economic egalitarianism. Economic egalitarianism would require people to see their participation in economic life primarily as a contribution to a collective enterprise. The market, by contrast, encourages people to see themselves primarily as individuals, and to see other economic actors primarily as competitors rather than collaborators. (Perhaps in doing this the market is merely exploiting and reinforcing what is already a natural tendency; but whether the market actually causes anti-egalitarian ways of thinking, or merely exploits and reinforces them, is not important here.)

I am not suggesting that there is any alternative to the market; nor am I denying that it is precisely *because* it harnesses our natural competitiveness that it produces such great riches—riches which can be used, by enlightened governments, to pursue collective aims. This is the conventional wisdom, and as a philosopher rather than an economist or psychologist I am unqualified to dispute it. All I am doing is pointing out the inconsistency inherent in 'market socialism': the inconsistency of wanting to carry on enjoying the economic benefits which arise from the way the market exploits motives which are competitive and therefore divisive, while at the same time telling people that they ought to be thinking of themselves primarily as equal members of some collective enterprise.

It seems the prospects for a distinctively economic egalitarianism are pretty dim. Now, the reason I am interested in economic egalitarianism is because for my purposes that encompasses egalitarianism about jobs. But if I am right, then many contemporary egalitarians who favour a wider economic egalitarianism might also have to rethink some of their most basic beliefs. They should perhaps start by reconsidering whether their egalitarianism is really compatible with their unquestioning conversion to the market. But the tension runs deeper than this. Modern egalitarians, like most modern philosophers (and indeed most modern politicians), tend to be *individualists,* in the sense that they tend to be suspicious of any argument which isn't ultimately grounded in an appeal to individual interests. There are obvious enough historical reasons for this—reasons for being suspicious of the alternative, which seems to be to say that the good of society comes first, and that whatever is good for society is good for the people in it.[13] But at the same time, if I am right, then it is especially limiting *for an egalitarian* to commit himself to the axiom that the only respectable kind of answer to the question of what makes a society a good society is one which appeals to individual interests. It is especially limiting because egalitarianism—at least, the kind of egalitarianism I have identified as the only remotely promising kind—depends on people thinking of themselves primarily as members of some collective enterprise, which means precisely not thinking of their relations with society in terms of what they as individuals put in and get out.

I am not suggesting that an egalitarian should recommend that people *always* think of themselves first and foremost as participants in some collective enterprise rather than as individuals. The point is that people must at least *sometimes* think of themselves in this way, if egalitarianism is to get off the ground; but that the axiom of individualism implies that it is somehow irrational for them *ever* to think of themselves in this way. This is why it is difficult to be both an egalitarian and an individualist. Egalitarians are probably led to embrace the axiom of individualism because they feel they are supposed to be on the side of the people against the establishment; but they need to find a different way of expressing that feeling. They also need to break free of the history of their movement. Their enemy is no longer the old conservative idea that society is more than the sum of its parts, and that everyone should know their place. It is the new conservative idea that society is nothing more than a neutral space in which individuals come together to further their individual aims.[14]

5. EQUALITY OF WHAT: WORK, OPPORTUNITIES, OR CHANCES?

In the last section, I outlined what I take to be the most promising kind of egalitarian argument, and showed how it could be extended from small groups to whole societies, using the example of the argument for equal votes. But I also noted the problems with trying to extend the argument one stage further, from political to economic equality. The main problem was one of consistency: the tension between wanting to carry on enjoying the economic benefits of the market, which requires that people see one another primarily as competitors, while at the same time saying that these economic benefits should be distributed more equally, which would require that people see their relations with others in a quite different way. Until we can resolve this tension, we still don't have an argument for economic equality—which includes equality in the sphere of jobs. Nevertheless, for the sake of completeness it is worth thinking about what the third and final step in the argument *would* look like, assuming the first two steps could somehow be made to work. The third step, then, deals with exactly what form of equality the argument would recommend, specifically in relation to jobs.

Given that even the most successful modern economies are blighted by, on the one hand, involuntary unemployment, and on the other, the fact that many of those who do have jobs feel compelled to work longer hours than they would like, the obvious line for an egalitarian would seem to be that the work should be shared out more equally. But it is generally assumed that this would have disastrous consequences for productivity, and therefore for overall economic performance. So egalitarians—or at least the kind who are worried about overall economic performance— tend to concede that full equality is impossible, and channel their egalitarianism into the demand for some other kind of equality—in other words, into some version of 'equality of opportunity'.

Of course, the kind of egalitarian who *isn't* worried about overall economic performance will complain that this equality of opportunity is no kind of egalitarianism at all, since however we understand it, it is merely a mechanism for redistributing existing inequalities. Now, I have discussed this objection a couple of times already, in earlier parts of the book. It is true that if you think the problem is inequality of outcome—that some people have jobs while others don't, or that some people have better jobs than others—then it will seem no sort of solution to fiddle with the way these inequalities are distributed. But this is not, I think, a good reason for opposing equal opportunity. Equal opportunity was never intended as a solution to the problem that some people have jobs while others don't, or that some people have better jobs than others. It was intended as an answer to a different and more constrained question: *given* that some people will always have jobs while others don't, and given also that some of these jobs will always be better than others, how should they be allocated? No doubt some egalitarians will insist that this is the kind of question which a true egalitarian would refuse to answer. A true egalitarian, they will say, would refuse to accept the constraints on the question—the assumption that some people will always be better off than others, and that the only remaining question is who they should be. But I think it is a mistake to dispute the constraints: I don't think this is a question we can simply refuse to answer. I observed in the Introduction that even if it was possible to arrange things such that everyone had an equal amount of work, it would be virtually impossible to arrange for everyone to have a share of every different *kind* of work; and some kinds of work will be intrinsically more desirable than others, even if we remove all disparities in pay. Significant inequalities would therefore remain—and we would still have to face the question of how they should be decided. A hard-line egalitarian might think that in refusing to say who should get the best jobs, he is keeping the moral high ground, but in fact he is being simplistic as well as utopian.

Moreover, it isn't as if there is no genuinely egalitarian way of answering the question of how jobs should be allocated. This, after all, is where 'equality of opportunity' is supposed to come in. What must 'equality of opportunity' mean, if it is to mean something genuinely egalitarian? Well, as I suggested in Section 1, the 'opportunity' part must be understood in a way which isn't purely formal, and which doesn't simply derive from the prior idea of competition. It makes no sense to apply an egalitarian principle (or for that matter any other distributive principle) to 'opportunities' in a formal or competitive sense, since opportunities in these senses are not limited goods. To have a formal opportunity is to be entitled to apply for a job, or to have the right to be judged on your merits, or some such thing. To have a competitive opportunity is to be entitled to compete—to have a place in the starting line-up. There is no limit to how many people can be given an opportunity in either of these senses; and we don't need a principle of equality, or any other principle of distributive justice, to tell us what to do with goods like this. We might talk about everyone having an 'equal' opportunity, but really we just mean that everyone should have as many opportunities as possible. This is a universalist or maximizing principle, not a principle of distributive justice.

If equality of opportunity is to mean something genuinely egalitarian, 'opportunities' must be understood in some more substantial way, as meaning something like prospects or literal chances of success. Chances of success *are* a limited good. In probabilistic terms, the sum of everyone's chances of getting any given job must add up to one; so the sum of everyone's chances of ending up with some kind of job must add up to the total number of jobs available. We can't give some people more of a chance without giving others less of a chance—unless we increase the number of jobs available. Given that chances are limited in this way, it at least makes sense to argue that they should be distributed equally. Whether it is actually a good argument, of course, is something else—and something we will come to in due course. For now, all I am trying to show is that this idea, that everyone should literally have an equal chance of success, is one way of understanding 'equal opportunity' which does make it look like a genuinely egalitarian principle, a principle for regulating the distribution of goods under conditions of scarcity.

I'm not saying that everyone who would describe themselves as believing in equal opportunity believes that everyone should literally have an equal chance of success. I'm not interested in whether this is the most usual interpretation of equal opportunity, or the best. I realize perfectly well that the 'opportunity' in 'equal opportunity' often does mean opportunity in some formal or competitive sense, and therefore that the overall view often does just mean that anyone should be entitled to apply for any position and be treated on their merits, or that everyone should start equal in the competition for jobs. Indeed, even when people explicitly say that everyone should have an equal chance, this shouldn't always be taken literally. Talking about people's 'chances' is itself often just a loose way of describing formal or competitive opportunities. (I hope it is obvious that this is just a loose way of talking—i.e., that giving everyone a formal or competitive opportunity doesn't literally give them an equal chance. If everyone is treated on their merits, for example, then unqualified or untalented people will have very little chance. Similarly, if there is a competition in which everyone starts equal, if this just means starting in the same position, or even having access to the same resources, it still won't give everyone an equal chance. This is obvious enough in a normal, athletic race, where if you gave everyone access to the same equipment and the same training, and started them all in the same place, they wouldn't all have the same chance of winning.)

So in reducing the vague notion of equal opportunity to the more precise idea of equal chances, I am not claiming to offer an analysis of what 'equality of opportunity' means. My point is that it can mean many things, but that it only counts as a genuinely egalitarian view if it means that everyone should literally have an equal chance of success. If it just means that everyone should have the opportunity to apply for any job, and should be judged on their merits, then it is a universalist principle, not a principle of distributive justice. To be a genuinely egalitarian position, it has to appeal to equality as a principle of distributive justice. (It also has to appeal to equality as a *distinct* principle. This is why the view that everyone should start in the same position doesn't count as genuinely egalitarian, even though it does involve equality as a distributive principle. It doesn't count as genuinely egalitarian because, as I argued in Section 1, it imposes equality as a means to an end—as a way of making sure that we get the best people, or of making sure that the winners deserve their success. The kind of equality it recommends just derives from some prior commitment to competition.)

I have said that I am not interested in whether the view that everyone should literally have an equal chance is the best or most usual reading of equal opportunity. Clearly, though, it is more than merely a theoretically possible reading. People do sometimes talk about equal opportunity in terms of everyone having an equal chance, and they do sometimes seem to mean this literally. At other times, the literal reading is left implicit, but is strongly suggested by some of the other things people say: for example, when they complain about factors like race or sex or class being correlated with success. If they think the mere existence of any such correlation is unfair in itself, this suggests that they really do care about the distribution of literal chances. (Thinking the mere existence of such correlations is unfair in itself is different from thinking that such correlations are indicators of possible injustice—indicators that employers might actually be discriminating against people on the basis of race or sex or class.) Moreover, the general idea here, that everyone should have an equal chance, is actually quite persuasive. The idea is that when people have an equal claim on something, but it isn't the kind of thing that can be shared, fairness demands that they each be given an equal chance. This certainly seems the natural way for an egalitarian to react to a situation where it is impossible to give everyone an equal share.[15] And it appears to be backed up by the way people actually behave in everyday situations where they have to decide who is to get some benefit, or to perform some unpleasant task, and sharing is not an option: they agree to draw lots, or, where there are only two of them, to toss a coin.

Of course, when it comes to jobs, no one seriously suggests that we should equalize people's chances like this, *directly*. Rather than demanding that employers draw lots among minimally qualified applicants, or that some wider randomizing procedure be applied across the job market as a whole, the usual suggestion is that we should try to equalize chances *indirectly*—by rearranging the background conditions such that there is some earlier point in people's lives at which they all have an equal chance. The suggestion is, for example, that we should look at the types of people (in terms of race, family background, geography, etc.) who currently tend to do well or badly in the competition for jobs, and shift the balance of educational resources in favour of those types who currently tend to do badly. This would move us closer to equality of chances. (Clearly this kind of approach only makes sense if we are trying to equalize people's *overall* chances, rather than trying to give them an equal chance on a job-by-job basis; trying to achieve *that* indirectly, by monitoring which groups or types do well at every kind of job and with every kind of employer, would be fantastically complicated. But I suspect that the version of the view which says we should be trying to equalize people's overall chances, taking account as it does of the quantity and quality of the options open to people, is anyhow the version that most egalitarians favour.)

This choice between direct and indirect intervention is something I first described in the Introduction. I noted that meritocrats face the same choice. But there are important differences between the way meritocrats and egalitarians tend to approach it. First, as I argued in Part 1, meritocrats tend to believe the state should promote merit *both* directly, by requiring employers to hire on merit, *and* indirectly, by trying to create the background conditions in which merit can thrive. Egalitarians, on the other hand, tend to favour the indirect approach as an *alternative* to the direct approach, at least when it comes to jobs. Moreover, if any meritocrat did offer the indirect approach as an alternative, that would probably be because he had realized that, since meritocracy is in fact based on efficiency rather than fairness, it could never justify direct intervention. Egalitarians, by contrast, would be confident that the argument for equality *could* justify direct intervention, if that was what they wanted to argue for. This suggests that they must have a different reason for only wanting to pursue equality indirectly. I have already touched on what this might be, when I observed that they seem to feel they have to find some way of fitting in egalitarianism around meritocracy. This is probably why they become indirect egalitarians. Rather than saying that everyone should actually have an equal chance at the point when they try to get a job, they suggest we rearrange the background conditions such that there is some earlier point in people's lives at which they have an equal chance. This way, we can combine equality at this earlier point with meritocracy at the point when the decisions are actually made.

Exactly how this kind of egalitarian interprets the idea of equal chances within this hybrid view depends on how they understand meritocracy. I distinguished the two possibilities at the start of Part 1. If they think meritocracy is just a matter of finding the best person for the job, they will argue that everyone should have an equal chance to become the best. In this way, they will say, we can combine fairness with efficiency.[16] If on the other hand they think meritocracy is about rewarding the deserving, they will argue that everyone should have an equal chance to become deserving. Again the point is to combine fairness, in the shape of equal chances, with some meritocratic value; only this time it is not efficiency but desert: everyone is to have an equal chance to earn the right to a job.

Either way, because on both versions the view demands that there be some point in everyone's life at which they literally have an equal chance of success (as opposed to merely starting in the same position), it does count as genuinely combining the values of meritocracy and equality. Unlike the kind of view I discussed in Section 1, the equality it recommends doesn't just derive from the idea of meritocracy itself. However, precisely *because* this view combines meritocracy with equality—and with a kind of equality that is essentially alien to meritocracy—it ends up looking slightly odd. There is something odd in the very idea of a race which all the runners literally have an equal chance of winning. Whichever way we choose to understand the idea of competition, it is about creating or recognizing *difference*—the difference between winners and losers. If what egalitarians really want to do is express people's fundamental equality, why choose to do this through a mechanism that is intimately bound up with the idea of there being winners and losers?

One possible answer is that there have to be winners and losers in the end: we are talking about a variety of egalitarianism which accepts that there are always going to be winners and losers in the sense that some people will get a job and some people won't, and some jobs will be better than others. What we should be looking for, according to this kind of egalitarianism, is a mechanism for deciding the winners and losers which also expresses the fact that *fundamentally* everyone is equal. Drawing lots is one mechanism which would do this, but it seems impractical—and wasteful, since it doesn't encourage people to put any effort into making themselves into better candidates. It seems that what we need is a mechanism which combines the randomizing element of drawing lots with the more practical and efficient idea of competition.

This suggestion raises a number of questions. First, there is the practical question of exactly how we are supposed to set up a meritocracy such that everyone has an equal chance. Trying to compensate for every single background factor which tends to make people's chances unequal would be a daunting task. We could start, as I suggested earlier, by doing some statistical analysis on certain broad groups, or types, of applicant, asking which of them tend to do well and badly in the job market, and then weighting educational and social resources towards those who are doing badly. But this could only inch us towards equality, rather than getting us there in one jump; moreover, each time we changed policy we would have to wait a long time before we discovered how much closer it has got us. The second question is whether this kind of hybrid mechanism would really be an appropriate vehicle for expressing people's fundamental equality—especially given what I said at the end of Section 4, about the tension inherent in thinking we can continue to exploit people's competitive motives while at the same time trying to create or preserve the kind of fraternal motives necessary for egalitarianism.

There are interesting questions, but I am going to leave them hanging, because I want to go back to the question of why we are supposed to be equalizing chances in the first place—never mind *how* we should be doing so. If the argument fails at the abstract stage, we won't even have to ask whether it can survive being combined with some form of meritocracy, nor whether, if it can, what would be the best way of combining it.[17]

The question is whether, even if egalitarians are right in thinking everyone has an equal claim on a job, they are also right to move so quickly from this premise to the conclusion that everyone should be given an equal chance. I have conceded that giving everyone an equal chance seems like a natural way for an egalitarian to react to a situation where it is impossible to give everyone an equal share. But its being a natural way to react doesn't make it the *right* way to react. The most promising kind of argument for equal treatment, I have argued, is the kind that builds on cases like that of a small and closeknit group who have to divide the spoils of some collective enterprise. There is a problem with trying to build on such cases when we are trying to justify equal chances rather than equal shares. The problem is that this particular kind of argument for equality involves the idea of fraternity, and fraternity doesn't obviously support the extension from shares to chances.

It is true that fraternity might sometimes seem to give people a reason to equalize chances. For example, in a life-and-death situation, a small and closeknit group might choose to express their fraternity—or what in such cases we might more naturally call their *solidarity*—by sticking together, such that either all survive or all die. But while this would indeed equalize their chances of survival, this is not what makes it expressive of their solidarity. What makes it expressive of their solidarity is the fact that it binds their fates together. Where equalizing chances would not bind their fates together, as is the case with drawing lots, it is less clear that it expresses solidarity. To bring this out we need to think about a case in which a small and closeknit group could respond to a crisis *either* by choosing to bind their fates together, *or* by choosing to give everyone separately an equal chance. Here is such an example. A shipwrecked crew find themselves sharing a lifeboat in a raging storm. The lifeboat is overcrowded and taking in water. If there were fewer on board—say half—it would almost certainly stay afloat until the storm blew over, when they would almost certainly be rescued. However, anyone who left the boat would definitely perish. If on the other hand they all stuck together, the boat would be far less likely to last out the storm—let us say their chances would then be one in three. Now, I don't think it would be unreasonable of them to choose to stick together, even though this would give each of them less of a chance (one in three) than if they chose to cut their numbers in half, drawing lots to see who had to leave the boat (one in two). If they did choose to stick together, I think we would say that they were expressing their solidarity. This seems to suggest that equalizing their chances separately would *not* express their solidarity; which in turn suggests that *merely* equalizing chances does not express solidarity. The implication for our purposes is that equal opportunity, understood as equal chances, would also not express solidarity or fraternity—since it gives everyone separately an equal chance.

But perhaps I am being too dismissive of equal chances. Perhaps all we need say is that, from the point of view of expressing solidarity or fraternity, the *best* thing is to bind people's fates together—for there to be at least some chance of everyone ending up in a good position—but that everyone having an equal chance is better than nothing. In other words, the best thing is for people's equality to be reflected in the outcome, but it is better that it be reflected in the procedure than not at all. In fact, perhaps we can go further. Presumably it is *not* better for equality to be reflected in the outcome if the only way it can be reflected in the outcome is by nobody getting anything—if there just isn't any possibility of everyone ending up in a good position. In this kind of case it would actually be better for equality to be expressed procedurally—for everyone to be given an equal chance. This certainly seems true of life-and-death cases: where it just isn't possible for everyone to survive, it is surely better to say that everyone should have an equal chance than to say that if not all can survive, then none should. And perhaps this idea can help salvage the argument for giving everyone an equal chance of getting a job. I have argued that with jobs, we are talking about precisely this kind of case: the whole debate takes place against the background assumption that it just isn't possible for everyone to end up with a job (and certainly not with an equally good job). Is it not better that people's equality be expressed procedurally than not at all?

Well, this might resurrect the argument for equal opportunity as equal chances, but it might also explain why traditional egalitarians feel such a lack of enthusiasm for this argument. At earlier points in the book I seemed to dismiss this lack of enthusiasm. But in fact, what I meant to dismiss was the idea that a true egalitarian would see equal opportunity as answering the wrong question. I still think this is not quite the right way to put it: we can't just refuse to answer the question of how jobs should be allocated. At the same time, traditional egalitarians are right to be concerned about the assumption behind the question, the assumption that there will always be winners and losers, and that it is just a matter of deciding who they are going to be. The point is not that this is an unreasonable assumption. The point is that it just isn't clear how this assumption can be squared with any substantial kind of egalitarianism: it isn't clear that egalitarianism *can* just be pushed back a step, from being a view about outcomes, to being a view about procedures. If equal opportunity is supposed to express our fraternity —to express the fact that we are all equally members of some collective enterprise—then we have to accept that it is a poor way of expressing this. Maybe it is the best way, or even the only way, but it is still not a good way, because it is about giving each individual *separately* an equal chance.

And is it even the best way? I have said that it is better for people's equality to be reflected procedurally—in their each separately having an equal chance—than in the outcome, if the only way it can be reflected in the outcome is by nobody getting anything. But small and closeknit groups do sometimes decide that if not all of them can have something, then none should. The most obvious kind of example is where the group as a whole must endure great hardship, but where it is not necessary for absolutely everyone to do so. Rather than drawing lots, or taking turns, a truly fraternal group might decide that it would be better for them all to endure together. Is this a reasonable thing to decide? It is harder to justify sticking together in this kind of case than in the lifeboat case, where if everyone stuck together there was at least a *possibility* of everyone ending up in a good position (even though it was true that sticking together would give each of them a smaller chance of ending up in that position than if they equalized chances separately). In the lifeboat case, we might expect a truly fraternal group to hold out for this possibility, however slight, instead of settling for expressing their equality in some purely procedural way. In the case of the group which has to endure great hardship, it is perhaps more difficult to argue for sticking together, since there is no suggestion that anything tangible could come out of this. But if it is possible to argue for sticking together even here, then perhaps we need to reconsider the jobs case. For some egalitarians might think that, of the two examples we have considered, the jobs case is closer to the lifeboat case, in that there is at least a possibility that if people stick together, something good might come out of it. This might be what explains the hostility to equal opportunity among those who still believe in class solidarity. For these people, the demand for equal opportunity—the demand that everyone should have an equal chance to escape from the working class—might well seem inadequate to express their solidarity. They might think that what they should really be fighting for is the possibility, however slight, that all might escape together.

The general thought here, that certain kinds of equality are better expressed by fighting for an equal outcome than by settling for some kind of procedural equality, also explains something else that any egalitarian view needs to explain. Why, when we are talking about something that *can* be shared, do we prefer to give everyone an equal share, rather than giving everyone an equal chance of receiving the whole amount? The idea that equal treatment expresses fraternity or solidarity looks as if it can explain this: it tells us that fraternity or solidarity are better expressed by an equal outcome than by any kind of procedural equality. What about the other egalitarian arguments I have discussed so far? Formal arguments, like the argument from insufficient reason or the so-called 'requirement of ethical consistency', fail this particular test. These arguments would seem to be satisfied just as well *either* by giving everyone an equal share *or* by giving everyone an equal chance of receiving the whole amount. This is precisely because these ways of arguing for equal treatment are purely formal: because they are so formal, they are unlikely to have any natural affinity with any particular version of equal treatment, and therefore cannot explain our preference for equalizing shares rather than chances in those cases where we could do either.

What about the other argument I discussed in Section 2, the argument that it is unfair for some people to be worse off than others through no fault of their own? Its supporters could try to argue that there is something internal to this argument which at least *implies* that it should be applied first to shares, and only then, if sharing is impossible, to chances. The fact that some people are worse off than others matters more, they might say, when we are talking about shares than when we are talking about chances. But this is a dangerous move. This way of explaining why we should apply equality to shares before chances plays into the hands of those opponents of egalitarianism, like Joseph Raz, who argue that much of the appeal of equality can be explained away by the fact that people's claims on things tend to be *diminishing*.[18] To say that someone's claim on something is diminishing is to say that the more they have of it, the weaker their claim. There are, I think, two kinds of reason why we might think people's claims on something are diminishing.[19] The first is where the thing in question is a means to a further end, and where the efficiency of an extra unit, as a means to that further end, varies inversely with how much the person already has. The second is where the thing in question has value in itself, but where the value of a given unit is thought to vary inversely with how much the person already has. These two kinds of reason tend not to be distinguished, because they often point in the same direction. Money is a good example of this. Its efficiency as a means typically decreases the more you have of it; but there is also the further point that people who have less money are typically in a worse position in respect of the things that really matter—for example, they are less likely to have their basic needs satisfied. So people's claims to more money are diminishing for the first kind of reason (because its efficiency as a means decreases the more they have of it); and their claims on what money will buy them are diminishing for the second kind of reason (because in general, the more money they have, the less things they still actually *need*, as opposed to want). Both points suggest that everyone having an equal amount of money would be better than everyone having an equal chance of becoming a millionaire.

As I say, the power and usefulness of this idea, of diminishing claims, creates a strategic problem for the kind of egalitarian who argues that it is unfair for some people to be worse off than others through no fault of their own. He needs to explain why we should give everyone an equal amount of money rather than giving everyone an equal chance of becoming a millionaire. He can explain this by invoking the idea of diminishing claims, which implies that inequality of shares is worse than inequality of chances. But this ends up undermining his whole position—the position that it is unfair for one person to be worse off than another through no fault of their own. Of course inequality *seems* unfair; but this might be not because equality is good in itself, but simply because people's claims are diminishing, in the two separate senses identified above.

It is important to see why believing that people's claims are diminishing is not a genuinely egalitarian position. It is not genuinely egalitarian because it does not imply that people's claims are essentially relative. True, it leads us to take an interest in relativities—in asking who has more and who has less; but that is not the same as being interested in relativities for their own sake. It tells us to take an interest in people's relative positions because we can *infer* from this, first, who would make the more efficient use of a given amount of money, and second, who it is more important to help. This is what really matters: how easy it is, and how important it is, to help any given person—and these things are true of any given person independently of the relation between their position and anyone else's. Moreover, while as I have said these two aspects of our concern will *usually* point in the same direction—towards equality—they won't always do so.

In a medical context, for example, the neediest cases might also be those where we can make the most difference, but this will not always be true. Sometimes, the neediest cases will be the least responsive, and then, instead of there being an unambiguous tendency towards equality, we will have to make a choice. The second kind of reason for thinking people's claims are diminishing—that the worse off people are, the more important it is to help them—will still favour equality, but the first kind of reason, which tells us to concentrate resources where they would make the most difference, will actually push us away from equality, if the neediest cases also happen to be those in which we would make the least difference.

It seems, then, that egalitarians should be wary of appealing to the idea of diminishing claims to explain why we should prefer to give everyone equal shares rather than chances. The problem is that once the idea of diminishing claims is brought in to the argument, it calls into question whether there is any need for equality as a distinct value. So from a strategic point of view, egalitarians would be better off trying to suppress the idea of diminishing claims. Of course, this would still leave a problem for the kind of egalitarian we have been looking at here, who believes that it is unfair for some people to be worse off than others through no fault of their own. It leaves him in the same position as the kind of egalitarian who believes in the argument from insufficient reason or the requirement of ethical consistency: namely, that of being unable to explain why we should equalize shares rather than chances in those cases where we could do either.

If we don't believe in equality as a distinct value—if we come to think of the tendency to favour equal shares as being fully explained by the idea of diminishing claims—what does this imply for equal opportunity? It implies that in the kind of case where it is impossible to equalize shares, and we can only equalize chances, we no longer have any reason to favour equality. We have no reason to favour equality because people's claims on *chances*, as distinct from their claims on goods themselves, are not diminishing. To see this, consider the following example. A military surgeon in a field hospital is faced with two urgent cases; he doesn't have time to treat both, and must decide which to treat. He estimates that the first man would have a 50 per cent chance of survival without treatment, and a 95 per cent chance with treatment; the second man would have a 25 per cent chance without treatment, and a 50 per cent chance with treatment. If we no longer believed in equality for its own sake—if we accepted that the natural tendency to favour equality merely reflects a deeper sense that people's claims are diminishing—what would we think about this case? Clearly the way to give the two men an equal chance is to treat the second. But treating the first would make more of a difference, and this is surely an impeccable reason for treating him. It might seem unfair, given that he already has more of what is being 'handed out' (i.e. he already has a greater chance of survival); but if so, we are being misled by our tendency to associate this case with the kind where people's claims are diminishing. We are thinking about increasing people's chances of survival as if it was like increasing their level of wealth, or nutrition, or well-being, where the argument for giving them more gets weaker, the more they already have— independently of whether other people are involved or not. This is not true of chances of survival. Chances of survival are of constant value right across the range from zero to one. There is the same reason to increase someone's chances of survival by a percentage point if his chances are currently 95 per cent as if they are currently 50 or 25 per cent. If no one else was involved, we would readily admit this. And this is, I think, fundamentally a point about *chances*, rather than about chances of survival in particular. Claims on chances are not diminishing.

I should emphasize that all this only creates problems for certain kinds of egalitarianism—specifically, the kinds I discussed in Section 2, not the more sophisticated kinds I discussed in Sections 3 and 4. The state of the debate, as I see it, is that anyone who wants to be an egalitarian has to explain three things: first, why there is sometimes a reason to give people equal shares; second, why there is sometimes a reason to give people equal chances; and third, why, when it is perfectly possible to do either, we should go for shares rather than chances. The kinds of egalitarian argument I discussed in Section 2—the argument from insufficient reason or consistency, and the argument that no one should be worse off than another through no fault of their own—cannot do all these things at once. By themselves they do not have the resources to answer the third question—to explain why we should deal in shares rather than chances where we can do either; and if they invoke the idea of diminishing claims to explain this, they risk undermining their answer to the first two questions.

On the more sophisticated kind of egalitarian view which I tried to refine in Sections 3 and 4, the position is as follows. Wherever we value equality for its own sake—whether we are talking about giving people equal shares *or* equal chances—that is because we think it *expresses* some fundamental respect in which people are equal. This argument is at its most persuasive when the underlying fundamental equality is based on people's shared membership of some collective enterprise—and on the fact that, as members, they see and relate to one another as equals. This kind of argument *can* explain why, in the case where we could equalize either shares or chances, we tend to go for shares: because that is a better way of expressing common membership. The weakness in the argument is its limited scope—and, in the particular context of equal opportunity, the limited nature of the support it can offer for the idea of equal chances. Where people do see themselves as members of some collective enterprise, equalizing chances is not just second best to equalizing outcomes, it is arguably not expressive of equality at all. And where people do not see themselves primarily as members of some collective enterprise—which probably applies to their participation in economic life—any tendency to favour equal treatment is best explained by the idea that people's claims are diminishing, which can *only* justify equality in the sense of equal shares, and definitely can't offer equal chances any support at all.

6. SO WHY DO WE BELIEVE IN EQUALITY?

It should by now be clear why I am opposed to equality—and therefore to equality of opportunity, to the extent that it has anything to do with equality, in any substantial sense. First and most importantly, because it is not clear that equality is something we should be striving for in this area. We just don't conceive of our relations with one another in the right way: we don't think of ourselves as partners in some common enterprise, at least not in the economic sphere. But second, even if we did conceive of our relations with one another in the right way, that would bring us to the next problem. Jobs cannot be shared, so we would have to argue for a different kind of equality: everyone having an equal chance. The problem here is that this kind of equality—everyone having an equal chance *to become unequal*—seems a poor way of expressing the fact that we are all equal partners in some common enterprise.

The obvious question, for someone who believes all this, is why the idea of equality still exercises such a powerful hold over our thinking. One possibility is that what really exercises this hold over our thinking is the *language* of equality. We talk about equality, but we mean equality in the sense of procedural justice: we mean only that whatever the rules are, they should be applied equally to everyone. Or else we talk about equality, but really our position is what we might call *universalist*. (We have encountered two kinds of universalist position in the discussion so far. First, there was the kind of person who says that everyone has *an equal claim on a job*, but who really just means that it would be nice if everyone who needed a job was able to get one. Second, there was the kind of person who says that everyone should have *an equal chance*, but who by 'chance' just means 'opportunity' in some formal or competitive sense, and by saying that everyone should have an *equal* chance just means that these formal or competitive opportunities should be extended to as many people as possible.) The final possibility is that although we talk about equality, what really concerns us is *adequacy*: that is, what concerns us is not the bare fact that some people are worse off than others, but that some people are in a position that is unacceptable, in some absolute sense. (Consider, for example, the view which I outlined at the end of the Introduction. I argued that instead of worrying about whether everyone is in an equal position, we should focus on making sure that as many people as possible have some control over their lives. A loose way of describing this view might be to say that 'everyone should be equally in control of their lives'. Clearly this would just be a loose way of talking: the view isn't really concerned with whether some people have more control over their lives than others. The point is that so long as people have *enough* control over their lives, that will encourage and enable them to live in the right way—to see their lives as stories they help construct, stories whose evolving shape reflects the good and bad choices they make along the way.)

All these possibilities suggest that it is just the language of equality which exercises a hold over our thinking. But there is a further possibility, which is that people are not merely confused by language, they really do believe in equality. The demand for 'equal life chances' in particular seems too robust and persistent to be explained away as resting *solely* on a misleading choice of language. Some people—perhaps even most of us, at some time or other—really do seem to believe that it would be good if everyone literally had an equal chance of success. We are probably encouraged in this by thinking about the way civilized people behave when they have to decide who is to get some benefit, or perform some unpleasant task, when sharing is not an option. Even when they have merely been thrown together by circumstance, people often agree to draw lots. Doesn't this imply that there must be *something* in the idea of equal chances? I don't think so. One of the things I have been trying to show is precisely that many otherwise sensible people are wrong about equal chances, so I am hardly likely to concede that just because people often agree to draw lots, they must have a good reason for doing so. Moreover, to the extent that they do have good reasons for doing so, we should be careful not to assume that these reasons have anything to do with *fairness*. For example, one reason why civilized people might propose drawing lots for something is because they think it would be *impolite* just to grab it for themselves; another is because they suspect that drawing lots would be a good way of avoiding an argument. Neither of these reasons has anything to do with fairness. Moreover, the second does not even apply in the kind of case we might expect the egalitarian to be most concerned with, the kind where some people are in a much stronger position than others—even if they don't have a stronger *claim*. Consider, for example, the kind of case where a group of people stumble across something valuable. None has any more claim to it than the others; but let us suppose that one of them is much stronger than the rest, and so could simply take it if he wanted. Why should he care about the fact that he *would* have agreed to draw lots, if everyone had been in an equally strong position? Even if he would, that would have been for reasons that were nothing to do with fairness; the question is why he is supposed to think that this constitutes a fairness-based reason to agree to draw lots now, when everyone is *not* in an equally strong position.[20]

Nevertheless, I think this is one of the reasons why the idea of equal chances oversteps its proper boundaries. Procedures like drawing lots or tossing a coin are introduced primarily as ways of avoiding conflict, and people then confuse them with *fair* procedures, applying them to cases of equal claims rather than to cases of equal bargaining positions. This, together with the possibility that people are just confused by language, and the possibility that they genuinely believe in arguments like the argument from insufficient reason, might seem enough to explain the otherwise surprising popularity of the idea of equal chances. But there is also a further reason—a further, conceptual confusion that some people at least are guilty of. They seem to run together the positive idea that everyone should have an equal chance with the negative idea that people's chances shouldn't depend on other people's prejudices. This is certainly part of the explanation behind the demand for equal chances in the sphere of jobs. When people say that everyone should have an equal chance they often just mean that their chances shouldn't depend on things like race or sex. But this same point might also help explain the wider popularity of procedures like drawing lots or tossing a coin: it might be a quite general truth that such procedures are often more to do with making clear that prejudice and favouritism are not influencing the outcome than with giving everyone an equal chance for equal chances' sake. Of course, there are other ways of making clear that prejudice and favouritism are not influencing the outcome. You could hand over the decision to someone who is thought to be above prejudice. Or, if you want to allay people's suspicions over one particular kind of prejudice, you could deliberately 'overcompensate'. But drawing lots or tossing a coin is often the cheapest and quickest way, and the one that sends the clearest signals.

How might we test this claim—that often the real reason we draw lots or toss a coin is to make clear that prejudice and favouritism aren't influencing the outcome, not because we believe that fairness demands that everyone be given an equal chance? Consider the following case.[21] Two coastal towns are in imminent danger from a volcanic eruption. There is a fishing boat close by, but it only has time to make one trip; moreover, given its small size, it could only rescue a small fraction of the people in either town. If we thought that fairness demanded equal chances for equal chances' sake, we would presumably think the fisherman should toss a coin to determine which town to head for, and then draw lots on arrival to see who gets a place in the boat. But there is a striking asymmetry between the fairly strong intuitive presumption in favour of his drawing lots on arrival, and the weak or non-existent presumption in favour of tossing a coin at the earlier point, when he must decide which town to head for. On my view, this asymmetry is easy to explain. This is one of those cases where the point of giving everyone an equal chance is not to express their fundamental equality—since, unless you are the kind of person who believes we are all God's children, it is not obvious why you would think the people all had an equal claim to be rescued. The point is simply to make clear that favouritism and prejudice are not influencing the outcome. If this is the point, there will be two reasons why it is unlikely to apply at the earlier stage where the fisherman must choose which town to head for. First, because the group who don't get chosen will probably never know that this choice was ever made; and second, because we are assuming that the fisherman knows nothing about what kinds of people are in the two groups. Both these factors change when it comes to deciding who gets a place in the boat: all concerned will know that their fate depends on this one man; and since he is now face to face with them, any prejudices he might have will come into play.[22] (If you want to test this explanation further, consider a modified version of the example, in which, first, the fisherman knows from the beginning that the two groups are divided along, say, racial lines; and second, those involved are aware of his actions throughout—perhaps via the kind of ghoulish live media coverage that events like this tend to attract these days. If I am right, there should now be a much stronger intuitive presumption in favour of his tossing a coin at the point when he must decide which group to head for.)

The same example can be used to illustrate a second advantage of my view. Those who believe in equal chances for equal chances' sake need to explain why tossing a coin or drawing lots is generally thought good enough even if a more elaborate procedure would in fact be required to generate equal chances. Suppose that, as is likely, the two towns did not contain exactly the same number of people (that would after all be quite unlikely). Tossing a coin and drawing lots on arrival would not then give everyone an equal chance: under this procedure, each of the inhabitants of the smaller town would start with a better chance than each of the inhabitants of the larger town. And yet if the fisherman did toss a coin and then draw lots on arrival, we would be unlikely to say he had treated anyone unfairly. This suggests that my explanation is correct: what matters to us is not whether he actually gives everyone an equal chance, but whether he was acting for the right reasons—or at least not acting for the wrong reasons. Even if he knew, for example, that the larger town was full of the kind of people he didn't like, we probably wouldn't credit him with sufficient cunning to have seen that tossing a coin would enable him to get away with securing a limited bias in favour of his prejudices without anyone realizing that this is what he was doing.

My explanation of why we do things like draw lots or toss a coin also explains what is wrong with a certain argument which is sometimes raised *against* such procedures. In the present example, the argument would take the form of saying that there is no need for the fisherman to worry about giving people an equal chance, since in the grand scheme of things they have already had their equal chance. He should simply head for whichever town is closer, since it is a matter of chance which town he happens to be closer to—indeed, it was a matter of chance that any of these people needed saving in the first place, since the disaster could just as easily have struck somewhere else.[23] Now, some people respond to this argument by saying that we can't be sure that such things really are a matter of chance: some people just live closer to possible disaster, and further from possible help, and so don't really have an equal chance. But while this is true, the real problem with the argument is much bigger than this. If we understand the point of tossing a coin in the way I have suggested, it will be irrelevant whether there was some *earlier* stage, before anyone had to take any decisions, when everyone had an equal chance. On my view, the point of tossing a coin in a case like this is not that it brings about a certain state of affairs—the state of affairs in which everyone has an equal chance—and that this state of affairs is good in itself. The point of tossing a coin is to say something about the way *you see* the state of affairs: it is to show that you are not going to make the choice for the wrong kind of reasons. It is therefore irrelevant whether equality already obtained at some earlier stage.

This is interesting for our purposes because the very same line of argument against giving everyone an equal chance is often heard in the debate over equal opportunity. The argument takes the form of saying that there is no need to intervene now in favour of the less talented or less privileged, to ensure that they have equal life chances, since they have already had their equal chance—it was a matter of chance whether they were talented or privileged in the first place.[24] Again, if all we really want to do is communicate something about the way we see things—what we see as relevant and not relevant—then we can dismiss this criticism as missing the point. The reason we are tempted to give everyone an equal chance *now* is because this would at least make clear that we didn't want to see people succeeding or failing because of other people's prejudices. Equally, of course, if this really *is* all we want, then we should probably not be talking about giving everyone an equal chance in the first place. In the case of the fisherman, drawing lots and tossing a coin are quick and easy ways of sending the message that favouritism and prejudice aren't going to affect the outcome. Moreover, nothing is *lost* by deciding to draw lots or toss a coin. In the jobs case, by contrast, ensuring that everyone has an equal chance is a lengthy, complicated, and costly way of sending the same message. Lengthy and complicated first, because we cannot equalize chances directly, so we must continually tinker with the background conditions, and second, because we would have to wait a long time before we discovered how much closer to equality this had got us; and costly because distributing educational and social resources in such a way as to equalize overall chances will probably involve getting a very low overall return on those resources. We should therefore think about other ways of sending the same message. We could simply require employers to be more open about the way they make their hiring decisions, and then target prejudice itself, rather than trying to eliminate it in passing by ensuring that everyone has an equal chance of success.

7. CONCLUSIONS

My aim in this part of the book has been to show that whatever other values might bear on the way jobs should be allocated, equality isn't one of them. It has been a long process, not least because of the great variety of ways and places in which the idea of equality comes into the debate. For example, I began by looking at the view that everyone should start equal in the race for jobs. I argued that this isn't really a genuinely egalitarian view, in the sense that it doesn't appeal to equality as a distinct value: it starts from a belief in competition, and the kind of equality it recommends just derives from that prior belief in competition. As such, it inherits the problems facing all competitive views—problems I discussed in Part 1. But it faces its own distinctive problems as well, arising from the ways in which it tries to combine the ideas of competition and equality. For example, many people simply assume that unless everyone starts equal, no one can be said to deserve their success; but despite its popularity, this idea doesn't stand up to scrutiny. Similarly, if we take the other view of competition, on which competition is not about rewarding people's deserts, but simply about recognizing and developing talent, it just isn't obvious that an initial period of equality is really necessary in order to identify people's natural talents. There might be easier ways of identifying them: we could devise tests that control for environmental differences without actually having to place everyone in the same environment.

Having dealt with these arguments for a derivative kind of egalitarianism, I moved on to those views that really do appeal to equality as a distinct value. These views face a different kind of problem. Most obviously, it is difficult to argue that people really have equal claims—that they each need, or deserve, a job to exactly the same degree. Moreover, even supposing egalitarians could succeed in establishing this, it is not clear where they could go from here. They tend to present unequal treatment as being wrong *because irrational*, rather than simply unfair in itself; and I tried to show how this whole line of argument is completely misguided. However, in the course of the discussion I did discover one kind of egalitarian view which avoids these problems. This kind of view says nothing about what people deserve, or need, or merit, or any other aspect of their claims which might admit of degrees. It focuses instead on the kind of claim which people either have or they don't, and everyone does. Having identified such a claim, it does not try to argue that this is the only thing that could possibly be thought relevant; instead, it simply argues that it is so much more important than everything else that it must be expressed in the way people are treated. It thereby avoids implying that unequal treatment is wrong because irrational: the idea is that equal treatment *expresses* people's fundamental equality, rather than being the only rational response to it. This kind of view is also truly egalitarian in the sense that it implies that people's claims are essentially relative. In this it is unlike many views which use the language of equality but which turn out to be *universalist*, or turn out to be concerned with *adequacy* rather than equality. Unlike these views, the idea that some kind of equal treatment is the only way to express people's fundamental equality continues to support equal treatment beyond the point where everyone's non-relative claims have been satisfied. And finally, it is alone among the egalitarian arguments I have considered in being able to explain everything that an egalitarian view has to explain. It can explain why, where something can be shared, everyone should get an equal share; it can explain why, where it cannot be shared, everyone should get an equal chance; and it can explain why it is better for everyone to get an equal share rather than an equal chance where they could get either.

So much for the strengths of this kind of egalitarian view. The problems start when we consider the various suggestions for the universal claim on which it is supposed to rest. What it needs is the kind of claim which people either have or they don't, which everyone in fact does have, and which is so much more important than everything else that their equality in this respect must be expressed in the way they are treated. The first few suggestions I considered—claims based on the fact that we are all equally human, or the fact that we are all equally conscious, or the fact that we are all equal in having the capacity to pursue a rational plan of life—all failed to satisfy the third condition: they just weren't obviously that much more important than everything else. At this point I started to look in a different direction: instead of building a theory on the kind of claim which we are each separately supposed to possess, I suggested that egalitarians might be better off building a theory on the idea that our most fundamental equality consists in our relations with one another. I argued that this kind of idea is probably what underlies the most convincing egalitarian arguments— such as the argument for equal votes. But it turns out that there are serious problems with trying to transfer the same kind of argument to jobs. First, not many people see the economic side of society as a collective enterprise. Indeed, the market, which is the driving force behind most successful economies, encourages us to see our relations with one another and with society in precisely the opposite way: in terms of what we as individuals put in and what we get out. Second, because even if we did see ourselves as participating in some collective enterprise, and took this to mean that we all had an equal claim on the benefits of a modern market economy, including the benefits of having a decently paid and at least minimally satisfying job, there would be a further problem. Jobs cannot be shared, so we would have to argue for everyone having an equal chance. This might seem like the natural way for an egalitarian to react to a situation where it is impossible to give everyone an equal share. But in fact, this kind of equality—everyone having an equal chance *to become unequal*—is a poor way of expressing the fact that we are all members of a collective enterprise.

All this explains why I think we need to abandon equality in favour of the more limited view I outlined at the end of the Introduction. Never mind whether everyone has an *equal* opportunity, or starting position: we should simply focus on making sure that they have *enough* opportunity, and a good *enough* starting position, such that they can be said to have some control over their lives. This view differs from the 'starting-gate' views discussed in Section 1, in that it is essentially positive where they are negative. It says, simply, that people should have some control over their lives; whereas starting-gate views tell us to make sure that people's success or failure is *not* affected by anything that is *not* under their control. My view also differs from all truly egalitarian arguments, in that the question which is central to it—whether someone has control over his life—is essentially absolute, whereas the questions that are central to all truly egalitarian views are essentially relational.

It might seem as if I am exaggerating the distinctiveness of my view, particularly in terms of how different it is from starting-gate views. It might seem that in fact my view concedes the basic thrust of starting-gate views, which is that social justice consists in establishing a certain kind of background, together with a certain set of rules, against which people can then be said to be entitled to what they earn. It might seem that my view accepts this basic framework, and merely contests what the background requirement should be—replacing initial equality with the condition that everyone should have some control over their life. But this would be a misinterpretation. I am not saying that unless everyone has some control over their life, no one can be said to deserve anything. I am simply saying that it would be a good thing if everyone had some control over their life. We should help those who need help, rather than trying to orchestrate the entire distribution of opportunities and resources as part of some grand scheme for isolating and rewarding everyone's relative deserts.

This suffices to distinguish my view from starting-gate views. I have already explained what differentiates it from truly egalitarian views: namely, the fact that the central question—whether someone has control over his life—is essentially *absolute*, whereas the questions that are central to fundamentally egalitarian views are always essentially *relational*. A more interesting issue, perhaps, is how my view compares with another of the positions in the contemporary debate, the so-called 'priority view'. This view says, roughly, that we should give priority to the worse off. It therefore seems on the face of it to be relational: it focuses not on how well or badly off people are in absolute terms, but on who is *worse* off. But we need to be careful here, since there are two ways of understanding the priority view. As John Rawls understands it, it *is* fundamentally relational, at least in part: it starts by arguing that justice requires equality, but then combines that with arguing that no one could reasonably object if we moved from equality to a state of affairs in which everyone was better off—even if they were better off to an unequal extent. The general principle we can infer from this, according to Rawls, is that we should strive to make the worst off as well off as possible.[25] Derek Parfit understands the priority view differently. He defines it simply as the view that 'benefiting people matters more the worse off these people are'.[26] On this way of understanding it, the priority view is nothing more than a generalization of the idea that people's claims are diminishing, and this idea is *non*-relational. The question of whether or not someone's claim is diminishing is independent of what position other people are in (indeed, it is independent of whether anyone else is even involved). Of course, we could argue that what Parfit's version of the priority view does is take an idea which is fundamentally non-relational—the idea that claims are diminishing—and turn it into a principle which has relational implications: the principle that we should give priority to the worse off. According to this principle, so long as I am worse off than you, I should be given priority; it doesn't matter how well or badly off we both are in absolute terms. However, this doesn't alter the fact that at a fundamental level, the underlying view is non-relational. It just so happens that, in practice, translating the view into action requires us to make comparisons between people. This is quite different from the way egalitarianism *logically* depends on comparisons between people.

How does my view—the view that we should try to make sure that people have some control over their life—fit in to this picture? Like Parfit's version of the priority view, and unlike both Rawls's version and pure egalitarianism, my view is fundamentally non-relational: it tells us that what matters is how people fare in absolute terms, not how they fare relative to one another. But it could be argued that, like Parfit's view, it too becomes relational as soon as we actually apply it. Since jobs are scarce, and since therefore people have to compete for them, there is a sense in which if we want to know whether someone has control over what kind of job (if any) he is able to get, we have to know what position he is in relative to his competitors. In terms of the contrast between relational and absolute views, then, there is no real difference between my view and Parfit's priority view: both are fundamentally non-relational, but require us to make comparisons when applying them. However, unlike Parfit's priority view, and unlike the idea of diminishing claims from which Parfit's view derives, my view does not suggest that people's claims vary in strength according to some smooth and continuous function. Both my view and Parfit's view imply that we should give some sort of priority to the badly off. But unlike Parfit's view, my view does not imply that, as we move up from the bottom end of the distribution, people's claims become gradually and smoothly weaker. Instead, it implies that, as we move up from the bottom end of the distribution, we reach a point—the point where a person can be said to have at least *some* control over what kind of job they can get—where two things change completely. First, people's claims become immediately far less urgent. Second, above this point, there is no longer the same need to make comparisons: if two people are both comfortably above this point—that is, if we can say of both that they have real control over what kind of job they can get—then we no longer need to take any interest in whether one of them is worse off than the other. It just doesn't matter whether one of them has *more* opportunities, or *more* capabilities; the point is that both have *enough.*[27]

In summary, then, what distinguishes my view from most current views is, first, that it is essentially positive rather than negative; second, that it is essentially absolute rather than relational; and third, that it is essentially concerned with a particular point at which people no longer count as being 'badly off', as opposed to making some general statement about how to treat claims all the way across the distribution. However, despite these differentiating features, I should emphasize that I make no claim to complete originality here. I hope that my view seems sensible; and if it does, then the chances are that someone somewhere has probably talked about it already. Moreover, I am not especially interested in straining to refine the view to such a level of detail, in terms of what implications it has in the present political and social context, that I might claim some kind of originality here instead. As I have said before, I am interested in the values which lie behind policy, rather than in policy itself. However, for what it is worth, I will say that I cannot see the view having many implications specifically for equal opportunity—certainly not in terms of direct implications for how jobs should be allocated.

It is not necessarily a problem, however, that this view has no direct implications for equality of opportunity as that is traditionally understood. It only seems like a problem because the view is being put forward as a straight alternative to egalitarian views—telling us that everyone should be in a *good enough* position, never mind whether *equal*. Given that this is the role it plays in the argument, we naturally expect it to have implications in all the same areas that egalitarianism does. But egalitarianism is actually peculiar, in that it has implications for almost everything. If you say that everyone should be in an equal position, that has implications for every single thing which affects the position they are in. If, by contrast, you say only that everyone should be in a good enough position, that acts as a *constraint* on things rather than a fully determining principle, and accordingly tends to have more limited implications.

One similarity between my view and egalitarianism is that both tend to favour indirect intervention—that is, intervention in the 'background conditions' of social and educational policy. Now, as a principle for guiding social and educational policy, simply saying that we should be trying to give people some kind of control over their lives might seem frustratingly vague. But it is a good deal more focused than saying, as is the current fashion among educationalists and politicians, that 'every child should have the best possible start in life'. (This is an example of the kind of universalism, as distinct from egalitarianism, which I discussed at the start of Section 2, and which offers absolutely no guidance for how we should distribute resources under conditions of scarcity.) Moreover, it does have at least one concrete implication, which is that instead of concentrating on the very worst cases, we should concentrate on cases where we have a chance to make a real difference. With some people, in some situations, it will be hard to see how we could ever provide them with the kind of opportunities which would give them real control over what kind of job they are able to get. Should we nevertheless sink everything into trying to do the best we can for them? An egalitarian, or a believer in the priority view, would seem to be committed to thinking we must. The only way they can escape this implication is by tempering their view by introducing some additional principle, such as the principle that resources should be used as productively as possible. They can then present such cases as yet another embodiment of the conflict between justice and efficiency. By contrast, my view implies that if there is a conflict here, it is of a different nature. As far as equal opportunity is concerned, we start with an idea of a certain kind of life—life as a story we help construct, a story whose evolving shape reflects the choices we make along the way—and we say that as many people as possible should get the chance to live that kind of life. But if for some people this is an impossible or hopelessly unrealistic aim, then they will have no claim on us in this regard. They will still have a claim on us in other regards—for example, they will still have a claim to live a *decent* life, if not a self-directed one. Almost every human being has the capacity to live a decent life, and we have the resources to make it possible for them to do so. So again there seems to be a conflict, this time between the demands of equal opportunity and the demands of decency. But there are two ways in which this way of seeing the conflict differs from the standard way. First, on this way of seeing it both sides of the conflict concern the claims of the individual; whereas on the standard view, where the conflict is between justice and efficiency, only one side directly concerns the individual. And second, one side of the conflict—the idea of decency—is completely external to the debate over equal opportunity. If we restrict ourselves to thinking purely in terms of equal opportunity, then people's claims depend not on how badly off they are, but on whether they are ever likely to be able to live the kind of life which equal opportunity sets up as the ideal. We might therefore be justified in not always treating all badly off people the same. This was, perhaps, the thinking behind UK grammar schools. These schools were set up fifty years ago to give the opportunity of a new kind of life to those children who were felt to be best placed to benefit from that opportunity. Twenty-five years later, the experiment was abandoned, on the basis that the schools did not and could not extend the same opportunity to everyone. If I am right, and inequality just isn't something we should be worrying about in this area, then this was probably a mistake.

But enough of politics, and policy. As I have said several times, it was never my aim in this book to set out a new theory of equal opportunity, in the sense of a fully worked out alternative to the dominant theories of equality and meritocracy. I wanted to do enough to suggest that there *are* alternatives to these theories; but beyond that, as I said in the Introduction, the intention was for these alternatives to remain in the background. The first priority is unashamedly destructive rather than constructive—namely, to shake free of certain pervasive but mistaken ways of thinking about equality of opportunity, in order that something better might eventually take their place. In this light, I hope this part of the book has shown why we should reject the idea of equality once and for all. Moreover, I hope it has explained why we should reject equality not just in the weak sense of saying that it is not the only thing we should be striving for in this area, but in the strong sense of saying that it just isn't something we should be striving for *at all*.

I accepted that anyone who wants to argue for this strong position is faced with a problem of his own: that of explaining why the idea of equality continues to exercise such a powerful hold on our thinking. But I found plenty of good explanations for this, without having to concede that there must be something to the idea of equality after all. The first explanation was that it might just be the *language* of equality that exercises this hold over us: we talk about equality, but really we just mean procedural justice; or else our view is what I called universalist; or else it is really about adequacy rather than equality, and so on. The second, more depressing possibility was that people aren't merely confused, they really do believe in equality—despite the fact that, as I have shown, all genuinely egalitarian arguments are either fallacious or inapplicable in this particular context. Finally, there were a couple of other possible explanations that apply specifically to the idea of equal *chances*. The first was that the idea of tossing a coin or drawing lots is really just a procedure for resolving conflicts, and people mistake it for a principle of fairness. The second was that people are guilty of running together, on the one hand, the positive idea that everyone should have an equal chance, and on the other, the quite different negative idea that people's chances shouldn't be affected by other people's prejudices. I argued that if this is all we really care about—if we just want to show that we don't want to see people's chances being affected by other people's prejudices—then we should pursue this idea directly, since equality is too clumsy and expensive a way of achieving it. But in order to pursue this idea directly, we need to think a bit harder about exactly *why* it is wrong for people's chances to be affected by other people's prejudices; that is, exactly why it is wrong for employers to discriminate on the basis of things like race or sex. This is where Part 3 takes up the argument.

NOTES

1. It is of course a generalization to imply that only those at the upper end of the income scale define themselves by their job. Miners and other kinds of skilled

craftsmen probably define themselves by their job in just the same way that doctors or lawyers or philosophers do. But the kinds of manual job of which this is true do seem to be dying out, and yet the link between work and self-respect remains—even where the only kind of work available is the kind that no proud man or woman would identify themselves with. This is the point I am trying to make here.

2. See Part 1 n. 2.

3. See P. F. Strawson, 'Freedom and Resentment', in *Freedom and Resentment and Other Essays* (London: Methuen, 1974).

4. My real target here is a general pattern discernible in the work of many contemporary egalitarians, rather than the specific formulations of any one of the writers I have named. Nevertheless, as a sample they are representative enough. For a representative sample of their work, see Cohen, 'On the Currency of Egalitarian Justice'; Dworkin, 'What is Equality?', Parts I and II, *Philosophy and Public Affairs* 10 (1981); Nagel, *Equality and Partiality*, esp. ch. 7, e.g. 71. I should say that these writers, Dworkin especially, would probably deny that their theories really involve the idea of *desert*, as distinct from the idea of *fault*: the explicit identification of these two ideas is mine not theirs. But I think the only reason they deny this is because they are reluctant to be labelled as 'desert theorists'. Their view is certainly very different from the standard kind of 'desert theory', the kind that says each person should be assessed according to his 'overall deservingness'—whatever that means—and then treated accordingly. I am not accusing them of holding this kind of view. All I am saying is that the role which the idea of 'fault' plays in their theory seems to be essentially the same as the role which the idea of desert plays in everyday thinking about these matters.

5. Or that it is unfair for some people to *end up* worse off for no good reason. Many egalitarians place a great deal of emphasis on this distinction, between arguments for equality of *treatment* (it is unfair to *treat* some people worse than others) and arguments for equality of *outcome* (it is unfair for some people to *end up* worse off than others). I do not place the same emphasis on it, since both kinds of egalitarianism count as making arguments for 'equal treatment' in the wide sense that I am using here. Both kinds have implications for how you should treat people, and in both cases those implications involve the idea of equality. They just involve it in different ways—one tells you to treat people equally, the other to make them equal.

6. Kymlicka is an example of someone who runs together the two questions I have separated here—the question of whether a theory puts forward certain universal moral principles and demands that they be implemented consistently, and the question of whether one of those principles is actually a substantial principle of equality. In his eagerness to represent all mainstream political theories as being at bottom egalitarian, Kymlicka defines egalitarianism

based on the first of these two questions rather than the second—and so ends up including libertarianism on his 'egalitarian plateau' (*Contemporary Political Philosophy*, 4). But while it is of course true that libertarianism, like almost every respectable view, puts forward certain universal moral principles and demands that they be consistently implemented, libertarianism need not and perhaps should not be thought of as resting on any more substantial idea of equality—especially not Kymlicka's suggestion, the idea that everyone's interests matter equally.

7. See Joseph Raz, *The Morality of Freedom* (Oxford: Oxford University Press, 1986), ch. 7.

8. Raz, *The Morality of Freedom*, 186. There are brackets around 'some of' in the original; I have omitted them because for present purposes this qualification is the most important thing.

9. Here I disagree with Rawls, whose egalitarianism *is* ultimately based on the idea that we all have the capacity to pursue a rational plan of life, and who does take this to motivate equal treatment not only in contexts where that means giving everyone the same non-competing rights, but also in contexts where it means giving everyone an equal share of scarce goods. (In *A Theory of Justice*, equal treatment in the sense of giving everyone the same non-competing rights is embodied in the first principle of justice, and equal treatment in the sense of giving everyone an equal share of scarce goods is embodied in the second.)

10. I first heard this suggestion in a paper given by Jeremy Waldron at Oxford in 1999 under the title 'Basic Equality'.

11. There is an interesting tendency among egalitarian socialists to equivocate between, on the one hand, the idea that the objective of socialism is human brotherhood, and on the other, the idea that the validity of socialism's objectives follows from a recognition of *existing* human brotherhood. I have no quarrel with the first idea, which implies that we should try to change the way people see their relations with their fellow human beings. My quarrel is with the second idea: my point is that the only sense in which 'human brotherhood' already exists is the purely formal sense (the sense in which it necessarily exists), and I can't see how the recognition of this purely formal brotherhood could by itself motivate equality in the face of all our other differences.

12. See e.g. Nagel, *Equality and Priority*, 63.

13. See Isaiah Berlin, 'Two Concepts of Liberty', in *Four Essays on Liberty* (Oxford: Oxford University Press, 1969).

14. Some might object that I am implying that individualism is inconsistent with valuing certain kinds of social relations, when in fact the two are perfectly consistent. (I am grateful to an anonymous reader for Oxford University Press for pointing this out.) Of course it is a good thing, these defenders of individualism might say, for people to conceive of themselves as participants in some

collective enterprise, *if this would be good for them*. The individualist's point is that this is the only way that a certain kind of social relations can be said to be good—if it is good for the people involved. It cannot be somehow mysteriously 'good in itself' without being good *for* anyone.

There is a sense in which what the individualist says here is true; but another sense in which he gets things backwards. The question is, if it is good for us to conceive of our relations with each other in a certain way, how exactly is it good for us? It might be good for us in some way that can be specified without saying anything about whether it is good *in itself*: it might just make us happier, say, or psychologically healthier. Or, it might be good for us in a way that cannot be described or explained without making reference to its being good in itself. On this second way of looking at it, it might *also* make us happier or healthier, but—and this is what I meant by saying the individualist has got things backwards—it makes us happier precisely *because* we realize it is the right way to relate to one another, as opposed to its being the right way to relate to one another because it makes us happier.

In case this distinction, between two ways in which something can be good for us, is not immediately clear or persuasive, consider the following example. Just as fraternity is good, so exploitation is bad. I happen to think it is bad not just for the person being exploited, but for the person doing the exploiting. In what way is it bad for him? Perhaps in some way that can be described or explained without relying on the fact that it is bad in itself—we might think that exploiting others will ultimately make him unhappy, or will be psychologically damaging in some other way—though it seems a little optimistic to think this will always be true. But whether or not it is true, there must also be another sense in which it is bad for him just because it is bad in itself: his life is the worse for being a life that involves exploiting others. What this implies is that if we want to believe that certain things are bad in themselves, we don't have to fall foul of the individualist's undeniably intuitive objection, that something can hardly be good or bad without its being good or bad *for someone*. We don't have to fall foul of this objection because what we are rejecting in individualism is not the connection it draws between things being good or bad and their being good or bad for someone, but the implication that this connection can only run one way. Individualism asserts that things can only be good or bad because they are, in some independently specifiable way, good or bad for someone, whereas I am saying that *sometimes* the connection runs the other way. Sometimes things are good or bad for people because they are good or bad in themselves. There might be no way of fully capturing why or how they are good or bad for people without making reference to their being good or bad in themselves.

So much for the general point. For present purposes, the important point is as follows. Individualism is consistent with promoting fraternity, but only in terms of the good effects it has on individuals, where those good effects can be specified individualistically. And the argument I have been considering in the text, that equal treatment expresses our fraternity, would no longer count as a truly egalitarian argument if it was based solely on the idea that fraternal social relations are good for us in ways that can be specified individualistically.

It is another question whether there would be much difference *in practice* between the two ways of valuing fraternity—the way which values fraternity in itself, and the way which values it individualistically. But I am interested here in the difference in theory rather than practice; and it strikes me that, in theory at least, egalitarianism must be at bottom a doctrine about *justice*, not simply about what would make us happier.

15. See e.g. Bernard Williams, *Moral Luck* (Cambridge: Cambridge University Press, 1981), 89; John Broome, 'Selecting People Randomly', *Ethics* 95 (1984), 45–6.

16. See e.g. Bernard Boxill, 'Equality, Discrimination, and Preferential Treatment', in P. Singer (ed.), *A Companion to Ethics* (Oxford: Blackwell, 1991), 333–4.

17. It is, though, something worth noting about the equal chances view that there is such a sharp contrast between how simple it is, conceptually speaking, and how horrendously complicated it would be actually to administer. It is conceptually simple in two important senses. First, it purports to encapsulate everything we need to know about social justice in a single principle. Second, it also tells us that we can ignore any complexities in the *causes* of injustice. For example, we can ignore the question of whether some kinds of people have worse chances than others because they have been treated unjustly: the mere fact that they have worse chances is an injustice in itself, regardless of its cause. So it is simple in theory; the complexity only comes at the point when we have to apply it—because there is no obvious limit to how much of our lives (educational background, family background, genetics, etc.) it is supposed to regulate.

18. *The Morality of Freedom*, ch. 9, esp. 236–44.

19. Raz doesn't explicitly distinguish these two reasons, but he is clearly more concerned with the second, which is philosophically the more interesting; he offers some powerful arguments in its support (ibid.).

20. Well, one reason, an egalitarian might say, is because anyone who finds themselves in a position to dictate the outcome should be able to see that it is just a matter of luck that they, rather than anyone else, happen to be the one who is in that position. But given that 'luck' here just means, as is usual in egalitarian arguments, anything the person can't be held responsible for (see Introd. n. 14), it might or might not be a matter of luck, in this particular example, that this particular person happens to be in a position to dictate the outcome. Perhaps the reason he is much stronger than everyone else is because he has been spending all his spare time working out, while the others were lazing

about; if so, then it isn't a matter of 'luck', in the egalitarian's own sense, that he is now in a position to dictate the outcome.

Note that I'm not actually supporting the idea that this fact, that he has been spending his spare time working out, gives him a stronger claim than the rest. I'm just saying that it means it is not a matter of luck, *in the egalitarian's own sense*, that he is now in a stronger position than the rest. My point is precisely that these two criteria that egalitarians employ—on the one hand, whether everyone has an equal claim, and on the other, whether their relative bargaining positions are a matter of luck—don't always coincide. (Of course, even if we concede, in the present case, that it is a matter of luck that this person happened to be in a stronger bargaining position than the rest, it still wouldn't necessarily follow that it is unfair of him to exploit that position. We would also have to believe the argument, discussed in Section 2, that no one should end up better off than another without deserving to—an argument which I hope I have already done enough to refute.)

21. Similar examples have been much discussed in the literature: see e.g. G. E. M. Anscombe, 'Who is wronged?', *Oxford Review* 5 (1967); John Taurek, 'Should the Numbers Count?', *Philosophy and Public Affairs* 6 (1977); and Broome, 'Selecting People Randomly'. My example differs slightly from theirs, since they believe in equal chances for equal chances' sake, whereas I do not, and my example is designed to bring out this difference.

22. Broome, who believes in equal chances for equal chances' sake, admits that his own intuitions let him down here. According to his theory, the fisherman should toss a coin to decide which town to head for, as well as drawing lots on arrival. But he admits, 'I cannot persuade myself that [this] is right. I cannot believe it makes any difference which [town] you go to'; and he concedes that this is a 'serious threat' to his theory ('Selecting People Randomly', 55). As for the further point about the asymmetry between our intuitions about whether the fisherman should toss a coin to decide which town to head for and our intuitions about whether he should draw lots on arrival, Broome doesn't appear to notice it.

23. See e.g. Charles Fried, *An Anatomy of Values* (Cambridge, Mass.: Harvard University Press, 1970), 227.

24. See e.g. Brian Barry, *Theories of Justice* (Hemel Hempstead: Harvester-Wheatsheaf, 1989), 223–5, including footnote. I am arguing here that the real problem with this general line of argument is not simply that we can't be sure that these things are in fact a matter of chance: the real problem is that if we understand the egalitarian impulse correctly, it no longer makes any difference whether these things are a matter of chance. But for the record, I think Susan Hurley is right when she suggests that the idea that talents in particular are a matter of chance is not merely questionable but logically impossible. If talent is in part genetic, then you can't say that it was a matter of chance that

you have the talents you do, since that amounts to saying that it was a matter of chance that you have the genes you do—which is, in logical terms, meaningless, if your genes are one of the things that determine who you are. (I heard Hurley make this point in a seminar at Oxford University in 1999.)

25. See *A Theory of Justice*, 76f.

26. 'Equality and Priority', in A. Mason (ed.), *Ideals of Equality* (Oxford: Blackwell, 1998), 12.

27. There are in fact two different senses in which we might say that someone has 'enough'. In the first sense, when we say that someone has enough, we are referring to what we take to be the minimum acceptable level of whatever is at issue. If we are talking about food, for example, then if someone is starving, or malnourished, then this is a clear case of having less than enough. In the second sense of 'enough', the point is not that it is necessarily bad or harmful to have less than this level, but that there is nothing good about having more. If we are talking about food again, then having enough in this second sense would mean having more than you could possibly eat (of all the kinds of food you might want to eat). The first sense is the one I have in mind in the text. For more on these ideas, see Harry Frankfurt, *The Importance of What We Care About* (Cambridge: Cambridge University Press, 1988), 152–6. Frankfurt ends up adopting a position closer to the second sense. See also David Wiggins's illuminating remarks on the related idea of need, in *Needs, Values, Truth* (Oxford: Blackwell, 1998), essay I.

PART 3

Discrimination

I. DISCRIMINATION, MERITOCRACY, AND EQUALITY

At the end of Part 2 I suggested that while we often *say* that everyone should have an equal chance of getting a job, we might only mean that their chances shouldn't depend on other people's prejudices; in other words, we might only mean that they shouldn't be discriminated against on the basis of things like race[1] or sex. I pointed out that as an idea this is really quite different to that of equal chances; and therefore that we should try to keep the two ideas separate. But I also noted that keeping these ideas separate raises the question of what exactly *is* wrong with discriminating against people on the basis of things like race or sex, if not that it leaves them with unequal chances.

The question of what exactly is wrong with discriminating against people on the basis of things like race or sex might seem like the kind of question only a philosopher would ask. Isn't it enough that we know discrimination is wrong, never mind exactly why? I don't think so. For one thing, there are different *ways* of discriminating on the basis of race or sex—different reasons why people do this. Some of these ways might be obviously wrong, others less so. Consider, for example, the kind of case where an employer discriminates against women not because he doesn't like them, but because he genuinely thinks they tend to be less good at the job. Is this wrong? And if so, is it wrong *in exactly the same way* as it would be wrong for him to discriminate against women because he didn't like them? We will have no way of answering such questions unless we have already thought about the 'obvious' question of why it is wrong to discriminate against certain kinds of people simply because you don't like them.

The second reason why we need to ask why discrimination is wrong is more basic. Even in the supposedly obvious cases, like the case where an employer discriminates against women simply because he doesn't like them, we don't in fact all agree that this is wrong; and we certainly don't agree about what is supposed to *follow* from its being wrong. First, there are the people who are actually doing the discriminating. Presumably at least some of these people don't agree that what they are doing is wrong. Second, there are the hard-line libertarians, who accept that discrimination might be wrong, but insist that employers are nevertheless perfectly within their rights to do it. Neither of these groups is very influential in philosophy or for that matter in society; but that is no reason to pretend they don't exist.

We should start, then, by asking ourselves what *exactly* is wrong with discrimination in the supposedly obvious cases—cases where an employer discriminates against black or female applicants on grounds of their race or sex alone, rather than because he thinks they tend to be less good at the job. Now, the next thing to notice is that as soon as we do ask ourselves this question, we realize that even those of us who agree that this kind of behaviour is wrong tend to disagree about *why* it is wrong. Many try to explain its wrongness by appealing to the idea of meritocracy; others by appealing to the idea of equality. We find meritocrats arguing that discriminating against black or female applicants is wrong because it fails to judge them on their merits; and egalitarians arguing that discrimination is wrong because it leaves people with unequal chances.

As far as egalitarianism is concerned, you might be forgiven for thinking that there is an even simpler argument than this: that discrimination is wrong because it *fails to treat people equally*. But we need to be careful about how we interpret this argument, since in this particular context when we talk about 'treating people equally' we are usually just talking about procedural justice. We are just saying that if there is some rule in place, then it should be applied equally to everyone. So 'treating people equally' might just mean treating them on their merits; in which case, what looks like an egalitarian view is really just a meritocratic view in disguise. The truly egalitarian approach is to argue that discrimination is wrong because it leaves people with unequal chances. Of course, if egalitarians want to argue this way, they have to deal with my earlier suggestion that the seemingly widespread support for this approach rests on a simple failure to distinguish these two ideas, the idea that people's chances shouldn't depend on other people's prejudices, and the idea that everyone should have an equal chance. They have to make absolutely clear that *this is what makes discrimination wrong*: the fact that it leaves people with unequal chances.

No doubt many of those who take one or other of these paths, seeking to explain why discrimination is wrong by appealing to either meritocracy or equality, do actually start out with a genuine commitment to these theories. But for some people at least the order is reversed: they are only tempted to endorse meritocracy or equality because they are looking for something to back up their feeling that there must be something wrong with discrimination. I hope that anyone who has read the first two parts of this book will now see that this is not a good idea. Equality just isn't something we should be aiming for in this area, so there had better be something wrong with discrimination besides the fact that it leaves people with unequal chances. As for meritocracy, while it might be a reasonable thing for any individual employer to pursue voluntarily, it isn't something we can legitimately *impose* on employers; so if discrimination is wrong only because it fails to treat people on their merits, the implication would be that although we might reasonably expect employers not to discriminate, we can't require them not to.

If we want to adopt a stronger position than this, we will have to come up with an argument against discrimination which is independent of meritocracy and equality. Committed meritocrats and egalitarians who are unmoved by what I said in Parts 1 and 2 will see this as creating unnecessary extra work. But even if I cannot convince them to abandon their views, they should realize that there are still certain advantages to coming up with an independent argument against discrimination. It would avoid some of the awkward implications that follow from appealing to either meritocracy or equality to explain why discrimination is wrong. One implication of appealing to meritocracy, for example, is that rejecting someone on the basis of race or sex turns out to be no *worse* than rejecting them for any other reason which is similarly unrelated to merit. This does not seem quite right. Similarly, the implication of appealing to equality is that discriminating on the basis of race or sex turns out to be no worse than any other way of behaving which leaves different kinds of people with unequal chances. Again this does not seem quite right: it does not seem to capture what is *distinctively* wrong with discrimination.

But perhaps in the case of equality at least, some might be tempted to disagree, and to embrace the implication that discriminating on the basis of things like race or sex is no worse than any other way of behaving which leaves people with unequal chances. Remember that according to one version of egalitarianism, it is not so much inequality in itself that is objectionable, as people being unequal *for no good reason*.[2] On this version of egalitarianism, the implication of arguing that discrimination is wrong because it violates equality is that it is no worse than any other way of behaving which leaves people with unequal chances for no good reason. And perhaps egalitarians will be prepared to embrace this implication. After all, it seems to resonate with another common way of describing what is wrong with discrimination: that it is wrong because it is 'arbitrary' or 'irrelevant'. As Peter Singer puts it: 'Why pick on race? Why not on whether a person was born in a leap year? Or whether there is more than one vowel in her surname? All these characteristics are equally irrelevant'.[3]

However, it strikes me that rather than offering independent support to the idea that discrimination is wrong because it leaves people with unequal chances for no good reason, the idea that it is wrong because it is 'irrelevant' or 'arbitrary' is merely guilty of the same mistake. One wonders whether Singer really means what he says here. Does he *really* think that discriminating against people on the basis of their race is no worse than discriminating against them on the basis of the number of vowels in their name? If we actually came across someone who discriminated against people on the basis of the number of vowels in their name, I suspect we would think them mad, rather than bad. If so, then introducing the idea that discrimination is objectionable because it is 'arbitrary' or not based on any good reason hasn't solved the problem. It doesn't actually make it any easier to accept what egalitarians are asking us to accept: that discrimination is no worse than any other way of treating people in a similarly unequal manner.

This is not the only awkward implication of choosing to appeal to a theory like meritocracy or equality to explain why discrimination is wrong. A second problem is that we are usually far more certain that race or sex is the wrong way to make a given decision than we are about what would be the *right* way to make that decision. Sometimes it is hard to see how an outsider could possibly comment on what an employer positively ought to be looking for. But if we end up condemning discrimination on the basis of either meritocracy or the idea that it is wrong for people to have unequal chances *for no good reason*, then we *are* effectively committing ourselves to imposing a positive answer as to how employers should be making their decisions.

Finally, the meritocratic route in particular has one last, even more troubling implication. If I was right in Part 1 when I argued that meritocracy has more to do with efficiency than fairness, then the price of explaining the wrongness of discrimination by saying that it fails to judge people on their merits is that the wrongness becomes disconnected from the idea that it is the people who are discriminated against who are being wronged. If discrimination is wrong purely because it is not meritocratic, and if not being meritocratic is wrong purely because it is inefficient, then the wrong is done not to the people who are being discriminated against, but to some third party—whether that is shareholders, consumers, or society as a whole.

Admittedly, this last implication doesn't apply to those who take the egalitarian route. To say that discrimination is wrong because it leaves people with unequal chances does at least explain why it is supposed to be unfair rather than merely inefficient. But the other implications remain serious enough; and there is also the strategic problem, shared across meritocratic and egalitarian approaches, that in falling back on either meritocracy or equality to explain what is wrong with discrimination we are falling back on something less secure than what we started with. We are more convinced that discrimination is wrong than we are about either meritocracy or equality.

What is the alternative to falling back on meritocracy or equality? Well, we could actually think about discrimination from first principles, rather than trying to fit it into some pre-established theoretical framework. Now, I have several reasons for favouring this approach. First, because it is not my style to fix on some single principle and then try to roll it out across the entire landscape of political morality. I think it is more fruitful to approach each particular problem in its own context, rather than trying to subsume it into some grand theory. Second, I have tried in the last few paragraphs to show how appealing to these particular theories in this particular context probably raises more questions than answers—in terms of implying that there is nothing special about discrimination, for example. And third, because I happen also to think that these theories cannot provide a secure base on which to build anything. Since all I have put forward in their place is the idea that we should try to make sure that people have some control over their lives, I have no choice but to consider the idea of discrimination separately. For unlike each of meritocracy and equality, the idea that people should have some control over their lives does not by itself rule out discrimination. It is possible that everyone could have some control over their lives, while at the same time being subject to certain kinds of discrimination. Given these three aspects of my position, I am committed to considering the issue of discrimination separately. But rather than seeing this as an inconvenience—as a case of having to scrape around and come up with some ad hoc explanation of why discrimination is wrong—I see it as an opportunity, a chance to look again at something we have been taking for granted for too long. It is precisely one of the problems with the theory-building tendency that we never do look at individual issues in context, we just spend our time wondering how we can twist them to fit into various ready-made frameworks.

However, there is one last thing I need to consider, a possible objection to the whole approach—to the very idea that we should, or even can, think about discrimination separately from meritocracy in particular. The objection runs as follows. Perhaps *in theory* we can separate the idea of non-discrimination from the idea of meritocracy, but in practice we wouldn't be able to prevent the first idea turning into the second. We might *start* by ruling out discrimination on grounds of race or sex, but the list of factors we would want to exclude would inevitably lengthen until it included factors too numerous to mention—sexual orientation, religious or political affiliation, age, class, and so on—in other words, until it reached the point where employers were not allowed to discriminate on any basis other than merit. The result would be to bring in meritocracy by the back door.

This is a 'slippery slope' argument, and the first thing to say is that I am not sure how slippery the slope would actually prove in practice. Suppose we tried to implement non-discrimination by requiring any employer who was accused of discrimination to demonstrate to some external, independent body that the decision in question was not in fact based on race, or sex, or whatever. There is a real difference, and one that is defensible not just in theory but also in practice, between a regulatory regime of this kind, and the kind where companies are told what to do in the first place. It just *isn't* obvious that the first kind of regulatory regime would inevitably collapse into the second. Moreover, if on occasion it did, that would be because what really lay behind the drive to keep adding to the list of proscribed factors was a suspicion of any factor unrelated to suitability for the job. In other words, it would be because the people running the system were closet meritocrats. In the end, this whole objection really boils down to the banal observation that one kind of policy can turn into another kind if it falls into the hands of people who believed in the other kind all along. This is supported by observing that exactly the same kind of slippery slope argument could be run by an egalitarian. He too might say: perhaps in theory we can separate the idea of non-discrimination from the idea of equality, but in practice we wouldn't be able to stop the first from turning into the second. We might start by ruling out discrimination on grounds of race or sex, but the list of factors we would want to see excluded from influencing people's chances would inevitably lengthen until it included not just things like sexual orientation, age, class, and so on, but also family background and anything else people can't be held responsible for—indeed, almost everything that does in fact influence people's chances. In which case, the result would be that equality had been smuggled in by the back door. But again, a regime of non-discrimination would only collapse into equality in this way if it was being run by people who thought that no one can really be held responsible for anything—in other words, if it was run by people who believed in equality all along.

Perhaps, however, it is possible to reformulate this line of objection in a slightly less aggressive way. Suppose we accept that the negative idea of non-discrimination wouldn't *necessarily* collapse into one or other of the positive ideas of meritocracy or equality. Nevertheless, it might still be true that promoting merit, to take one of the two examples, is the simplest and most reliable way of eliminating discrimination. If the regulations are framed any more specifically, it will be too easy for employers to evade them, by simply lying about their motives. An employer who was accused of discriminating on the basis of race or sex could simply deny that these were his motives. He could claim that he hired people on the basis of personal likes or dislikes, and that it just so happened that this resulted in him employing disproportionately few black or female applicants. It is tempting to think that the easiest way of getting round this problem is to make his motives irrelevant, by forcing him to measure up to some unambiguous, externally imposed standard, such as meritocracy. Then all we have to do is show that he is not hiring the best applicants: *why* he isn't hiring them is no longer relevant.

There are two problems with this line of argument. The first is that what it attacks—the idea that it is possible to establish people's motives—is absolutely central to our systems of law and morality. If motives are morally relevant, we cannot just decide to ignore them because they are hard to establish. There are already plenty of other areas—cases of unfair dismissal, for example—in which courts or tribunals are required to establish employers' motives. The second problem is equally fundamental. This whole line of argument rests on the implicit assumption that one particular social goal—the goal of eliminating every last trace of discrimination—must be given priority over all other aims. Presumably, the idea here is that discrimination is an injustice, and that justice takes absolute priority over everything else. Unless we impose meritocracy, some instances of discrimination will continue to slip through the net; and tolerating this means tolerating injustice, which is unacceptable. Now, the most obvious weakness in this argument is the crude idea that justice takes absolute priority over everything else. A more subtle approach would seek to balance the acknowledged value of eliminating injustice—here, in the form of discrimination—against the disadvantages of imposing meritocracy when we don't really believe it is intrinsically justified. The most obvious disadvantage is the encroachment on employers' freedom. Many employers would never have considered discriminating on grounds of race or sex, but now they would be suffering along with everyone else under a system which allowed them no discretion in how they take their decisions. There is also the wider problem that we might come to forget that we only embraced meritocracy in the first place as a way of eliminating discrimination. We might start to accord it a wholly unwarranted intrinsic significance, with the result that it will be difficult to resist precisely where resistance is most required—in areas where it is absolutely vital to preserve some wider notion of 'relevance', encompassing all the different kinds of thing that a reasonable person might reasonably take into account when making a decision.

2. SO WHAT EXACTLY *IS* WRONG WITH DISCRIMINATION?

It seems there are good theoretical reasons for trying to separate the idea of non-discrimination from the wider ideas of meritocracy and equality; and that there is no good reason for thinking this separation would prove unworkable in practice. So for the remainder of the discussion I am going to treat discrimination as a separate problem. What exactly *is* wrong with discriminating on the basis of things like race or sex, if not that it violates some principle of meritocracy or equality? One suggestion is that it is unfair to discriminate against people on the basis of their race or sex *because these things aren't their fault*. In one sense, this explanation is like those that invoke meritocracy or equality, in that it too appeals to some wider principle—in this case, the principle that it is wrong for the way you treat people to be based on things which aren't their fault. But my objection to invoking meritocracy or equality was not simply that it involved appealing to some more general principle. True, I did argue for a more particularist approach, one which did not assume that everything in this area would end up being explained by a single principle. At the same time, however, we might wonder how else the wrongness of anything could ever be *explained*, if not by moving to some higher level of generality. I also objected specifically to *these particular* ways of generalizing what is wrong with discrimination—to the fact that they try to explain what is essentially a negative idea, that people should not be treated differently on the basis of things like race or sex, by appealing to a positive idea, about how employers *should* be treating applicants. In this respect, this new suggestion is in better shape. It seeks to explain the negative idea of non-discrimination by appealing to an idea which, though more general, is still negative: the idea that people should not be judged on the basis of things which are not their fault.

Of course, in saying that this idea is in better shape than the egalitarian approach I am assuming that it is truly separate from that approach. Clearly it is separate from the kind of egalitarianism I have been discussing here—the kind which argues that people should not have unequal chances *for no good reason*. But the separation becomes blurred if we go back to one of the kinds of egalitarianism I discussed in Part 2, the view that no one should be worse off than another *through no fault of their own*. Saying that people should not be judged according to things which aren't their fault, and saying they should not end up worse off than others through no fault of their own, might seem like only slightly different ways of making the same point. But in fact there are at least two respects in which the view I am considering here is distinct from the view I discussed in Part 2. The first is that here, the idea of fault is being deployed on its own, rather than as part of a wider theory which also involves equality. However, the idea of fault seems to be interchangeable with that of responsibility: to say that people should not be judged according to things which are not their fault appears to be the same as saying that they should not be judged according to things for which they cannot be held responsible. And we saw in Part 2 that for many contemporary political philosophers, the idea of responsibility is linked inextricably with the idea of equality—which is perhaps why they don't see how this view, that people should not be judged according to things which are not their fault, could be anything other than a kind of egalitarianism. They argue that everyone should be equal *unless they are responsible for being unequal*; and when it comes to explaining what would count as being responsible for being unequal, they invoke equality a second time, and argue that only if everyone started equal can they be said to be responsible for any inequalities that subsequently arise. In fact, there are two possible routes to this final position. One is to start with a principle of equality, and then bring in the idea of responsibility to qualify that: that is, to start by saying that everyone should be equal, and then introduce an exception to that rule, saying that inequalities are acceptable providing people are responsible for them. The other is to reverse the two steps, starting with a commitment to responsibility, saying that the question of what people are responsible for is the only fair or rational basis for determining who should get what, and then combining that with the argument from insufficient reason—the argument that where there is no good reason for one person to have more than another, they should have the same.[4] Both ways end up in the same position, arguing that everyone should be equal unless they are responsible for being unequal. But although there might be no difference in terms of where they end up, the *motivation* behind them is different. When I was discussing this kind of argument in Part 2, I was interpreting it as if it took the first route, the route which starts with the idea of equality. In the present context, we should interpret it as taking the second route, the route which starts with the idea of responsibility, and brings in equality, if at all, later. If we look at it this way, we will see that there is no *need* to bring in equality. What is essential to the position is the idea that the question of what people are and are not responsible for is the only fair or rational basis for determining who gets what. There is then some further question about what conditions have to be in place for people to be held responsible for anything; and equality might or might not be put forward as one of the conditions. For our purposes here it doesn't matter, since the previous idea, that what people are and are not responsible for is the only fair or rational basis for determining who gets what, is by itself enough to rule out discrimination. Almost everyone will agree that someone's race or sex is not something he can be held responsible for—whether or not they agree in more general terms about the conditions of responsibility.

The second respect in which the view I am discussing here differs from all those discussed in Part 2 is that it focuses primarily on the way people treat one another, rather than on states of affairs. If the same idea was applied to states of affairs, it would yield something like the following principle: that *people's prospects should not depend on things for which they can't be held responsible*. By contrast, because, as I have been interpreting it, it applies to how people treat each other, it ends up implying something quite different: that *the way you treat people should not be based on things for which they can't be held responsible.* Saying that it is unfair for the way you treat someone to be based on things for which they can't be held responsible is quite different from saying that things for which they can't be held responsible should not affect their prospects in any way. The latter idea is much wider, as there are countless ways in which a given factor could affect someone's prospects without being consciously present in the way anyone treats them. Moreover, while the wider idea does seem to be inextricably linked to egalitarianism, the former, narrower idea does not: it seems to have a life of its own. Consider, for example, how we think about blame and punishment. Most of us think it is unfair to blame or punish people for things they could do nothing about. But we don't generally see this as part of some wider egalitarianism: as far as blame or punishment are concerned, we wouldn't necessarily say that people should be treated absolutely equally unless they are responsible for being unequal. We might just say that it is wrong to blame or punish them for things they could do nothing about, and leave it at that.

The question is whether the narrower idea also applies to the way employers treat job applicants. One way of answering this is to argue that it applies to how people treat each other *in any context.* But there is something profoundly wrong in this suggestion—in the idea that it could *never* be acceptable, in any context, to treat people differently on the basis of things they can do nothing about. For example, whether or not someone is funny, or sexy, is generally something they can do nothing about; but I am surely not being *unfair* if I like some people more than others, or find them more attractive, because they are funny or sexy. Now, the kind of person who argues that the responsibility principle does apply everywhere will probably respond to this example by reminding us that the responsibility principle only tells us what is unfair, not what we should do about it. On this view, I am being unfair if I favour people who are funny or sexy; but this is not to say I should be forcibly prevented from behaving like this. There are good reasons for thinking the state should not even be trying to eliminate unfairness in this kind of context. There are no such reasons for holding back from trying to eliminate unfairness in the context of job allocation. The responsibility principle can *apply* universally without universally justifying intervention.

I agree that we cannot refute the universalist ambitions of the responsibility principle simply by coming up with an example where that principle doesn't seem to justify intervention. However, I disagree that this is all my last example shows. If you really think about the reasons why you like people or find them attractive, I suspect you will be struck not just by the thought that the state should keep out of this part of your life, but also by the absurdity of thinking that what you are doing is unfair. It would be absurd to try to stop *yourself* from liking people because they are funny or sexy—never mind whether the state should try to stop you. But in case this point does need reinforcing, consider the fact that most of us prefer to have sexual relations either just with women, or just with men. What we are doing is treating people differently according to whether they are male or female—which means according to something they can do nothing about. Suppose you are a man who happens to prefer to have sexual relations only with women, but you come across a man who wants to have sexual relations with you. If you refuse, are you being unfair? Surely not; and yet the reason you refuse is because he is male, which is something he can do nothing about. (It is no answer here to say that the real reason you refuse is because you simply don't find him attractive, because this too is probably something he can do nothing about. And of course, if the reason *why* you don't find him attractive is because he is male, we are back where we started anyway.)

The important point behind all this is that even if your sex is something you can do nothing about, it remains one of the things that *makes you who you are*. It is an odd idea to suppose that it could somehow be unfair to behave towards people in a way that simply takes them for who they are— even if 'being who they are' is something they can't always do anything about. Now, I am aware that saying this goes against the grain of recent 'progressive' thinking. But even by 'progressive' standards there are few things more obviously half-baked than this, the idea that we should judge and treat others not on the basis of the way they are, but on the basis of the way they would like to be. It is difficult to imagine how we could even make sense of our lives, and our relations with others, if we took this idea seriously.

This is enough to establish that the responsibility principle does not apply universally—and therefore that we can't simply *assume* it applies to the way employers treat applicants. It remains an open question how we should classify this case: whether we should classify it along with punishment, where the responsibility principle clearly does apply, or whether it makes more sense to classify it along with personal life, where the responsibility principle clearly does not apply. How might someone argue for classifying it along with punishment? First, he might argue that decisions about jobs, like decisions about punishments, are in some sense part of the public realm. Second, he might argue that decisions about jobs, like decisions about punishments, are made by people who are in a position of power over the rest of us—and who should therefore be held to higher standards.

Both these arguments are undermined by testing them on the case of blame. Both imply that although the responsibility principle applies to punishments, it does not necessarily apply to blame. Decisions about punishments are part of the public realm, and are whereas decided by people who are in some kind of position of power over the rest of us, whereas decisions about blame do not necessarily satisfy either of these conditions. And yet blame quite clearly *is* regulated by the responsibility principle. Even in a private context we still think it unfair to blame people for things they could do nothing about. Of course, this comes as no surprise, given the obviously close relationship between blame and punishment. But it proves that the responsibility principle is not restricted to the public realm, nor to decisions made by people who are in a position of power over the rest of us.

A better explanation of where the responsibility principle does and does not apply is to say that it applies only in those cases where people are supposed to be treated according to what they *deserve*.[5] This explains why the responsibility principle applies to decisions about both punishment *and* blame: both are decisions about what people deserve. It also explains why the responsibility principle does not seem to apply when we are talking about the reasons we find people attractive: few of us think that physical or emotional attraction have to be deserved to be appropriate. If this is the right explanation, the question becomes whether decisions about jobs are decisions about what people deserve. I have already set out my position on this, in Part 1. I pointed out that this certainly isn't what we naturally think: we don't naturally think of jobs as rewards. To the extent that we think about desert at all in this area, we only really think about it in relation to how much people get paid. We want to feel that people are getting paid what they deserve, and it can seem as if the only way we will be able to feel this is if we can say that they deserved to get the job in the first place. I tried to show that the second part of this view might be a mistake.[6] But the important point for present purposes was that once we separate out the issue of pay, there is much less motivation for thinking that jobs themselves should be allocated according to desert. If this is right, then there is also much less motivation for thinking that decisions about jobs should be regulated by the responsibility principle.

Meritocrats will certainly welcome this, since the responsibility principle would rule out meritocracy: people's merits are not something for which they can be held wholly responsible. However, those of us who reject both meritocracy *and* the responsibility principle are left without an explanation of why discrimination is wrong. The responsibility principle at least seemed to be on the right track: it explained why discrimination is wrong by appealing to a principle which is general but also negative, and which can therefore explain why it is wrong for employers to make decisions on the basis of things like race or sex without implying any positive view about how they *should* make decisions. I am going to recommend an alternative explanation which shares the same basic shape. This is that discrimination is wrong, when it is wrong, because it involves treating people with unwarranted contempt. This too appeals to a principle which is general but also negative: the principle *that it is wrong to treat people with unwarranted contempt*. Now, the first thing to say about this, as a possible explanation of why discrimination is wrong, is that not all kinds of discrimination obviously express contempt. Even discrimination based on race or sex cannot *always* be said to express contempt—let alone all the other kinds of behaviour that are commonly described as 'discrimination'. I return to this point below. The second point is that even when a given instance of discrimination does express contempt, we cannot simply assume that this contempt will be unwarranted. For example, discriminating on grounds of religious affiliation is often thought to be just as wrong as discriminating on grounds of race or sex; but some religious doctrines might actually be deserving of contempt, either in terms of the bizarre beliefs they involve, or in terms of their unsavoury social implications.

However, we cannot afford to reject this explanation of why discrimination is wrong purely on the basis that it does not completely fit our existing intuitions about which kinds of discrimination are wrong and which are not. There might not be a principle which fits all our intuitions. We need to find the one that makes the best of our intuitions—i.e. that explains and justifies our deepest convictions about which kinds of discrimination are wrong while at the same time not having unacceptable implications in other areas.[7] The idea that discrimination is wrong because it expresses unwarranted contempt does just this. It explains and justifies our deepest convictions about discrimination: it explains, for example, why it is wrong to discriminate against black or female applicants because you think them mentally or morally inferior. Such discrimination clearly expresses contempt, and the contempt it expresses is of a kind that is unlikely ever to be warranted. It is unlikely to be warranted because it is directed not at some specific feature or belief of the person in question, but at the whole person; and because it is directed not just at them as an individual, but to everybody of the same race or sex. The contempt principle explains our convictions about this central case of discrimination without having alarming implications elsewhere, either for other aspects of the equal opportunity debate, or for the way we think about our personal lives. This, then, is the principle on which I intend to base the rest of the discussion.

3. A LIBERTARIAN OBJECTION

Before I start to explore the contempt principle further, I need to deal with a couple of possible objections. The first concerns a potential misunderstanding which is especially likely to arise in relation to the issue of race. To pre-empt this, I should make clear that what I am arguing is that the contempt principle explains what is wrong with racial *discrimination*. I am not for a moment suggesting that it captures what is wrong with the worst kinds of racially motivated *behaviour*. Of course it does not begin to do justice to the terrible crimes perpetrated in places like Rwanda or the Balkans to say merely that the victims were treated with contempt. But we need to separate two things here: the way the victims were chosen, and what was done to them. My concern is purely with ways of choosing between people, since when we are talking about discriminating against certain kinds of job applicants, nothing positively bad is being done to anyone— they are merely missing out on something good. If there is supposed to be something wrong with this kind of discrimination, it must consist in the way people are being chosen. Of course, if instead I was discussing the morality of international intervention in places like Rwanda and the Balkans, I would be less interested in the way people are being chosen and more interested in what is being done to them. The main reason for intervening in places like Rwanda or the Balkans is nothing to do with the fact that the victims were selected on the basis of race. It is that people are being treated as no human being should ever be treated. Beside this fact, the reason why they were singled out—because of their race or their religion or their political views or whatever—pales into insignificance.

The second kind of objection is more serious. It comes from the libertarian, who is prepared to concede that discrimination might be morally wrong—and even wrong in itself, not just because it violates some wider principle of meritocracy or equality—but who insists that employers are nevertheless quite within their rights to do it. To understand the libertarian position, we need to go back to an idea I first discussed in the Introduction, the idea that private sector employers have property rights over jobs. According to this idea, since they are the ones who are going to pay the wages, their deciding who they want to employ is analogous to any other instance of deciding how they want to spend their money. The libertarian agrees with this, but takes it to have much wider implications than I did, since he regards property rights as virtually inviolable. For the libertarian, there is only one legitimate reason for restricting someone's property rights, namely, to ensure that they don't violate the rights, to property or person, of anyone else. This is why, even if discrimination is morally wrong, employers might still be within their rights to do it. They have a property right to allocate jobs as they see fit, so while it might be morally wrong to allocate them on the basis of things like race or sex, as long as this does not actually violate anyone's rights, they are perfectly entitled to do it.

We could respond by arguing that while the idea of property rights might rule out some conceptions of equal opportunity, such as meritocracy, it doesn't rule out non-discrimination. That is, we could argue that discrimination precisely does violate people's rights—at least if it is the kind of discrimination which involves treating them with unwarranted contempt. However, it is a good question whether people really have the *right* not to be treated with unwarranted contempt—especially when we bear in mind that we are only talking here about treating people with unwarranted contempt in the way you choose between them. If you required black applicants to lick your boots before you were prepared to offer them a job, then you would certainly be treating them with contempt in a way that violated their rights. But with discrimination we are talking about expressing contempt purely in the way you choose between people. If you simply discriminate against black applicants, all you are doing is making sure that they miss out on being chosen for something good, as opposed to singling them out for something bad. A libertarian will argue that merely expressing contempt in *this* way—refusing to *favour* a certain kind of person, rather than singling them out for bad treatment—can't be said to violate their rights. There are only two ways of violating someone's rights, on the libertarian view: by depriving them of something they are entitled to, or by causing them harm without good reason. Discriminating against applicants on the basis of things like race or sex doesn't qualify under either heading. It doesn't deprive them of anything they are *entitled* to (as opposed to something they merely want, or are qualified for), and it can't be said to cause them *harm* (as opposed to merely *not helping* them).

The libertarian might try to push home this argument by means of various analogies. Suppose, he might say, I have only contempt for Indians, and because of that, I would never consider going to an Indian restaurant. I might even quite like Indian food; I just don't want Indians to benefit from my custom. I am surely not guilty of violating anyone's *rights*. True, the way I am behaving—expressing contempt for a whole section of the population, for no very good reason, and in a way that actually frustrates my own desires—is pretty pathetic. But I am not actually harming anyone, except in the purely relative sense that I am leaving them less well off than they might have been, if they had enjoyed my custom. Nor am I depriving anyone of anything they are entitled to. No restaurateur is *entitled* to my custom: if their restaurant is good, and yet I refuse to go there, for no very good reason (or even for a bad reason), that might be a foolish or small-minded way to behave, but I am nevertheless perfectly within my rights to do it.

Why is the jobs case supposed to be different? We might try to argue that what makes it different is the relative seriousness of the interests at stake. But then the libertarian will simply come up with other analogies. Suppose, he will say, I shun a former friend on discovering she is Jewish. Clearly this is a dreadful way to behave, and in terms of seriousness—how upsetting or damaging it is for the person concerned—it might well be on a par with being rejected for a particular job. Yet the libertarian is surely right that it would be absurd for the state to try to regulate the way I choose my friends. In this particular example, my right to do what I like is not a *property* right, it is a right of a different kind; but according to the libertarian, the basic picture is the same. Because in shunning a friend I am withholding a benefit rather than causing harm, and because no one is *entitled* to that benefit, the fact that I am doing it for foolish or even reprehensible reasons isn't enough to justify intervening. It is the same with private sector jobs, the libertarian will argue: unless we hold some positive theory about what applicants are entitled to—unless we believe they are entitled to an equal chance, or entitled to be judged on merit—then the fact that employers make their decisions for foolish or reprehensible reasons will not be enough to justify intervening.[8]

These are powerful analogies. However, I am going to ignore them for the moment—in part because they are so powerful—and focus on the argument that lies behind them. The argument seems to fall into four parts. First, the libertarian tells us that we must start by assuming that employers have some kind of right to hire as they see fit; second, because of that, we cannot rule out discrimination unless we can show that it violates other people's rights; third, we cannot show that something violates people's rights unless we can show either that it deprives them of something they are entitled to, or that it causes them harm; and fourth, discrimination does neither of these things.

If we want to challenge the libertarian position, clearly we need to challenge one of these four claims. The first way, then, is to start from somewhere different than assuming that employers have the right to hire as they see fit. Top-down theories of equal opportunity, as I suggested in the Introduction, seem to do just this: indeed, they often seem to start from the diametrically opposing assumption, talking about jobs as if they are sitting there in a big pile waiting for society to decide how they ought to be distributed. However, I rejected this approach; on this issue at least, I sided with the libertarian. The next way to challenge the libertarian is to contest his second claim, arguing that even though employers do have some sort of rights in this area, these rights are not as stringent as he imagines: in particular, he might be wrong to assume that the only legitimate reason for restricting them is to ensure that employers don't violate the rights of anyone else. We could argue instead that many different kinds of consideration can sometimes override employers' rights. For example, we might decide we wanted to reduce the amount of racial tension in society, and we might think that one way of achieving this would be to require large and prestigious employers to reflect the racial make-up of society at every level in their organization. There need be no suggestion here that any individual from any one of the different racial groups has the *right* to a job; we might just decide that it would be a good idea, from society's point of view, for some of them to be given a job—a good enough idea to warrant placing restrictions on employers' right to hire as they see fit.

This is an interesting line of argument, but I am not going to pursue it any further here; the reason being that although it might be interesting, it doesn't have anything specifically to do with *discrimination*. Reducing racial tension is a quite separate aim from eliminating discrimination. Intervention has to be based on the rights of individuals if we are supposed to see it as a response to discrimination—and if we want it to reflect our intuitions, which are that discrimination is wrong because it wrongs the individuals concerned, not (or not just) because it contributes to an unhealthy society.

The next possible way of attacking the libertarian position is to contest the third claim, that there are only two ways of violating someone's rights —by depriving them of something they are entitled to, or by causing them harm without good reason. Again, this is not the route I intend to take: this part of the position strikes me as unobjectionable. The interesting questions are what counts as depriving someone of something they are entitled to, and what counts as causing them harm. This brings us to the fourth and last possible way of disagreeing with the libertarian. This is to contest his final claim, that discrimination doesn't count either as depriving anyone of anything they are entitled to, or as actually causing anyone any harm— which probably means contesting the way he understands these ideas. This is the route I am going to pursue in the remainder of this section.

To take the idea of harm first, the libertarian's point is that since discrimination is a matter of omitting to give someone something, as opposed to actively doing something to them, it cannot count as harming them; harm must be an active notion. One way of replying to this would be to insist that there *is* something employers are actively doing to certain kinds of applicant when they discriminate against them: they are actively pursuing a certain policy towards them. However, I think this simply misses the fundamental point here. Pursuing a given policy is indeed something employers actively do, but it is not something they do *to* any particular person who falls under the policy. If we accept that there is a morally significant difference between actively harming someone and merely omitting to give them something, the question must be whether the policy itself is a policy of harming people, or a policy of merely omitting to give them something. And a policy of discrimination does look like a policy of merely omitting to give people something. 'We might happen not to hire any black or female applicants,' employers might say, 'but there is nothing to prevent them starting up their own firms. We wouldn't do anything to stop that—at least, we wouldn't treat them any differently than we treat our existing competitors. That proves we aren't actually trying to do black or female applicants any harm. We have just decided that they aren't going to get any help *from us*, which is a different thing altogether.'

This leaves the question of whether discriminating against a certain kind of applicant counts, *purely in virtue of the contempt it expresses*, as actively doing them harm, or whether it is merely a particularly unpleasant way of omitting to give them something. But I am not sure what to say about this question, so I intend to leave the idea of harm behind, and focus instead on the other possibility, that discrimination might count as depriving people of something they are entitled to. This might at first seem like the least promising place to take a stand against the libertarian argument, given the way I have set the discussion up. That is, it might seem that I can hardly criticize discrimination on the basis that it deprives people of something they are entitled to, given that I have made such a big thing of the need to consider the issue of discrimination by itself—as opposed to considering it against the background of some positive theory about what people are entitled to, such as meritocracy or equality. But this is not quite fair. What I was really objecting to about meritocracy and equality—besides the fact that they are wrong—was the fact that meritocrats and egalitarians don't seem to think about discrimination separately at all. It was this, rather than the fact that their theories say something about what applicants are entitled to, which I found so objectionable. If we can come up with a view about what applicants are entitled to which is tied specifically to the issue of discrimination—such as the view that applicants are entitled to be treated with some minimum degree of respect—this would be quite consistent with what I was saying at the start of the discussion.

The problem is that while this seems like a good reply to the libertarian argument, it doesn't immediately give us a satisfying answer to the associated analogies—that of the man who refuses to go to Indian restaurants because he dislikes Indians, or the man who shuns a former friend on discovering she is Jewish. These analogies seem to tell against even this more limited suggestion, the suggestion that people are entitled to be treated with some minimum degree of respect, just as much as they tell against any other way of arguing against discrimination. But this might be because we are following the libertarian in misinterpreting what his examples actually show. The libertarian thinks that by giving us examples where, although someone is clearly engaging in the most straightforward kind of racial discrimination, we wouldn't dream of saying the state should intervene, he has shown that this kind of discrimination can't be wrong. But this does not follow. The reason we wouldn't dream of intervening in the way people choose a restaurant, or in the way they choose their friends, is not because we think there is no such thing as being unfair in this kind of context. It is because we see powerful opposing arguments against intervening, arguments which outweigh the value of eradicating unfairness.

This same general point—that there is a difference between saying something is unfair and saying we should do something about it—came up in Section 2, when I was discussing the responsibility principle. I decided there that this point alone could not rescue the responsibility principle's universalist ambitions. But in the present context I think it does help to defuse the libertarian's analogies. It is an important thing to realize about the libertarian that he denies precisely this point, that there is a gap between saying something is unfair and saying we should do something about it. For the libertarian, unfairness (which for him means the violation of people's rights) is not only a necessary condition of intervention, it is also a sufficient condition.[9] If discriminating on grounds of race does violate people's rights, then we should be trying to eliminate it everywhere, in private life just as in the job market. And if on the other hand we decide that people should be free to choose a restaurant or choose their friends in whatever way they see fit—even in ways that are racist—then evidently we must think that racist choices by themselves don't violate anyone's rights; and so for consistency we must take the same view about the way employers allocate jobs. Or so the libertarian argues.

We can avoid this dilemma by rejecting the assumption which underlies it, the assumption that unfairness is always a sufficient reason for intervening. If instead we maintain that there is a difference between saying something is unfair and saying we should do something about it, we will then be able to say—as surely seems right—that even though racist behaviour is equally *unfair* whether it occurs in the job market or in private life, it is not an equally good idea to try to stop it. There are many arguments against trying to stop it which only apply in private life. For example, one of the reasons why it would be crazy to try to eliminate unfairness in the way people choose their friends is because this would be self-defeating. If the state started to regulate the way people chose their friends, friendship as we know it would cease to exist. And if the reason we wanted to intervene in the first place was because we saw how important friendship was to people, and therefore how important it was that they not be treated unfairly in this area, it would be strange to insist on this even after we realized that the price of eradicating unfairness was to destroy the very thing we started by thinking was so important. Something like the same problem might even apply to the way people choose a restaurant. Perhaps the reason we object to the idea that the state should interfere in such choices is because we think a certain kind of spontaneity would disappear. We can generalize across the two examples and say that there is something in the very nature of personal life which tells against the idea that it could be *regulated*—whereas there is no such problem with regulating the way employers choose employees.

There is also a second, different kind of explanation why intervention might not be a good idea in the context of people's choice of restaurants or friends while at the same time being perfectly reasonable in the context of job allocation. This is that intervening in the way people choose a restaurant or in the way they choose their friends is a threat to their privacy. To understand this argument properly, we need to separate the idea of privacy from the idea of freedom. The idea of freedom cannot justify our reluctance to eradicate racism in private life, since 'freedom' is a morally loaded notion: it is generally understood as being something which is inherently good. (This is why the onus is always on those who want to restrict people's freedom to *justify* the proposed restriction.) If 'freedom' is inherently good, it cannot include the freedom to be racist in your choice of restaurant or your choice of friends, since there is nothing good about being free to make such choices.[10] However, the idea of *privacy*, as distinct from freedom, can still explain our reluctance to intervene. The reason we are appalled at the idea that the state might try to interfere in the way we choose a restaurant or the way we choose our friends is not so much that we think it is a good thing for people to be free to make racist choices, as that we think everyone should enjoy a certain amount of space in which they can make choices without anyone watching them, and without having to justify these choices to anyone in authority. Of course, a world in which people were no longer even tempted to make such choices would be a better world. I suspect we would not think that a valuable element of diversity would have disappeared. But so long as people are tempted to make such choices, and so long therefore as eliminating them would require us to police people's behaviour, a world in which they were eliminated would not necessarily be a better world.

One reason, then, why the libertarian analogies are falsely compelling is because they focus on an area where intervention would be invasive—and which is therefore disanalogous to job allocation. This is supported by considering those few, exceptional cases where decisions about jobs do introduce issues of privacy: these issues then influence our attitude to intervention in just the way we should expect. We are more likely, for example, to think people should be free from interference when they are hiring someone to work in their house, than when they are hiring someone to work in an office. To flesh out the example a little, consider the case of a wealthy but reactionary old man who wants to hire a live-in servant. Suppose he has no intention of hiring a woman. No doubt if he was required to come up with a *reason* for this, he might be able to do so—perhaps by detailing the delicate tasks involved in the job—but this seems beside the point. It would still seem inappropriate to intervene even if he made no secret of the fact that he just didn't like women. The equal opportunity zealots, of course, will disagree. But while they are right to think that sexism is *just as unfair* when it is carried out on a small scale by a private individual as when it is carried out on a large scale by a big corporation, this just tells us about the reasons *for* intervening: it might be the reasons *against* intervening which really make the difference.

There are two ways, then, in which we can explain why intervention seems to be unjustified in the libertarian's two examples, while still being justified in the case of jobs. The first is that in the libertarian's examples, intervention would be self-defeating—regulation would destroy, or at least alter, the very thing it was trying to regulate—whereas it is not self-defeating in the case of jobs. The second is that privacy, which is highly relevant in the libertarian's two examples, is not so relevant in decisions about jobs. Even if employers' hiring decisions were subjected to close scrutiny, they would continue to enjoy plenty of space in their lives as a whole where they could make decisions without anyone watching them.

If we want to support non-discrimination rules in employment while opposing them in personal life, this has to be the right way to do it: to argue not that discrimination is somehow less unfair in a personal context, but that although it might be equally unfair, there are good reasons against trying to stop it in personal life which do not apply in employment. This implies, as must surely be right, that while it is indeed absurd to suggest that we should be *legally* required not to do things like shun a friend on discovering she is Jewish, we are nevertheless *morally* obliged not to do so. (If instead we argued that the reason the state shouldn't intervene in private life was because discrimination was somehow not so bad in this context, this would imply that we don't even have as much reason to stop *ourselves* behaving this way, never mind whether the state should be trying to stop us.)

Although my main aim in this section has been to answer the libertarian's objections, it has been interesting along the way to see how much the equal opportunity zealots have in common with their libertarian opponents, even though they come from opposite ends of the political spectrum. They share the same simplistic view of the relationship between unfairness and intervention—the view that where unfairness exists, that is always a sufficient reason to intervene. They differ only in how wide is their conception of unfairness. The libertarians have a narrow view of unfairness, and therefore tend to want to intervene nowhere; the equal opportunity zealots by contrast have a wide view of unfairness, and therefore tend to want to intervene everywhere. If the debate is set up along these lines, the libertarian will end up gaining a lot of supporters through the kind of analogies I have been discussing. I hope I have shown why the debate should not be set up along these lines, and at the same time, why the analogies are not as threatening as they appear, precisely because they rest on this simplistic view of the relation between unfairness and intervention. When the libertarian's objection to non-discrimination is stripped of these supporting analogies, and contrasted not with the position of the equal opportunity zealot but with the more reasonable alternative of believing in intervention in some contexts but not others, it is exposed for what it is: namely, the bare and unsupported assertion of the unqualified right of employers to treat applicants with contempt.

4. DOES EVERY KIND OF DISCRIMINATION EXPRESS CONTEMPT?

It is time to return to the main thread of the discussion: the attempt to understand exactly what is wrong with discrimination. I have suggested that discrimination is wrong, where it is wrong, because it involves treating people with unwarranted contempt. I have tried to explain how this view can answer the libertarian's objections. But the view itself remains quite vague. In particular, I have yet to say anything about exactly which kinds of discrimination it rules out. I have already noted that there are many different kinds—many different reasons why an employer might discriminate on the basis of a factor like race or sex. How many of these can really be seen as expressing contempt? I suspect the answer is not as many as we might think.

If we start with the kind of discrimination which is based on some theory about the 'moral worth' of black applicants, this does seem to express contempt. But what about the kind where the employer is not making any *judgement* about black applicants—he just doesn't *like* them, or they make him feel uncomfortable? If this really is just a matter of preference, it doesn't obviously seem to express contempt. Equally, what about the kind where an employer discriminates against black applicants because he genuinely believes they tend to be less good at the job? Again, this doesn't obviously express contempt. He might think someone's suitability for the job had absolutely no bearing on their worth in any more general sense. Next, what about the kind where, rather than discriminating against people of other races, an employer who is himself a member of some minority race discriminates in favour of members of his own race? We can imagine him thinking about members of his own race in the way that other small employers might think about members of their family. When employers use their position to help their family, even if we don't agree with what they are doing (probably because we are still intuitively attached to meritocracy, or to the idea that other possible candidates should have an equal chance), we wouldn't naturally think of it as expressing contempt for everyone who is *not* a member of their family. Indeed, in this case we probably wouldn't even describe what they are doing as discrimination. But then we have to ask ourselves why we take a different view of the minority employer who wants to help members of his own race.

We could go on like this, finding yet more cases where something we might naturally classify as 'discrimination' doesn't actually seem to express contempt—and therefore isn't wrong, on the view I am defending here. But before we get carried away, I should admit that there might be some artificiality in trying to separate all these different kinds of discrimination. There is, for example, no very precise boundary between discriminating against a certain kind of person on the basis of sheer dislike, and discriminating against them on the basis of some theory about their moral worth. Indeed, the problem might not just be one of vagueness. It might be better to think of the difference between these two kinds of discrimination as lying along a continuum, rather than falling into two separate classes. After all, people seldom have *nothing* to say in support of their dislikes—so it might be misleading to talk as if there is any such thing as sheer dislike.

However, this does not matter for present purposes. The point is that to the extent that we talk about 'sheer' dislikes—and sometimes this way of talking does seem to be helpful, even if it exaggerates the contrast between this kind of dislike and the kind which is based on some theory—there is no good reason for denying that some instances of discrimination could fall in this category. Nevertheless, some people do deny precisely this. Kurt Baier is one example; his reasoning is that 'if it is true, as is now fairly widely believed among scientists, that racial antagonism is never innate but always culturally determined, then entirely ungrounded racism, i.e., racism not based even on a crude racist theory, will be rare or nonexistent'.[11] But this is a *non sequitur*. Baier is guilty of running together two separate contrasts: first, the contrast between dislikes that are *innate* and dislikes that are *acquired* (or in Baier's terms 'culturally determined'), and second, the contrast between 'sheer' dislikes and dislikes that are based on some kind of theory. Suppose we agree with Baier that racial dislikes are never innate, but always acquired. Dislikes can be acquired but nevertheless still 'sheer' in the sense meant here—in the sense of not being based on any kind of belief or theory.

Why is it important whether dislikes are 'sheer' or are based on some theory? I have been implying that discriminating on sheer dislike is less bad than discriminating on the basis of some theory, because it doesn't obviously express contempt. Of course, even if it is less bad, it could still be wrong. But is it even wrong at all? It surely can't be wrong merely to *feel* sheer dislike. The idea must be that while it is not wrong to feel it, it is wrong to *act* on it. But before we rush to this conclusion, we should think about the number of different ways in which you might act on sheer dislike. For the purposes of the present discussion, we need to focus not on the kind of case where you *harm* someone on the basis of sheer dislike—which would seem to be clearly wrong—nor even the kind of case where you take something away from someone on the basis of sheer dislike. The proper parallel to discrimination in employment is the kind of case where sheer dislike merely causes you not to give someone something—and something they are not entitled to. Perhaps even this is still wrong. Suppose you have something that would make someone else very happy but is worthless to you, and yet you don't give it to them, simply because you don't like them. There does seem to be something wrong with this. But in fact, this is still not the proper parallel to what is going on in hiring decisions. As I made clear in Section 3 of Part 1, it is in the nature of these decisions that there is a limited number of jobs on offer, and employers have to choose who is going to get one and who is not. Some people are going to miss out whatever happens. It is not like the case where you could give something to someone but don't, because you don't like them, and instead give it to no one. The question is whether it is wrong to make the *choice* between people on the basis of sheer like or dislike. One way to think about this would be to imagine a world in which sheer likes and dislikes evened themselves out—that is, in which it was not the case that some groups, or individuals, were more disliked than others. I wonder whether we would still object to employers acting on their sheer likes or dislikes, if we lived in such a world.

It is possible to come up with a general principle which suggests we should. For example, there is the principle I discussed in Part 1, that it is wrong to act without good reason when serious interests are at stake. But the problem is that this principle cannot explain what is *distinctively* wrong with acting on sheer dislikes when those dislikes have a racial or sexual dimension. Racial or sexual discrimination turns out to be no worse than any other way of treating people irrationally. If we are not happy with this implication, then we must appeal to a different explanation of why discrimination is wrong—such as the explanation I have been defending, that it is wrong because it involves treating people with unwarranted contempt. But then we cannot take it to cover the kind of discrimination which is based on sheer dislike, since this kind of discrimination does not obviously express contempt.

I am not necessarily suggesting that actual legislation should be sensitive enough to take account of the difference between the kind of discrimination which is based on some racial theory and the kind which is based on sheer dislike. This difference might be just too hard to establish in practice. But if it is, we must be clear what we are doing. We must admit that in including discrimination based on sheer dislike among the kinds which are prohibited, we are prohibiting something which in itself is unobjectionable. There is also a wider implication here, which is that there is always more to assessing employers' behaviour than simply asking whether it is discriminatory. We need to ask what kind of discrimination it is—and sometimes the difference between different kinds will be less easy to ignore. Consider, for example, the difference between the kind which is based either on some racial theory or on sheer dislike, and the kind which is based on a belief about people's suitability for the job. Again, I am not suggesting this will be an easy difference to establish in practice. If an employer holds some theory about the wider moral worth of black applicants, that will generally involve ascribing certain properties to them (intelligence, character, etc.) which will be relevant to many jobs. So although the theory is probably what is driving his choices, he could equally say that he was discriminating against black applicants because he believed them to be less good at the job. Even if he was completely honest it would be difficult to pull the two kinds of belief apart, either in terms of which came first, or in terms of which had the greater influence on any given decision. Nevertheless, the point is that it is at least *possible* to separate these two kinds of reason for discriminating against certain kinds of applicant. It is at least conceivable that an employer might discriminate against people of a certain race on the basis of some view about their moral worth, while at the same time admitting that this had nothing whatever to do with their suitability for the job. (Indeed, we can imagine an anti-Semitic employer admitting that the morally undesirable characteristics he associated with Jewishness—cunning, say, or miserliness—would actually be a positive asset in the job.) But equally, it must be at least conceivable that an employer might discriminate against people of a certain race solely on the basis of a belief about their suitability for the job, without making the link between this and any view about their wider moral worth, and without disliking them in any way.

This last kind of case is the one that interests me. But I should emphasize again that it interests me *in theory*, not in practice. I am not suggesting that it is ever easy to *prove* that a particular case of discrimination is based purely on a belief about suitability, uncontaminated by any kind of racial theory or dislike. I am interested only in whether if we *could* prove that a particular case of discrimination was based purely on a belief about suitability, we would still think it wrong. Now, I realize that merely to suggest that certain kinds of behaviour could be discriminatory without being wrong will be seen by some as a contradiction in terms—and something close to an apology for racism. But I am not trying to be provocative, other than in the sense of trying to make people think twice about something they probably take for granted. It is true that once we do think about it, we run the risk of coming up with an answer which will be welcomed and exploited by racists and other undesirables. Given half a chance, almost every racist employer will be trying to argue that their discriminatory preferences are really based on some belief about suitability, rather than on a view about people's global worth. But this unsavoury prospect doesn't justify pretending that these two kinds of discrimination are morally equivalent, and it certainly doesn't justify pretending that there isn't even a question to be answered here. It is never a good enough excuse for refusing to think about something that you are afraid of where you might end up, or of the company you might end up in.

5. IS IT UNFAIR TO USE STATISTICAL JUDGEMENTS WHEN DEALING WITH PEOPLE?

I intend to focus, then, on the kind of discrimination which is based purely on a belief about suitability for the job. I suggest we start by distinguishing two ways in which an employer might think a factor like race was relevant to suitability. First, he might believe that *everyone* of a certain race has certain characteristics which make them flatly unsuitable—or at least which make them less suitable than everyone else. Second, he might believe that people of a certain race merely *tend* to be unsuitable or less suitable. I am going to pass fairly quickly over the first of these. This is not because I doubt that such cases exist. It is because where they do exist—where an employer really does believe that *everyone* of a certain race is simply unable to do a given job—the best explanation is probably that he also holds some wider view about their worth; in which case we don't need a separate account of why this kind of discrimination is wrong. We only need a separate account if we are thinking about the kind of discrimination which is based *purely* on a belief about people's suitability. So we should focus on the second type of case, where an employer believes that people of a certain race merely *tend* to be unsuitable, or less suitable, since these cases are more likely to reflect the kind of discrimination which is based *purely* on beliefs about suitability.

Of course, even here we will probably never entirely shake off all doubts over whether the employer's beliefs about suitability are really driven by some more general feeling of contempt or dislike. Even if we restrict ourselves to thinking about the kind of employer who believes that black applicants merely *tend* to be less good at the job, we might wonder how many of these employers are, when it comes down to it, simply racist. They might say their policies are based on suitability, but this is because they know they wouldn't get away with being straightforwardly racist. Or perhaps they are racist without even realizing it: they genuinely think they are discriminating on grounds of suitability, but the reason they believe that black applicants tend to be less good at the job is because they subconsciously discount evidence of them doing well and overreact to evidence of them doing badly. Now, I am not denying that one or other of these explanations might well be true of many employers who say they believe that black applicants tend to be less good at the job. But I don't think we can assume this will be true of *all* of them; indeed, I suspect that making this assumption is just a way of avoiding the difficult question of whether, if there *is* such a thing as discrimination based purely on beliefs about suitability, it is wrong in itself. I think we need to confront this question. So I suggest we think about the kind of case, however hypothetical, where it is the employer's *sole* motivation for discriminating against black applicants that he believes they tend to be less good at the job; where that belief is true (and surely there must *sometimes* be a correlation between being black and being below average in terms of the qualities directly relevant to the job); and where the employer believes it *because* it is true, that is, where prejudice played no role in his arriving at the belief.

The first thing to say about this kind of case is that the employer need not deny that some black applicants might be more suitable than some white applicants. To think that such exceptions undermine his position is to misunderstand him, since he is operating on the basis of a *rule of thumb*. Anyone who relies on a rule of thumb is explicitly accepting a certain reduction in accuracy in the interests of speed or cost. To illustrate this, consider the topical question of whether homosexuals should be allowed to serve in the armed forces. There is an argument for excluding them as a rule of thumb, which runs something like this. First, it is undeniable that a professional relationship between two homosexuals of the same sex (or, for that matter, two heterosexuals of different sexes) is more likely to be complicated by a sexual element than is a professional relationship between two heterosexuals of the same sex. Second, it is generally a bad thing for the professional relationship between two members of a fighting unit to be complicated by the presence of a sexual element, especially given that lives are at stake. The implication is that, as a rule of thumb, fighting units of more than two people should be composed of hetero-sexuals of the same sex. This rule is in no way invalidated by the observation that many homosexuals emerged with impeccable service records from previous conflicts. It explicitly accepts the possibility of exceptions: it merely argues that *on average* the armed forces would be better off not employing homosexuals. Of course, it also makes a difference that the aim now is to recruit a relatively small professional army, whereas in times of war the aim is often to recruit as many able-bodied and otherwise under-employed people as possible. So it does not follow, from believing that this is a good rule of thumb for today's armed forces, that it was a mistake for them to tolerate homosexuals in World War II.

I am not for a moment suggesting that this is the actual reasoning behind the bans on homosexuals that continue to apply in the armed forces of countries like the UK. There is little doubt that many of those responsible for these bans simply dislike homosexuals, or even hold them in contempt. Of course, the real question for our purposes here is whether they *could* have argued for the ban as a rule of thumb; I am suggesting they could. However, given that this is not their actual argument, this raises the question of why I chose this particular example in the first place. It might seem as if I must have chosen it deliberately to outrage any 'progressive' readers. But in fact this is not so. I chose it because it nicely illustrates an interesting modern tendency, the tendency to focus exclusively on the interests of the individual who wants to get a certain kind of job, and forget entirely the interests or rights of everyone else who is involved—including those whom the job exists to serve. The campaigners talk about homosexuals having the 'right' to serve in the armed forces; but it strikes me that no one has the right to do any particular job. This is clear enough in the case where someone possesses a characteristic which makes them directly unsuitable: then, even if their possessing that characteristic is not their fault, they do not have the right that the criteria be waived simply because they really want the job. The question, of course, is whether this argument can be carried over from the case where someone is *individually* unsuitable, to the case where they merely belong to a type who *tend* to be unsuitable. This is precisely what is at issue here. But the issue is obscured by talking about whether different groups have the 'right' to get a certain kind of job.

Whatever you think of this particular example, the more important point is the general one, that we cannot simply insist that employers are always wrong about there being a correlation between suitability and sexual orientation, or between suitability and race, or suitability and sex, and so on. Many people do take precisely this line, insisting, in the face of all evidence to the contrary, that there aren't any such correlations—or at least that there *wouldn't* be, in an ideal world. But what does 'an ideal world' mean here? Presumably, one in which there had never been any discrimination, nor any other kind of economic or social injustice. But I don't think we can be sure that even in this 'ideal' world factors such as race or sex or sexual orientation wouldn't still be correlated to some extent with being good or bad at a particular job. Of course, we could simply *define* 'an ideal world' as one in which there were no such correlations. But this just takes us back to the wider egalitarian view that everyone should have an equal chance, whereas we are supposed to be trying to think about what's wrong with racial or sexual discrimination independently, precisely without having to fall back on a wider egalitarianism.

So we cannot simply insist that there are no correlations between suitability and sexual orientation, or between suitability and race, or suitability and sex, and so on. But perhaps the real question is not whether such correlations exist, but if they do, how *strong* they are. A more subtle way of objecting to rules of thumb would be to argue that even if such correlations exist, they are never strong enough to outweigh the reduced accuracy which comes from relying on a rule of thumb.

This argument, like others I have discussed in this book, attempts to base a moral objection to a certain way of behaving on the prior claim that this way of behaving is *irrational*. Arguments of this kind rest on a general principle which I identified in Part 1, the principle that it is wrong to behave irrationally when serious interests are at stake. Now, as I have already noted, arguing that a certain way of behaving is wrong *because* irrational has awkward implications, even if the charge of irrationality can be made to stick. Most obviously, it implies that this way of behaving is no worse than any other way of treating people irrationally. If you are the kind of person who gets exercised by the idea of racial rules of thumb, I doubt this is what you really think: I doubt you think that this way of classifying people is no worse than any other way which is similarly irrational. You are more likely to think that it is *unfair*, in some distinctive way, rather than simply irrational. But if so, you cannot merely argue that whatever correlations do exist are probably too weak to make it rational to rely on a rule of thumb. This cannot be the real reason behind your opposition.

Just for the record, however, I want to consider whether the charge of irrationality can be made to stick. The first thing to say is that it cannot be made to stick in the abstract. The question of whether it is rational to rely on a rule of thumb can only be assessed in the particular case. Moreover, it depends on many other factors besides the strength of the correlation: for example, it depends on what other information is available; also on the relative importance of accuracy and speed. Clearly many people fail to see this. They argue, for example, that *even if* intelligence did vary with race, it could never be rational to use race as a proxy for intelligence, since the variation in intelligence within different races far exceeds the variation in mean levels between them. But while this might seem a plausible enough objection, in fact it just isn't something that can be argued in the abstract. At the extreme, if an employer was looking for intelligence, and the *only* thing he knew about the applicants was their race, then it would be perfectly rational to discriminate on the basis of race (again assuming, for the sake of argument, that intelligence does in fact vary with race). Of course, it will seldom be true that the only thing an employer knows about applicants is their race; but the example suffices to establish the general point, which is that the question of whether it is rational to rely on a racial rule of thumb just isn't something that can be settled in the abstract. If you want a more realistic example, consider whether it might sometimes be rational for an employer to use a racial rule of thumb as a screening device. Suppose he was blessed with so many good applications for a job that he was unable to give them all due consideration. If there was a correlation between race and suitability, would it really be *irrational* for him to use a racial rule of thumb to get the pile of applications down to a manageable size? Would it be more rational to take a purely random sample? You could argue that either would be irrational, because it would result in him overlooking some good candidates. But he already *knows* he is going to overlook some good candidates; that is why he is looking for a screening device in the first place. The question is whether using a rule of thumb as a screening device would lead him to overlook *fewer* good candidates than would the alternatives; and if the alternative is taking a random sample, the answer is yes it would.

Of course, you could argue that the reason why it would be better to take a random sample is because that would be *fairer*, even if not more rational. But remember that the kind of argument we are examining here is the kind which tries to base a claim about fairness on a prior claim about rationality—that is, which tries to argue that discrimination is unfair *because* irrational. Evidently we have abandoned this kind of argument, if we are now conceding that a random sample would be no more rational than a rule of thumb, yet somehow fairer. However, perhaps it was not a very promising argument to begin with. I suspect that rationality was never the real issue here. After all, companies rely on averages in all sorts of contexts without anyone complaining that they are being irrational. Of course, this might be because we just don't *care* whether they are being irrational when they are dealing with things as opposed to people. But I suspect this is not the whole story. Suppose a company regularly has to choose between two types of investment—call them Type *A* and Type *B*. Suppose it knows that over the last twenty years, Type *A* investments have outperformed Type *B*s—but it does not know why. On this basis, and this basis alone, it always chooses Type *A* investments over Type *B*s. This is surely unobjectionable. But I think that what this example shows is not merely that we wouldn't *care* if a company was being irrational in its investment decisions; I think it shows that we wouldn't dream of suggesting it was being irrational purely on the basis that it relied on averages rather than individual comparisons.

Moreover, people seem to object to the use of averages in hiring, especially when they concern things like race or sex, far more than they object to other hiring procedures which are more obviously questionable from the point of view of pure rationality. I am sure they would persist in thinking the use of racial averages unfair even if they became convinced that it was perfectly rational. They are merely using the idea of rationality to attack something they feel to be wrong. The appeal to rationality is purely tactical: they know that if they can succeed in persuading us that a certain way of behaving is irrational, most of us will stop; whereas if they try to persuade us that it is immoral, we might just think—so much for morality. But deep down it is the moral argument they really believe in.

Why then do people think the use of averages in hiring is unfair, if not because of some prior view about its irrationality? Because they are confused, in at least two different ways. First, they are guilty of running together, on the one hand, a specific objection to those rules of thumb which are based on things like race or sex, with, on the other, a more general objection to the very idea of using a rule of thumb, or any other kind of statistical judgement, when dealing with people. Second, this more general objection is itself the product of confusion. Here too people are guilty of running together two distinct ideas: first, the idea that a person's prospects should depend on facts about him rather than on facts about some group of which he happens to be a member; and second, the idea that it is wrong to treat people differently according to differences for which they are not responsible.

So we have confusion built on confusion: all people really want to object to are rules of thumb which are based on things like race or sex, but they end up ruling out the use of all statistical judgements; and the way they do this is by arguing that the use of such judgements violates the responsibility principle, when what they really mean is that a person's prospects should depend on facts about him rather than facts about some group of which he happens to be a member.[12] As far as the second confusion is concerned, I hope it is clear that these are quite distinct principles. For example, it is quite possible, and not at all inconsistent, to permit statistical judgements while at the same time affirming the responsibility principle. The idea would be that it is permissible to rely on statistical judgements just if the property you are *ultimately* selecting for, even if indirectly, is something for which people can be held responsible. This would imply, for example, that while it is wrong to discriminate on the basis of race if your reason for doing so is the belief that race is correlated with IQ, it is not wrong if your reason is that race is correlated with involvement in violent crime. It is wrong in the first case because people can't be held responsible for their IQ; it is not wrong in the second because people can be held responsible for their involvement in violent crime. It doesn't matter that in either case people can't be held responsible for their race, since that is not what you are ultimately interested in.

Again, whether or not you agree with this particular example, you should focus on the general point it is designed to illustrate, which is the difference between two principles: the responsibility principle, which restricts the kinds of thing we are allowed to regard as ultimately relevant, and the principle that a person's prospects should depend on facts about him rather than on facts about some group of which he happens to be a member, which restricts the *ways* we can pursue the things we regard as relevant—that is, which tells us we cannot pursue them indirectly, by relying on statistical judgements. The question is whether the second principle has any independent weight, once it has been disentangled from the first. To answer this we need to think about the mirror image of the position I described above. That position affirmed the responsibility principle while denying the principle that a person's prospects should depend on facts about him rather than on facts about some group of which he happens to be a member. If we really want to focus on the latter principle, we need to think about the kind of position which affirms it while saying nothing at all about responsibility. On this position, the problem with classifying people according to their race is not that they aren't responsible for their race. It is that they aren't being treated *as individuals*; they are being treated merely as members of some group. I think this finally gets to the heart of most people's hostility to rules of thumb. After all, many of those who think it unfair to classify people according to race also think it unfair to classify people according to their religious or political views; and people clearly *can* sometimes be held responsible for being members of a religious or political group. So it must be the idea that a person's prospects should depend on facts about him rather than on facts about some group of which he happens to be a member, rather than any concern about responsibility, which is really doing the work.

The idea, then, is that classifying people according to their race, or their sex, or their religious views, fails to treat them as individuals; that is, fails to take seriously the fact that each of them is an individual rather than merely a member of this or that group.[13] But what exactly does it mean to take people seriously *as individuals*? Presumably it is supposed to mean that, as a matter of fairness, employers should give full consideration to every claim. Now, sometimes fairness does seem to require that everyone's claim be given full consideration. But does this principle really apply to the case of jobs? That depends on whether, when we talk about people's 'claims' on jobs, these are really the kind of claim which demands full consideration. The principle of full consideration might only apply to 'claims' in the strong, moralized sense of the word. I made the point in Part 1 that not all reasons for giving someone a job count as an aspect of their 'claim' in this strong, moralized sense. This distinction between claims and reasons applies in other contexts as well. Suppose, I argued, that a number of patients are awaiting treatment; all are equally needy and equally deserving, but some are cheaper to treat than others. If resources are scarce, then the fact that some are cheaper to treat is a good *reason* for giving them priority, since this would enable more to be treated overall. But we wouldn't naturally say that it gave them a stronger *claim*. This is important here, because I suspect that the principle we are considering, the principle that it is unfair not to give full consideration to every claim, is only meant to apply to 'claims' in the strong sense, and not to every single factor that might be relevant to a given decision. So in the medical example, we might have good reason to give priority to those who are cheaper to treat, but if we simply didn't think about that aspect of the problem, this might be an oversight, but it wouldn't be *unfair*. Other examples are even clearer. Suppose I am thinking about how I should distribute some scarce good. If a number of people each deserve or need it, then if I fail to give full consideration to their claims, perhaps I am being unfair. But suppose instead that the thing I am distributing is a personal possession of mine, and desert and need don't seem to come into it. Fairness surely doesn't require me to give full consideration to everyone's 'claim'—in other words, to consider every possible reason for giving it to every possible recipient. I can surely just give it to whoever I feel like.

How does the case of job allocation relate to these examples? When we talk about people's 'claims' on jobs, we generally mean claims of merit rather than desert or need. I argued in Part 1 that merit, in the narrow sense of being good at the job, is not a moral claim. If you are the best person for the job, that might be a good reason for someone to give it to you, but it doesn't give you a moral claim on it. So while fairness might well demand that people's *claims* be given full consideration, it doesn't obviously demand that their *merits* be given full consideration; in which case it isn't obviously unfair for employers to rely on rules of thumb after all.

I suspect that, at this point in the argument, most people simply won't accept that being the best person for the job doesn't give you a moral claim on it. They will insist that merit is a moral matter; or they will argue that because it is so important to people whether they get a job, this gives them the right that their claims be given full consideration.[14] Either way, they will then be able to appeal to the principle that every claim must be given full consideration, thereby justifying their opposition to rules of thumb. So perhaps we ought to look more closely at the principle itself. In order to focus on the principle, and not be distracted by the question of whether it really applies in the case of jobs, I am going to shift the discussion back to the medical context. If we stick to discussing people's claims on life-saving medical treatment, there can be no question about the moral status of these claims. The principle of full consideration must surely apply here if it applies anywhere.

If it did apply here, it would suggest that if any patient was rejected for life-saving treatment on the basis of a rule of thumb, they could complain that they had been treated unfairly. Their claim was not given full and thorough consideration, and so they were not treated as an individual. Is this right? I suspect that whether we would say they had been treated unfairly would depend on the reason why the doctors were relying on a rule of thumb. For example, one possible rule of thumb might be a gener-alization about which types of patient tend to respond better to treatment. Perhaps nobody yet knows why some types of patient—women rather than men, for example—tend to respond better. Should we insist that until doctors do know why, until they are able to get beyond the patterns and identify exactly which patients will respond better, they are forbidden to treat men and women differently? I would argue against this. If doctors know that some types of patient tend to respond better than others, then when resources are scarce, they should give these types of patient priority, whether or not they know *why* they tend to respond better. Moreover, I would argue that if and when doctors do behave like this, they are not treat-ing anyone unfairly, even though it is true that they are not treating their patients 'as individuals'. It is a doctor's duty to try to save as many lives as possible, given the resources available to him. He cannot afford to ignore statistical information about various types of patient if that is the best, or even the only, information he has.

However, this kind of case is not perhaps the best analogy to the case of jobs. The reason why employers rely on rules of thumb is not because statistical information is the best or only information they have, but simply because getting more information is expensive or time-consuming. The question we should be asking is whether we would still be tolerant of doctors using rules of thumb if they were doing so purely because this was quicker or cheaper than assessing patients as individuals. But perhaps even this is not the proper analogy. We might still tolerate this, but only because we would be assuming that the reason why doctors want to save time or money is because, given a limited budget and staff, spending time and money on assessing cases individually would take resources and staff away from the actual business of treatment, and so would result in fewer people being treated. So the reason we forgive the use of rules of thumb is because we think the doctors are trying to do the best for their patients, given the constraint of limited resources. Their only motivation for not wanting to assess patients individually is to save time and money *which will then be used to treat more patients.* To the extent there is any unfairness here, we would therefore probably say that it lies not in the way the doctors decide who gets treated, but in the fact that they don't have enough resources to treat everyone in the first place. By contrast, when an employer uses a rule of thumb, he isn't trying to do his best for the applicants. He is trying to do his best for himself.

He could argue that what he is doing has the *effect* of helping applicants: if it makes him more efficient, it might lead him to employ more people, or give his existing employees greater job security. But no one would believe that this was his *reason* for using the rule of thumb in the first place. He might also try arguing that, like doctors, he is operating under an external constraint—which in his case is that his recruiting policies must be economically viable. He might thereby hope to achieve what the doctors manage to achieve: to pass the blame on to the situation, rather than the way he is reacting to that situation. But again, this defence simply won't be convincing. Few employers operate in markets so competitive that if they tried to treat their job applicants more as individuals and less as statistical types, they would actually go out of business

Where have we got to? It seems that if you want to object to statistical judgements you can accept that their use is sometimes justified, even when dealing with people, while continuing to insist that it is never justified in the jobs case, where the underlying motive is purely to save money. But even this more cautious view faces problems of consistency. The real reason we object to statistical judgements is because we want to oppose the use of racial rules of thumb; but what are we going to say about, for example, the fact that employers rely on examination results? Remember that it is the bare fact of relying on statistical judgements which is supposed to be the problem, not specifically the fact that the judgements relate to things like race or sex. Employers presumably don't think performance in examinations is somehow worthy of reward in itself; rather, they believe that those who fail to attain a certain level of performance *tend* not to make good workers. Most people wouldn't dream of suggesting that employers are behaving unfairly here, in specifying a set of minimum examination requirements and then refusing to consider anyone who doesn't meet them. But this is a clear example of classifying people according to a statistical judgement. If instead employers treated applicants 'as individuals', they would probably discover that at least some of those who do not meet the stated requirements are nevertheless worthy candidates. The employers are not unaware of this possibility; they have simply decided that it is not enough to warrant the extra cost of treating applicants 'as individuals'.

Even if we stick to thinking about statistical judgements involving race, there are inconsistencies in our attitude to companies using such judgements in hiring as opposed to, for example, in the way they treat their customers. Suppose a company decided that its target customers were predominantly black, and therefore that it should base its marketing strategy on black culture, black icons, or whatever. This would be an example of relying on a statistical judgement, since its target customers aren't all black, they merely *tend* to be black. It is failing to treat its target customers 'as individuals'. But few of us would think of suggesting that anyone was being treated unfairly here.

Why do these inconsistencies go unnoticed by those who argue against the use of race-based or sex-based rules of thumb in hiring? In the last example, that of a company which fails to treat its customers 'as individuals', the answer is fairly clear. We tend to assume that companies should treat job applicants with a certain degree of respect; we are less likely to think the same way about how companies should treat their customers. But is this justified? The relationship between a company and its potential employees strikes me as being fairly similar to the relationship between a company and its potential customers, in terms of being driven by self-interested, economic motives on both sides. The main difference is that in the case of the customer relationship we are more prepared to embrace the market and its implications. We are more prepared to embrace the fact that companies are generally motivated by profit, rather than by the desire to treat the people they deal with 'as individuals'.

As for the inconsistency of not objecting to employers relying on examination results, I can think of two possible explanations of this. The most obvious is that people only really object to the use of statistical judgements when they involve things like race or sex. They are opposed to race-based or sex-based rules of thumb because they think of them as just another form of discrimination. When they are forced to say exactly what is wrong with them, they pick on the fact that they involve statistical judgements; but since they are just looking for a way of rationalizing their feelings, it is not surprising if their answer ends up being inconsistent with some of their other views. The second explanation is the one I mentioned right at the start of the discussion of rules of thumb. This is that people only really object to the use of statistical judgements when they involve things for which people can't be held responsible. It is worth saying something more about this, since to the extent that this is the right explanation, it suggests that people really are seriously confused. Besides the fact that they aren't sure what they object to, they also end up in a position which probably represents the exact opposite of the way they ought to incorporate the responsibility principle into their views. If the responsibility principle is one of their fundamental moral principles, they should apply it to what employers are ultimately interested in, rather than to what employers merely pick on as being *correlated* with what they are ultimately interested in. Suppose, for example, an employer is using examination results as a guide to intelligence. It would be reasonable enough for anyone who believed in the responsibility principle to object to the employer discriminating on grounds of intelligence, since how intelligent people are is in large part something they aren't responsible for. But if they object to him discriminating directly on the basis of intelligence, can they really think it acceptable for him to discriminate on the same basis indirectly, by relying on examination results? The idea would have to be that this at least introduces a slightly larger element of responsibility: people are *more* responsible for their examination results than for how intelligent they are. But this surely gets things backwards, from the point of view of the responsibility principle. If you take that principle to rule out the employer's ultimate criterion, of intelligence, that cannot be rectified simply by introducing a proxy criterion, of examination results. Consider the following analogy. If you believe in the responsibility principle, you will presumably think it wrong to discriminate against people who come from a certain social class, since this isn't something for which they can be held responsible. But suppose an employer discriminated against people from a certain social class indirectly, by requiring applicants to conform to certain standards of dress or accent. This would introduce an element of responsibility—people are more responsible for the way they dress or speak than for their social class—but introducing this element of responsibility surely doesn't make the overall aim of the policy any more acceptable.

Now, in saying how I think people ought to incorporate the responsibility principle into their overall position, I don't mean to endorse that principle—indeed, I have already vigorously opposed it. I am merely trying to show that *if* you believe in the responsibility principle, it doesn't necessarily follow that you should also object to the use of statistical judgements. The two are quite separate, and it is perfectly consistent to adhere to the responsibility principle while rejecting the principle that it is unfair to use statistical judgements when dealing with people. The only reason for believing in the latter principle remains the quite distinct and much more general idea that everyone's claim should be given full consideration; and I have suggested that there are good reasons for doubting whether this idea can really apply in any economic context, given that it embodies a kind of principled thoroughness which is quite incompatible with the profit motive. We cannot simply turn round and condemn the profit motive when it affects the way employers treat applicants, while being happy to tolerate or indeed praise it in other areas. Of course, we can decide to start condemning it everywhere, but then we will be faced with the problem that what started out as a limited debate about the fairness of using statistical judgements will have turned into a much wider debate about the morality of the whole system of private enterprise. Throughout this book I have urged against allowing the debate to explode in this way.

It seems, then, that we cannot simply condemn the use of statistical judgements in hiring—even when they relate to things like race or sex, and even when they are motivated simply by the desire to save time or money. It is true that if we permit the use of statistical judgements, this will open up the possibility that racist employers will try to pass off their racism as if it was based on beliefs about average suitability; and if we are worried about this, we might decide not to permit the use of statistical judgements after all. But I am not concerned with such pragmatic questions. I have been talking about what we should think about different kinds of discrimination in principle, not what we should do about them in practice.

6. GIVING IN TO PEOPLE'S PREJUDICES

There is, however, a slightly more interesting reason why we should be wary of concluding that employers should be allowed to discriminate on the basis of something like race or sex provided they can show that it is correlated with being good at the job. This is the troubling class of cases in which the reason *why* race or sex is correlated with being good at the job is because of people's prejudices. Consider the following example. A company realizes that its customers, who are predominantly white, tend to prefer to do business with white staff. Depending on how strong this preference is, it might be rational for the company to discriminate against black applicants on the basis that, for this reason alone, they tend to be less good at the job. In one sense, this kind of case seems like the kind discussed in the last section: the employer is discriminating on the basis of race not because he dislikes blacks or thinks them mentally or morally inferior, but simply because they tend to be less good at the job. Obviously, however, there is an important difference. In the kind of case discussed in the last section, it was assumed that the *reason why* black applicants tend to be less good at the job was nothing to do with anyone's prejudices: it was just a brute fact about the different average capabilities of different races. Here, by contrast, it is the fact that other people are prejudiced which makes it true that black applicants tend to be less good at the job. In giving in to their prejudices, the employer acts as the vehicle through which those prejudices are translated into effect.

Does this make what he is doing unfair? He will try to argue that, if we look at it from his point of view, this kind of case really is no different from the kind discussed in the last section. In both kinds of case, the employer is simply relying on a statistical judgement about what kinds of people tend to be better and worse at the job. And while the present case might be different in that it involves prejudice, the prejudice is nothing to do with him. There is undoubtedly some force in this reply; and perhaps we wouldn't naturally describe what the employer is doing as unfair. However, he cannot claim to be completely innocent. He is knowingly acting as the vehicle through which prejudice is translated into effect, and this must be morally significant. At the very least he is left with *dirty hands*. But perhaps this is not the kind of wrongdoing that warrants state intervention. We might think that whether he keeps his hands clean is a matter for his conscience alone.[15]

Other examples are more complicated. Consider the fact that female applicants under the age of forty are more likely than their male rivals to take a large amount of time off, or to leave permanently, on having a child. This might make it rational for employers to discriminate against them. Small employers in particular cannot afford to hire and train people if they are going to leave after a couple of years, and for them it might not be rational to take the risk.[16] (They could try asking applicants whether they expected to have children, and if so, how they expected that to affect their work; but they couldn't really assume that people would answer this kind of question truthfully, nor would they be able to hold them to their answers.) However, even if we thought it was perfectly *rational* for employers to discriminate against women on this basis, we might be uneasy about it from a moral point of view. Suppose we think that at least part of the explanation why mothers tend to take more time off work than fathers is because of prevailing attitudes concerning the appropriateness, or value, of women pursuing careers. Suppose we also think these attitudes are unfair. We might then think that, in discriminating against women on this basis, employers are behaving in just the same way as a company which appeases its racist customers by refusing to hire black staff. They are treating prejudice as if it was part of the scenery, and as a result, they are left with dirty hands.

However, as I say, this case is in fact more complicated than that of the company which refuses to hire black staff. In both cases, prejudice is part of what makes it true that black or female applicants tend to be less suitable. But in this second case, the way prejudice becomes relevant is different: it becomes relevant at least in part through being internalized in the choices women make. No doubt it also has a direct influence: some fathers might coerce or implicitly shame their partners into shouldering an unequal share of the burden of bringing up their children. To the extent that prejudice does have this kind of direct influence, the situation *is* exactly the same as in the previous case. But to the extent that prejudice becomes relevant through being internalized in the choices women make, it is not the same. Asking employers to dissociate themselves from people's prejudices would then effectively ensure that women can make certain choices without having to face up to the costs of those choices. This is something that liberals, who are supposed to believe in people facing up to the costs of their choices, might be reluctant to do.[17]

Clearly this is a controversial position to hold. Some will argue that it is all very well to say that *individual* women should face up to the costs of their choices, but that this is not what is going on here: what is going on here is that women *as a whole* are being forced to face up to the costs of the choices made by only some of them. But this simply takes us back to the argument discussed in the last section, the argument for treating people 'as individuals' rather than as members of some group. I rejected that argument. There are also good reasons for doubting whether, even if it was generally sound, it would really apply in the present kind of case. Consider again the previous case, of the employer who refuses to hire black staff on the basis that his customers don't like them. Suppose he simply hires white staff, when in fact his customers would have no problem with, say, staff of Asian appearance. Would we say that in rejecting Asian applicants, he was treating them unfairly *relative to black applicants*—because he was treating them as if they faced the same handicap, when in fact they do not? I doubt it: if anything, I suspect we would say he was treating black and Asian applicants equally unfairly. This suggests that the problem is not the general one that, like most employers, this employer is failing to treat applicants as individuals—since this would apply as much to the difference between black and Asian applicants as to the difference between white and non-white applicants. The problem is more specific: it is, as I suggested earlier, that he is acting as the vehicle through which prejudice is translated into effect. And if we think *this* is the real problem with such cases, then we will recognize a significant difference between the case where an employer refuses to hire black staff because his customers don't like them and the case where he discriminates against women because their careers are more likely to be disrupted by children. For in the latter case, as I have said, it is the choices women make as much as the choices the employer makes which act as the vehicle through which prejudice gets translated into effect.

This is a delicate area, and I want to make sure that my position here is understood. I am not saying we should allow employers to discriminate against women on the basis that their careers are more likely to be disrupted by children. There are plenty of good reasons for not allowing them to do this. My point is that the way to understand these reasons is not to treat this kind of case as if it was just another example of sex discrimination. The principal reason for preventing employers from discriminating against women on the basis that their careers are more likely to be disrupted by children is simply that society owes a debt of gratitude to those who spend their time bringing up children. One of the most obvious ways we can pay this debt is to ensure that they don't suffer in terms of their careers, if they want to have careers. This is why we should require employers to make allowances for the fact that women are more likely to leave or take time off to have children. But in doing this, we are not denying that, in itself, expected length of unbroken tenure is a perfectly acceptable basis for choosing between people—and even for choosing between different *types* of people.

A libertarian, of course, would reject this way out of the problem. We saw earlier that the libertarian argues that we cannot intervene in the way employers make decisions unless we can show that they are behaving in a way that violates other people's rights. I have been arguing, contrary to this, that we can intervene in the way employers make decisions as a way of paying the debt of gratitude that society owes to those who spend their time bringing up children. On this way of looking at things, there need be no suggestion that any individual woman has the *right* not to be discriminated against on these grounds; we have a duty to ensure that they are not discriminated against, but this is not necessarily the same thing.[18]

Now, this way of arguing offends against the libertarian's general strictures on intervention, but I have already explained why those strictures are wrong. A less doctrinaire objection would be to concede that we do have some sort of duty to those who spend their time bringing up children, but to insist that because this duty falls *on society as a whole*, and not on employers in particular, we should therefore restrict ourselves to intervening in ways that place the burden of fulfilling this duty on society as a whole, rather than on employers in particular. Again, I have already shown what is wrong with this kind of objection. It is a quite general point that there is no reason why the burden of fulfilling a given duty should not fall disproportionately on a particular person or group, simply because they happen to be in a position to do something about it, and not because independently of that they have any more reason to do something about it. So none of these various objections succeeds. It seems we can argue for this position, that employers should not be allowed to discriminate against women on the basis that they are more likely to leave or take time off to have children, without having to imply that the *reason* they shouldn't be allowed to do this is because it is just like any other kind of sex discrimination.

7. IS DISCRIMINATION WRONG IN ITSELF, OR BECAUSE OF ITS EFFECTS?

So far I have been concentrating on the question of whether discrimination is *wrong in itself*. Before I close, I want to consider whether discrimination might be wrong in another way, *because of its effects*. The first thing to say here is that this contrast can be a tricky one to draw. Suppose we ask ourselves whether the kind of discrimination which expresses contempt, for example, is wrong in itself, or merely because of its effects. Surely what makes it wrong, we might think, is the fact that it makes people miserable; so it is wrong because of its effects. But this is too quick. Everything depends on *why* it makes people miserable, and why we think it matters that it makes people miserable. Suppose the reason it makes people miserable is precisely because they know they are being treated unfairly. Suppose, moreover, that the reason we think it matters is because we think they are *justified* in feeling miserable. In this case, while we might talk about discrimination being wrong in terms of its effects—because it makes people miserable—we are not saying that it is wrong in terms of its effects *as opposed to* being wrong in itself. The reason it has the effects, and the reason we think the effects are morally significant, is because it is wrong in itself. It therefore makes no sense to say that we have to *choose between* saying that discrimination is wrong in itself, or wrong because of its effects.

Nevertheless, there is an interesting contrast to be drawn here somewhere: we just need to be more careful about how we draw it. As a way into the problem, I am going to return to a related contrast I identified in the Introduction, between what I described as *bottom-up* and *top-down* theories of equal opportunity. Suppose we just wanted to stop employers treating certain kinds of applicant with unwarranted contempt. This would be a bottom-up view. It focuses first on the way employers are supposed to treat people, and only indirectly has implications for what the overall distribution of jobs should look like. Clearly some think the order of priority should be the other way round. Their interest in things like race or sex is *primarily* to do with how these factors show up in the overall distribution of jobs, and only derivatively to do with how they actually figure in employers' deliberations. They object to the fact that blacks tend to do worse than whites, or that women tend to do worse than men, but they aren't really interested in whether this is because employers are actually discriminating on the basis of race or sex, or because of some other reason. This is an example of a top-down view: it starts with a view about what the overall distribution should look like, and derives implications for how employers should behave from the effect their behaviour has on the overall distribution. On this view, the question of whether certain kinds of discrimination are wrong *in themselves* is not a very interesting one. If employers discriminate against black applicants, that will tend to leave people of different races with different chances, and is therefore wrong. But equally, if employers select on the basis of some other factor, which merely happens to be *correlated* with race, that too will tend to leave people of different races with different chances, and is therefore equally wrong. From a top-down point of view, the two are morally equivalent.

I happen to think the bottom-up approach must be the right one—that is, that as far as things like race and sex are concerned, we should focus primarily on the way employers actually treat people, not on the resulting distribution. But I also want to argue, as a separate point, that those who take the other side—who are concerned primarily with how things like race and sex show up in the overall distribution—have no business saying that their position has anything to do with discrimination. It is not discrimination they object to, but its effects; and these effects can equally be brought about by other causes. This second point is merely terminological, and therefore less important than the first. But it is not entirely trivial. The fact that top-down as well as bottom-up theories talk about discrimination is the source of much unnecessary confusion. For example, most people probably start off with the vague conviction that discrimination is a bad thing, without having pinned down exactly why. The top-down theorist then comes along and points out that discrimination leaves different kinds of people with different chances. From there it seems an easy step to conclude that anything which leaves different kinds of people with different chances must be (1) a form of discrimination and (2) wrong. Clearly I disagree with (2)—the substantive conclusion that anything which leaves different kinds of people with different chances must be wrong. This was what I was trying to prove in Part 2. But (1) is what I am interested in here—the terminological claim that anything which leaves different kinds of people with different chances must be a form of 'discrimination'. It strikes me that if all you really object to is that different kinds of people have different chances, it is an unnecessary distraction to use the word 'discrimination'. 'Discriminate' is an intentional verb, and yet the entire thrust of your argument is that intention is irrelevant: anything which leaves different kinds of people with different chances is wrong, whether it is something employers do intentionally, or unintentionally, or even some deep structural feature of the situation.

The general confusion is reinforced by the tendency to talk about discrimination in vague terms such as that 'people's prospects should not depend on their race' or that 'no one should suffer because of their race'. These constructions are ambiguous between bottom-up and top-down views—between the narrow view that employers should not intentionally discriminate against people on grounds of race, and the wider view that there should be no correlation between race and any kind of disadvantage. The use of such ambiguous constructions encourages the false assumption that these very different views are somehow both concerned with the same basic problem, that of 'discrimination'. So when people talk about 'discrimination' we need to realize that they don't necessarily have anyone's behaviour in mind; they might just mean that there exists some correlation between being a member of a certain group and suffering a certain kind of disadvantage.

A good example of this is the debate over physical disability. The physically disabled suffer certain disadvantages. Many aspects of everyday life, and not only working life, are more difficult for them. But this is not because anyone has deliberately constructed our world in such a way as to make life difficult for them. Indeed, many of the things that put them at a disadvantage are not man-made. But even if we restrict ourselves to considering those that are man-made (buildings, cities, transport systems, and so on), I am sure that the people who designed these things were trying to make things *better* for the disabled—to the extent they were thinking about the issue of disability at all. They might have failed, especially if the criterion of success is whether they made things just as easy for the disabled as they are for the able-bodied, but this does not make them guilty of *discrimination*. Yet people continue to make exactly this point—simply that life is more difficult for the disabled—by saying that they suffer from discrimination.[19]

There are, of course, two possible explanations of why people talk in this way. One possibility is that they are deliberately trying to stretch the meaning of the word 'discrimination'. They themselves hold the wider view that disability should not be correlated with any kind of disadvantage, but realize that it will do them no harm if this view is sometimes confused in the public mind with the narrower, less contentious view that it is wrong to discriminate intentionally on grounds of disability. So they *deliberately* favour vague constructions like 'no one should suffer because of their disability'.[20] The second possibility is more interesting. They might be guilty neither of deliberately confusing the two views, nor of being the naïve victims of such a ploy. They might actually believe that there is no real distinction between the two views. For example, they might hold the kind of 'top-down' theory I described earlier in the section: they might really believe that the only thing wrong with intentionally discriminating against disabled people is that it leaves them with unequal chances. It follows from this that anything else which similarly causes disability to be negatively correlated with chances of success is also wrong, and wrong in exactly the same way. If they really think there is no difference between all such cases—if they really think it makes no difference whether intention is involved—then they won't think there is anything misleading about using the same words to describe them.

If this is what is going on, then mere terminology and conceptual clarity are not the real issue here. The real issue is a substantial one: whether the top-down theorists are right in saying that the only thing that matters is how jobs are distributed overall across different sections of the population, or whether I am right in insisting that it also matters how employers actually treat people. If the top-down theorists are right, then this part of the book has been a waste of time. There is no point in trying to understand the various different senses in which employers might discriminate against black applicants if it doesn't even matter whether they are doing it deliberately.

This, then, is the real confrontation between top-down and bottom-up theories over the issue of discrimination. As a way of illustrating it, I want to go back to a distinction I first made in Section 3, between employers who discriminate *against* the members of other racial groups, and employers who discriminate *in favour* of members of their own group. A top-down theorist would not recognize that there is any distinction to be made here. From a top-down point of view, to discriminate in favour of members of your own group just is to discriminate against non-members: whichever way we describe it, the *consequences* are exactly the same, and top-down views focus on consequences alone. But from a bottom-up point of view, motives matter, and there does seem to be a difference of motive between discriminating *against* or discriminating *in favour* of a certain kind of applicant. Certainly there are other contexts in which this distinction seems important. For example, if gentlemen prefer blondes, is that the same as discriminating against brunettes? I would say not. Perhaps some men do discriminate against brunettes—perhaps they have had bad experiences at their hands in the past—but I suspect that most men who prefer blondes do just that: they simply prefer blondes, rather than seeking to do down brunettes. But if we accept this distinction when we are talking about the kinds of women men find attractive, why should we deny the same distinction when we are talking about how employers behave towards people of different races? Well, there are at least two ways in which someone might try to argue that the two kinds of case are not analogous. The first is to say that it makes a difference whether the preference we are talking about is based on race or hair colour; the second is to say that it makes a difference whether we are talking about jobs or personal life. I will consider them in order.

The first point, that it makes a difference whether the preference we are talking about is based on race or hair colour, really just boils down to the assertion that when it comes to race there isn't any such thing as a genuinely positive preference. There might be men who genuinely prefer blondes, as opposed to disliking brunettes, but there aren't any white employers who genuinely prefer white applicants, as opposed to discriminating against black applicants. But this is bare assertion. Alternatively, the idea might be that, although there are some white employers who genuinely prefer white applicants, in practice we would never be able to know who they were. Other employers whose preferences were in fact negative would try to pass them off as positive if they thought this would make them easier to get away with. But if this is the argument, we can ignore it, given that our purpose here is to consider what we should think about different kinds of discrimination in principle, not what we should do about them in practice. From this point of view, the fact that we won't always be able to *tell* positive racial preferences from negative ones doesn't justify carrying on as if genuinely positive racial preferences simply don't exist.[21]

What about the second point, the point that it makes a difference whether we are talking about jobs or personal life? It is certainly true that when we are talking about jobs, people are more likely to think that consequences alone are relevant. Decisions about jobs are generally thought of as being 'public' rather than personal; and the kind of hard-headed theory which denies that motives are relevant can seem more persuasive when applied to public as opposed to personal morality. Nevertheless, this is a mistake. Motives are equally indispensable to moral assessment whether we are thinking about personal or public matters. The only reason people ever deny that motives are relevant is probably because they are confusing the claim that motives make a *difference*—that causing a certain bad effect intentionally is *worse* than causing it unintentionally—with the much stronger claim that motives make *all* the difference—that causing bad effects is perfectly all right so long as it is done unintentionally. The stronger claim is clearly false. Often it is wrong to cause bad effects even if you do so unintentionally. But even then it is still *different* from bringing those effects about intentionally. This point is especially obvious in personal life. Consider the example of a married man who has an affair, and as a result causes great distress to his wife. There are at least three possibilities here: first, he did it deliberately to cause distress to his wife; second, he knew it would cause her distress, but this was no part of his intention (if it hadn't caused her distress, he would have felt relieved rather than frustrated); and third, he genuinely thought she wouldn't find out. In one sense we might think these differences don't matter: what he is doing is still wrong whether the effects are intentional, known but not intentional, or even unintentional. But in another sense these differences do matter. Having an affair with the deliberate aim of causing your wife distress is surely *worse* than merely knowing that it will probably cause her distress; and arguably, doing it when you *know* it will cause her distress is worse than doing it when you might expect her not to find out. Now, precisely what is at issue here is whether the same kinds of difference also apply in 'public' contexts, when we are talking about companies rather than individuals. But if we consider areas other than hiring—pollution, say—we do tend to think it makes a difference whether something was done deliberately, or knowingly but not deliberately, or unintentionally. Even if we think it is wrong in all three cases, the first is surely worse than the second, and the second worse than the third. It strikes me that the same must be true in the case of hiring: there must be a difference between, first, deliberately hiring disproportionately few black applicants; second, pursuing a policy which you know has that effect but where it is no part of your intention to have that effect; and third, pursuing a policy which has that effect but without even realizing it. Even if you are the kind of person who thinks that all three are wrong—because you think that anything which leaves people with unequal chances is wrong—you surely have to accept that the first is worse than the second, and the second worse than the third.

The fact that these kinds of difference *are* morally significant, even in a public context, means that there will always be a place for a bottom-up approach—that is, for an approach which focuses on the way employers treat people rather than on what the overall distribution of jobs is supposed to look like. This kind of approach isn't necessarily inconsistent with *also* believing in some kind of top-down theory; it just means accepting that the top-down theory doesn't tell us everything. However, we do have to ask ourselves whether we even need a top-down theory at all. Why should we still care about how factors like race or sex or disability show up in the overall distribution, once that issue has been separated from the question of whether employers are actually discriminating along these lines? Imagine the following scenario. No employers are actually discriminating on grounds of race, but some are discriminating on the basis of factors which, while perfectly respectable in themselves, are significantly correlated with race. These employers end up employing disproportionately few black applicants. Is there anything wrong with this? They are behaving in a way that leaves black applicants worse off than white applicants, but they are not guilty of treating them badly. If it is *only* a question of consequences—if the sole charge is that they are behaving in a way that leaves black applicants worse off than white applicants—then the problem is that *every* way of choosing between people will leave some groups worse off than others. It seems arbitrary to object to this fact in the context of race, or sex, or disability, without going all the way, and arguing that no one should be worse off than anyone else—that is, without going all the way to equality.

For example, is it not similarly unfair for *mediocre* applicants to have worse prospects than others? Of course, a certain kind of egalitarian will reply that this is not at all unfair: what is unfair, he will say, is not the bare fact that some kinds of people are worse off than others, but that they are worse off for *no good reason*. Mediocre applicants are worse off for good reason. Now, we have seen this kind of egalitarian argument several times before, and I am not going to rehearse its general weaknesses here. Its specific weakness in the present context is that the very same argument actually justifies the fact that black applicants tend to be worse off in the scenario I just described. If, as I assumed, the reason why black applicants tend to be worse off is because employers are selecting on the basis of a relevant criterion which merely happens to be correlated with race, then this is a good reason for their tending to be worse off.

It seems, then, that if you really want to object to the fact that race or sex or disability are correlated with chances of success, the only way to do this consistently is to embrace an *unqualified* egalitarianism—not the weaker idea that people should be equal unless there is good reason for them to be unequal, but the stronger idea that people should be equal, full stop. You cannot just argue for equality as the default position, in the absence of good reasons for people being unequal; you have to argue for it as a positive ideal. Now, I have already argued at length against equality as a positive ideal. I am more interested here in whether there is any other, more coherent way of being concerned about how things like race and sex and disability show up in the overall distribution, one that does not simply collapse into egalitarianism. In fact, I think there is. We need to go back to an idea I introduced at the end of the Introduction: the idea that everyone should have some control over their lives. If this is what we believe, then clearly there is cause for alarm if certain groups have very bad prospects. People in these groups will be unlikely to think of their lives—at least their working lives—as something they have the power to control, to shape through their voluntary choices. Clearly this is something to be concerned about; and equally clearly, there is no danger of this concern collapsing into egalitarianism. It is fundamentally concerned with asking whether people are in a *good enough* position, never mind whether *equal*.

The only remaining question is whether this alternative idea could ever support anything like a quota system for black or female or disabled applicants. The difficulty would be in justifying the group-based aspect of such a system. Even if it is true that black applicants, say, are less likely to have any real control over what kind of job they can get, this is not true of every individual black applicant. The best black applicants will be in a better position than many white applicants. It will be true that there is a disproportionate number of black applicants who need help. But shouldn't we try to deal with this problem in a way that specifically targets those who actually need help, rather than simply targeting the whole group on the basis that its members are more *likely* to need help?

Against this, we could argue that a quota system might be a reasonable rule of thumb—a cheap and easy way of giving help to those who need it. I have already argued that there is nothing inherently wrong with rules of thumb, even when they concern things like race; we could now use this result to argue that there is nothing inherently wrong with a quota system, and to point out that the argument for quotas is not defeated by simply observing that not all black applicants need help, since this is already factored in to the argument. The idea would be that simply giving preference to all black applicants is so much easier, or cheaper, or less invasive, than trying to find out exactly which black applicants need help, as to outweigh the fact that it will inevitably mean extending help to some who don't need it. Equally, of course, if you are the kind of person who earlier *objected* to rules of thumb, on the grounds that they fail to treat people 'as individuals', then you cannot now turn round and argue for a group-based policy for supporting disadvantaged groups, since the description 'disadvantaged' applies only to the average position of the group, not to every individual member.

However, my earlier argument that there is nothing inherently wrong with rules of thumb only establishes that a quota system cannot be dismissed out of hand, simply on the grounds that it is group-based. We still need an argument for thinking that a group-based policy would be justified in this particular context. And to make the argument, it is not enough merely to point out that black applicants are more likely to need help than white applicants. We also need to say something about the actual proportion of black applicants who need help. Even if black applicants are twice or three times more likely to need help than white applicants, if the proportion who need help is relatively small, then a group-based policy will still be hard to justify. Suppose, for example, we estimate that 10 per cent of the working population are in the kind of position where they lack any real control over what kind of job they are able to get. That would mean 20 or 30 per cent of black applicants are in this position; but it still might be inefficient to target all black applicants in order to reach that 20 or 30 per cent.[22]

However, perhaps we can argue for a group-based policy in a more imaginative way. We need to go back to the original reason why we were interested in how factors like race and sex and disability show up in the distribution of jobs. We were concerned that an unusually large proportion of certain sections of the population are not in a position to lead the kind of life which we are saying they ought to be leading: the kind where they see their lives as stories they help construct, stories whose evolving shape reflects the good and bad choices they make along the way. But clearly, whether people think like this will depend not just on whether it makes sense for them as individuals—whether they do in fact have any real control over what kind of job they are able to get—but also on how their parents think, how their friends think, and on the attitudes prevalent in the wider community. In which case, if a certain group genuinely functions as a community, perhaps it will be worthwhile to pursue a group-based policy, as a way of having an impact at the level of the whole community as well as on individual members.

Clearly much more needs to be said about this argument. For present purposes, I just wanted to explore what kinds of initiatives would make sense within the overall framework I have set out—in particular, whether there is a way of being concerned about things like race and sex and disability without simply collapsing into egalitarianism. The answer is that there is. At the same time, we should note that if we do end up making this kind of argument for quotas, there will be no special reason why we should restrict it to black or female or disabled applicants. If some other group—demarcated by geography, psychological make-up, or whatever—should also turn out to include a relatively high proportion of people who need help, and also functioned as a community in some genuine sense, it would have exactly the same claim to be included in a quota system. But this should come as no surprise, given that this particular argument for helping disadvantaged groups is not essentially connected to the issue of discrimination—that is, it is not connected to whether the groups in question are, or have been historically, the victims of intentional discrimination. Like any top-down argument, it focuses on the position people are in, rather than on why they are in that position. On this way of looking at things, the fact that there are all sorts of different reasons why people might end up needing help is beside the point. It simply doesn't matter whether they need help because of discrimination they have suffered in the past, because of congenital factors, or because of sheer accident. Top-down views are focused on improving the present, or the future, not on rectifying the past.

8. CONCLUSIONS

In this last part of the book, I have tried to explain why I think discrimination is wrong, without falling into the confusions inherent in standard ways of thinking about the problem. The standard ways are to explain why discrimination is wrong either by appealing to equality or meritocracy, or by grouping things like race or sex or disability under the more general heading of 'factors for which people cannot be held responsible'. I have argued that all these explanations are mistaken. True, we need to come up with some kind of general principle, or else we won't have succeeded in *explaining* why discrimination is wrong. But we are better off restricting ourselves to a principle which, though general, is narrower and more focused than equality or meritocracy or the responsibility principle. In other words, we need to come up with a principle which doesn't try to bundle up the explanation of why discrimination is wrong with the explanation of all sorts of other aspects of equal opportunity. I suggested one such principle: that it is wrong to treat people with unwarranted contempt.

This approach immediately opened up questions about different *kinds* of discrimination. For example, does it imply that race discrimination is wrong only if it is based on some racial *theory*? Or does it also cover those cases where an employer simply doesn't *like* black people? Finally, and most importantly, does it also cover the kind of case where an employer believes, rightly or wrongly, that a factor like race is actually relevant, in the sense of being usefully correlated with being good at the job?

I devoted most of the discussion to the last case, the kind of discrimination which is based ultimately, even if only indirectly, on some belief about suitability. I reached two main conclusions. First, we cannot simply *assume* that employers' beliefs about the relation between suitability and things like race or sex are false—especially if we are considering beliefs about *tendencies* or *averages* rather than about what every single black or female applicant is like. Second—and this echoed a point made several times already in the book—even if employers' beliefs *are* false, then while this means they are making a mistake, it is not clear why we should regard their mistake as a moral issue. And if we can't turn it into a moral issue, then it will be hard to justify intervening. That is, it will be hard to justify prohibiting employers from using race-based or sex-based rules of thumb if all we can say against such rules is that they are lazy or irrational.

I ended the discussion by looking at the possibility of a different kind of objection to discrimination: that it is wrong not *in itself*, but because of its effects. I dismissed this objection, making the point that while it is perfectly legitimate to be concerned about the effects of employers' behaviour as well as being concerned about whether the way they behave is wrong in itself, this concern really has nothing to do with discrimination. If employers hire disproportionately few women or blacks, that fact by itself does not mean that they are *discriminating against* women or blacks. But this was really a secondary conclusion; the most important conclusion was that even if employers *are* discriminating against women or blacks—even if what they are doing *is* rightly described as 'discriminatory'—it is still not necessarily wrong. I noted that, to some readers, this will seem close to a contradiction in terms; I hope I have made them think again.

NOTES

1. I should admit from the start that I am not using the term 'race' very precisely. In particular, it may be that the kind of discrimination I have in mind would be better described as discrimination on the basis of *colour* or *ethnicity* rather than race. Even if people think they are discriminating according to race, the choices they make might actually correspond better to differences in colour or ethnicity. But this wouldn't change anything of substance in the discussion that follows.

2. See pp. 99–101 above.

3. Peter Singer, *Practical Ethics* (Cambridge: Cambridge University Press, 1993), 22. Singer is talking about a different context here, but the basic point is the same.

4. See again pp. 99–101 above.
5. In the strict sense, the sense in which to say that someone deserves something is to say they have actually done something to *earn* it. See again Part 1 n. 2.
6. See again Part 1, Sect. 2.
7. Here I follow Rawls, in method if not outcome: see *A Theory of Justice*, 20.
8. This outline of the libertarian position is not taken directly from the writings of any particular libertarian thinker. Robert Nozick's *Anarchy, State, and Utopia*, the most influential and interesting modern libertarian text, does not explicitly address the question of discrimination. But it does address the question of where the state can and cannot legitimately intervene; and in answering this question, Nozick does rely on analogies between the decisions we make as economic agents and the decisions we make in our private lives (see e.g. 150, 262–4, 269). These analogies are taken very seriously by some of Nozick's opponents: see e.g. Phillippe Van Parijs, *Real Freedom for All* (Oxford: Oxford University Press, 1995), 130.
9. See e.g. Nozick, *Philosophical Explanations* (Oxford: Oxford University Press, 1981), 498–504.
10. See Raz, *The Morality of Freedom*, ch. 14.
11. 'Merit and Race', *Philosophia* 8 (1978), 122–3.
12. Examples of writers who fail to separate these last two principles include James Fishkin, *Justice, Equal Opportunity, and the Family* (New Haven: Yale University Press, 1983), 24–9; and George Sher, 'Predicting Performance', *Social Philosophy and Policy* 5 (1987), 190–3.
13. This is a line of objection I have come across countless times. See e.g. Singer, *Practical Ethics*, 30–1 ('members of different racial groups must be treated as individuals'), Fishkin, *Justice, Equal Opportunity, and the Family*, 24 ('a fair assessment of an individual's qualifications . . . should not rest simply on statistical inferences derived from the behaviour of other persons . . . who happen to share some arbitrary characteristic with him or her'); also Noam Chomsky, 'The Fallacy of Richard Herrnstein's IQ', in *The IQ Controversy*, ed. N. Block and G. Dworkin (London: Quartet, 1977), 295–7, and Stephen Jay Gould, *Ever Since Darwin* (Harmondsworth: Penguin, 1991), 247.
14. I discussed the second kind of argument at pp. 45–6 above.
15. A good discussion of the idea of 'dirty hands' can be found in Michael Stocker's *Plural and Conflicting Values* (Oxford: Oxford University Press, 1990), 19–26. Admittedly, the kind of case I am discussing here differs from what is perhaps the standard case of dirty hands. The standard case is characterized by Stocker as one in which a person is 'immorally coerced into participating in another's immoral project'. In the present case, although we might say that the employer 'had no choice' (if, that is, we believed him when he said that hiring black staff would actually put him out of business), we would not naturally say that he was being *coerced*. His customers are not threatening him, saying they will

withdraw their business if he employs black staff; he merely knows that this is what they will do. Nor is it obviously appropriate to speak of his being coerced 'to participate in an immoral project', since his customers' position might be insufficiently well worked out to be described as a 'project'. Nevertheless, the problem he faces is the problem I take to be central to the idea of dirty hands: the problem of 'how to act morally in immoral situations' (ibid. 22).

16. Clearly this would depend not only on the *relative* probability—how much *more* likely women are to take extended leave than men—but also on the *absolute* probability. For example, if women were three times as likely as men to take time off, but the proportions were only 10 and 3 per cent respectively, this would not be much of a risk. But I am going to assume, for the sake of argument, that at least sometimes the absolute probability will be high enough to make this kind of discrimination rational. I am going to assume this simply in order that we can get on to the more interesting question of whether, even if this kind of discrimination is rational, it might nevertheless be immoral.

17. See Introd., n. 4. Some liberals would deny that this aspect of liberalism applies in this kind of case. They would argue that women's choices are *contaminated* by the fact that they are partly conditioned by prejudice. On this view, as soon as prejudice becomes involved at all in the way people's choices are formed, those choices no longer have any moral significance. Now, one question this raises is whether there is any such thing as a pure and 'uncontaminated' choice —that is, a choice which is not even partly conditioned by other people's attitudes, prejudiced or otherwise. But the more fundamental problem with the whole idea of 'contamination' is that it takes what started out as a positive idea—the idea that what happens to people should reflect the choices they make—and twists it into something quite different and negative, into the idea that nothing else but pure and 'uncontaminated' choice should have any influence on people's lives. (See again pp. 28–30 above.)

18. See Raz, *The Morality of Freedom*, ch. 7.

19. Here is an example of the kind of thing I have in mind, chosen at random from *The Times*: 'Having no access to so many places which the able bodied take for granted is an obvious form of the discrimination which disabled people face every day'.

20. You might be forgiven for thinking that this kind of talk is harmless enough, even if it is strictly misleading. But consider the following case. American hospitals, faced with a shortage of life-support machines for premature babies, used to prioritize babies according to birth-weight. They did this because of the strong correlation between birth-weight and survival rates—and because there was no obviously better way of saying which babies are more likely to survive. But amazingly, the disabled lobby successfully challenged this policy in the courts (see Dan Brock, 'Justice and the A.D.A.', *Social Philosophy and Policy* 12 (1995), 12). They argued that it was 'discriminatory', on the grounds

that disabled babies tend to have lower birth-weights. Perhaps what they were really trying to say was that doctors don't value disabled babies as much as other babies, and were merely hiding behind the excuse of birth-weight. And perhaps they were right. But if we actually take their argument at face value—as saying that the birth-weight rule is wrong *in itself* just because birth-weight is correlated with disability—it is surely crazy. (Even if you don't agree that it is crazy, you should be aware of what it has achieved, which is to ensure that a smaller proportion of premature babies now survive.)

21. Moreover, we probably can come up with a few general guidelines about when racial preferences are likely to be positive and when they are not. Most obviously, we might expect positive racial preferences to be more common among employers who come from minority groups. Positive racial preferences are based on a positive desire to help members of a certain group, usually your own group. They therefore generally presuppose a certain degree of solidarity in the group, a kind of solidarity which I argued in Part 2 is more likely to be found in a small and relatively closeknit group than in a large, disparate, and heterogeneous one. (Of course, one thing that can generate and sustain solidarity even in a large and otherwise heterogeneous group is persecution by outsiders. It could be argued that women, for example, sometimes indulge in genuinely positive discrimination in favour of other women, for precisely this reason, even though they are not a minority.)

22. Cf. n. 16.

Conclusions

This is not the kind of concluding chapter that exhaustively recapitulates what has gone before. Readers who feel the need for recapitulation would be better served by returning to the arguments themselves. As for those who have picked up the book and turned straight to this point hoping for a summary of the main conclusions, they will be disappointed. But if there is a single message coming out of the book as a whole, it is that things are often more complicated than they first appear, and that any view which lends itself to simple summary is likely to be wrong. Indeed, theories such as equality or meritocracy, which purport to explain everything with a single idea, are not only wrong but also unhelpful: their influence makes us assume that even if they *are* wrong, the right answer will have the same basic shape. Whereas in fact, among the loose confederation of ideas that travel under the heading of 'equality of opportunity', those that turn out to be worth defending—non-discrimination, and the idea that everyone should have some control over their lives—are not complete theories in themselves, nor do they obviously fit together to create a complete theory.

Some will see this as a disappointing position in which to find ourselves at this stage; but I think they are making a mistake. Of course, it is tempting to assume that there must be one overarching idea or principle which will make sense of everything—or at the very least, to assume that even if we do have disparate aims and principles, these should fit together to form a complete theory. But as I observed in the Introduction, this desire for simplicity or consistency is in fact utterly misplaced. We are behaving as if the virtues of simplicity and consistency play the same kind of role in moral or political theorizing as they play in scientific theorizing, when clearly they do not. What scientific theory does is theorize about the way the world is. By contrast, what moral and political theory does is theorize about *what we ought to do*. Perhaps when we are theorizing about the way the world is, there is reason to believe that a simple theory is more likely to be the right theory—though I must admit I have never understood exactly what this reason is, if not the belief in a rational creator. But either way, this reason will certainly not transfer to moral and political theory, that is, to theorizing about what we ought to do. Whatever advantages there are to simplicity in this context are practical rather than theoretical—such as, for example, the fact that a simple theory is easier to explain, and harder to corrupt.

As for consistency, there is of course good reason to think that, if we are theorizing about the way the world is, then everything we say must be consistent with everything else we say. If two of our beliefs turn out to be inconsistent, this tells us that at least one of them must have been false all along. But the same does not apply when we are theorizing about what we ought to do. 'What we ought to do' just means what it is right, or healthy, or decent, to want to do; and there is no obvious reason why we should expect everything that it is right, or healthy, or decent, to want to do, to be consistent with everything else that it is right, or healthy, or decent, to want to do. To take just one example, consider the kind of situation in which you want to be truthful to someone, but also want them not to be unhappy, and realize that telling them the truth would make them unhappy. The undeniable fact that such situations exist does not undermine the thought that both these aims—being truthful, and not making people unhappy—are aims we ought to have. The same is true of our political aims: the fact that there are situations in which all our aims cannot be satisfied together does not for a moment suggest that at least one of those aims must not have been right all along.

Nevertheless, many philosophers persist in modelling the way we are supposed to think about our aims on the way we think about our beliefs. They present moral conflicts, whether personal or political, as opportunities to refine the set of aims with which we face the world—either by eliminating one of the conflicting aims, or by placing them in some kind of hierarchy. But there is absolutely no reason to think that this is the right way to react to moral conflicts—even if you believe that there is such a thing as moral truth. Conflicting moral aims simply aren't in competition in the same way as conflicting accounts of the way the world is. When two aims conflict, only one can be pursued, but this is not the same thing at all as saying that only one can be true. Once we realize this, there is no longer any obvious reason to pursue consistency in the set of aims with which we face the world. Progressively eliminating all sources of conflict among our aims might make us *feel* better, but will not make us into better people. Indeed, since the effect would be to narrow down the range of situations in which we actually need to *think* about what we ought to do—as opposed to simply reaching for the relevant principle—there is good reason to suspect that it would make us into worse people.[1]

We should not assume, then, that all our political aims should derive from a single principle, or even that they should fit together into a coherent theory. Yet this does not mean throwing up our hands, and saying that anything goes. I hope this book exemplifies the kind of work that philosophy can still do, even after it has abandoned the attempt to provide us with a complete theory which tells us everything we need to know. I remind the reader what I said at the start of the book, which was that philosophy cannot always take us all the way to the truth, but that this is no reason for losing faith in it: it just means we need a new and more realistic sense of what it can achieve. First, it can clarify the possible aims we might adopt, and help us eliminate those that are based on confusion or logical error. Then it can help us draw out the implications of those that remain, so that we can see whether we really find them so attractive after all. This is the approach I have taken in this book, in relation to those of our aims that bear on the way jobs are allocated. I have tried to clarify the different aims we might find ourselves with in this area. I have tried to show that although we take many of them for granted—we assume that they must be at least part of what we should be striving for, even before we are sure about exactly what they imply, or how they fit together—in fact they are often either confused, fallacious, or simply short of any real argumentative support. When we clear them away, we are left with something far less ambitious than most of us would have expected. We are left with the idea of non-discrimination, narrowly construed, together with the equally limited idea that we should try to do what we can to give people some control over their lives.

I describe this position as 'unambitious', but this is not why we should adopt it—I am not suggesting that meritocracy and equality are somehow *too* ambitious. This is a common enough view: that what we need is a compromise between principle, in the shape of equality or meritocracy, and practicality; but this is not what I am arguing. Not because I don't believe in compromise (after all, I have just been arguing that our aims won't always be jointly achievable) but simply because I don't see this particular view as representing any sort of compromise, especially not one that involves the ideas of meritocracy and equality. To see it like that would imply that equality and meritocracy are genuine values, and I have argued that they aren't genuine values at all.

Some will no doubt say, of the position I have defended, that it is what they meant by 'equality of opportunity' all along. They will be wondering why the book has the title it does. Clearly the disagreement between them and me is not very great: the question is only whether I am right in thinking that they are in the minority, and that most people would have expected equality of opportunity to add up to more than this. Moreover, they would probably agree with me if I suggested that we might be better off dropping the slogan of 'equal opportunity' in favour of something less misleading. The old slogan does have the peculiar quality of managing to appear at once both radical and unthreatening; but this advantage is more than outweighed by its debilitating vagueness, and by the associations with the ideas of meritocracy and equality—precisely the ideas we most need to escape from if we are to stand any chance of working out a new and better understanding of what we should be trying to do in this area.

In the end, of course, the question of what slogan we should use—how we should package the ideas we believe in—is not a question philosophy should be trying to answer. The question philosophy should be trying to answer is what we should be striving for, not what we should call it, and this is the question I have tried to answer in this book. For what it is worth, however, if I was forced to come up with a new slogan, I might suggest *Opportunity for All*. The only problem with this slogan (at least in a British context) is that it has already been appropriated by the present Labour government—a government which for all its talk of modernizing is a good example of what happens to people when they fail to break free of the ideologies of equality and meritocracy. Admittedly, in the case of equality their situation is complicated. They have deliberately moved away at least from the rhetoric of equality; but evidently some of them feel embarrassed by this, which they see as the abandonment of one of their party's historical commitments. As a result, when they face questions about, for example, how educational resources are to be allocated, where once we might have expected them to talk about equality, now all we get are trite pronouncements such as that '*every* child should have the best possible start in life'.[2] In one way, this kind of thing is even worse than equality: at least equality is a meaningful position, whereas this is no sort of position at all. It is no help at all to be told what our politicians *would* do, in an ideal world, in which they had the resources to give everyone as much as they needed. What we need to know is what they *are* going to do, in *this* world, where resources are scarce, and where they have to take hard decisions about who or what is going to take priority. However, as I say, I suspect that their evasiveness merely reflects the fact that they have been driven to abandon equality more by the realization that it is politically unsellable than by any serious attempt to rethink their principles. As a result, they still don't seem to be able to make up their mind what they think: whether all they really object to is the fact that some people are so *badly* off, or whether they genuinely object to anyone being *worse* off than anyone else.

In the case of meritocracy, the situation is more straightforward. The government are clearly enthusiasts, at least in theory. As I write this, they are starting a new election campaign with the promise 'to build a new society based on merit'.[3] I would like to think that some of them might read this book, and think again. But it is one of the problems with political philosophy—and one of the things the discipline is not entirely honest with itself about—that there is no real mechanism, formal or otherwise, through which its ideas can have any impact on the actual practice of politics. This is the main reason there is so little in this book about how its conclusions relate to contemporary politics: because this just isn't the role that political philosophy plays in our society, and because it is useless and frustrating to pretend otherwise. Of course the ideas in this book have implications for what politicians ought to do and say, but in the end it remains a work of philosophy rather than of politics or policy. It is a book about the values that lie behind policy—an attempt to contribute to a kind of debate which in contemporary politics and journalism is either absent, or being carried on at such a crude level as to make one wish it were absent. In times like these it is the responsibility of private intellectuals as much as professional philosophers to keep the discussion alive. This book is for those private intellectuals, if there are any left out there.

NOTES

1. Influential examples of philosophers who think we should see moral conflicts as an opportunity to refine our aims include, in the context of personal morality, R. M. Hare (*Moral Thinking*, Oxford: Oxford University Press, 1981), and, in the context of political morality, Rawls (*A Theory of Justice*, Oxford: Oxford University Press, 1971). The alternative view, which I have tried to defend here, is associated with the work of Bernard Williams (see e.g. 'Conflicts of Values', in his *Moral Luck*, Cambridge: Cambridge University Press, 1981) and David Wiggins (*Needs, Values, Truth*, Oxford: Blackwell, 1998). Wiggins puts it well: 'Not only

was the world not made for us or to fit our concerns; we have not made our moral concerns simply in order to fit the world, or even to perfect the accommodation between our very best intentions and that which we shall definitely, despite contingency, be able to achieve. Even if we had the power and the foresight to do this, we might still despise to do so' (*Needs, Values, Truth*, 176).

2. See virtually any speech or interview given by the then Minister for Education, David Blunkett, during 2000 and early 2001.

3. In a speech given by the Prime Minister, Tony Blair, on 8 February 2001, reported in most British newspapers the following day.

References

Anscombe, G. E. M. (1967), 'Who is Wronged?', *Oxford Review* 5.

Baier, Kurt (1978), 'Merit and Race', *Philosophia* 8.

Barry, Brian (1989), *Theories of Justice*, Hemel Hempstead: Harvester-Wheatsheaf.

Berlin, Isaiah (1969), 'Two Concepts of Liberty', in *Four Essays on Liberty*, Oxford: Oxford University Press.

Blackburn, Simon (1998), *Ruling Passions*, Oxford: Oxford University Press.

Boxill, Bernard (1991), 'Equality, Discrimination, and Preferential Treatment', in P. Singer (ed.), *A Companion to Ethics*, Oxford: Blackwell.

Brock, Dan (1995), 'Justice and the A.D.A.', *Social Philosophy and Policy* 12.

Broome, John (1984), 'Selecting People Randomly', *Ethics* 95.

Chang, Ruth (1997), *Incommensurability, Incomparability and Practical Reason*, Cambridge, Mass.: Harvard University Press.

Chomsky, Noam (1977), 'The Fallacy of Richard Herrnstein's IQ', *The IQ Controversy*, ed. N. Block and G. Dworkin, London: Quartet.

Cohen, G. A. (1989), 'On the Currency of Egalitarian Justice', *Ethics* 99.

—— (1992), 'Incentives, Inequality and Community', *Tanner Lectures on Human Values* XIII.

Dworkin, Ronald (1981), 'What is Equality?', Parts I and II, *Philosophy and Public Affairs* 10.

Fishkin, James (1983), *Justice, Equal Opportunity, and The Family*, New Haven: Yale University Press.

Frankfurt, Harry (1988), *The Importance of What We Care About*, Cambridge: Cambridge University Press.

Fried, Charles (1970), *An Anatomy of Values*, Cambridge, Mass.: Harvard University Press.

Gould, Stephen Jay (1991), *Ever Since Darwin*, Harmondsworth: Penguin.

Hare, R. M. (1981), *Moral Thinking*, Oxford: Oxford University Press.

Kymlicka, Will (1990), *Contemporary Political Philosophy*, Oxford: Oxford University Press.

Lucas, J. R. (1993), *Responsibility*, Oxford: Oxford University Press.

Nagel, Thomas (1991), *Equality and Partiality*, Oxford: Oxford University Press.

Nozick, Robert (1974), *Anarchy, State, and Utopia*, New York: Basic Books.

—— (1981), *Philosophical Explanations*, Oxford: Oxford University Press.

Parfit, Derek (1998), 'Equality or Priority', in A. Mason (ed.), *Ideals of Equality*, Oxford: Blackwell.

Rawls, John (1971), *A Theory of Justice*, Oxford: Oxford University Press.

Raz, Joseph (1986), *The Morality of Freedom*, Oxford: Oxford University Press.

Sher, George (1987), 'Predicting Performance', *Social Philosophy and Policy* 5.

Sindler, Allan (1978), *Bakke, DeFunis, and Minority Admissions: The Quest for Equal Opportunity*, New York: Longman.

Singer, Peter (1993), *Practical Ethics*, 2nd edn., Cambridge: Cambridge University Press.

Stocker, Michael (1990), *Plural and Conflicting Values*, Oxford: Oxford University Press.

Strawson, P. F. (1974), 'Freedom and Resentment', in *Freedom and Resentment and Other Essays*, London: Methuen.

Taurek, John (1977), 'Should the Numbers Count?', *Philosophy and Public Affairs* 6.

Tawney, R. H. (1931), *Equality*, London: George Allen and Unwin.

Temkin, Larry (1993), *Inequality*, Oxford: Oxford University Press.

Van Parijs, Phillippe (1995), *Real Freedom for All*, Oxford: Oxford University Press.

Walzer, Michael (1983), *Spheres of Justice*, New York: Basic Books.

White, Stuart (1997), 'What Do Egalitarians Want?', in J. Franklin (ed.), *Equality*, London: Institute for Public Policy Research.

Wiggins, David (1998), *Needs, Values, Truth*, 3rd edn., Oxford: Blackwell.

Williams, Bernard (1981), *Moral Luck*, Cambridge: Cambridge University Press.

Young, Michael (1958), *The Rise of the Meritocracy: 1870–2033*, London: Thames and Hudson.

Index

Printed in the United Kingdom
by Lightning Source UK Ltd.
103864UKS00001B/39